What Leaders are S.
Persecution of Chris

"Members of the clergy have fallen apart in my presence as they told how wives and daughters had been raped . . . How many more Christians will have to suffer and die before we realize that it is our job to try to stop these atrocities? We are so often caught up with our own petty problems that we don't make time to think about the Christians who are bleeding and dying across the world."

Luis Palau, President
Luis Palau Evangelistic Association

"It is imperative that we as a church marshal the power of prayer. We cannot sit by as if nothing is happening. Get on the phone, write letters, and let those in authority know what you believe. We have been confused, intimidated, and silent too long. We must stand and be counted."

Joseph M. Stowell, President
Moody Bible Institute

"NAE has prepared a document which clearly describes this situation and calls on all Americans to respond and to stand in defense of innocent human life. The declaration, the *Freedom of Conscience Statement*, is not a political statement, but a statement appealing to the very basis of American life. And that is freedom of conscience."

Don Argue, President
National Association of Evangelicals

"The Bible is very clear about what we are asked to do for those who are victimized because of their faith. We are called upon to pray for them and lay claim to the civic privileges that God has given to us. It is our turn to speak up. The silence of many on behalf of the few ultimately diminishes and could destroy all of us."

Ravi Zacharias, President
Ravi Zacharias International Ministries
and author of *Deliver Us From Evil*

"These persecutions are intense and horrifying. In many famine-stricken areas, the government will only allow relief agencies of the radical Islamic groups to go in, and they insist that anyone who wants to eat must convert to Islam. If you don't convert, you don't eat. You die. Somehow we must reach out and bring pressure to stop this intolerance and hatred."

William Armstrong
Former U.S. Senator, Colorado

"We need to shake awake those who are in power, to bring their attention to these injustices. And where we have a voice, speak out . . . Once you know, then you're accountable. And I would say, now we know. Proverbs 3:23 and 24 says, 'Don't withhold to do good when it's in the power of your hand to do it. And don't say to your neighbor in need, "Come back tomorrow and I'll help".'"

Jack Hayford, Pastor
Church on the Way

"Persecution of Christians around the world is growing and intensifying. Very severe beatings, burnings, lootings, and electric shock . . . Crucifixions of Christians in the Sudan . . . Many would like to sweep it under the carpet and pretend it doesn't exist, but it's true. It's happening."

Peter Torry
President of The CenterPoint Group,
former President of Open Doors with Brother Andrew

"We must feel a sense of moral outrage that Christians, in this day and age, are being sold into slavery, and are being tortured for their faith."

Charles Colson, Chairman
Prison Fellowship Ministries
and author of *The Body* and *Gideon's Torch*

Advance Comments About "Their Blood Cries Out"

"*Their Blood Cries Out* is an encyclopedic compilation of modern-day accounts of religious persecution against Christians throughout the world. With gripping detail, it gives a thorough record of the oppression faced by millions of Christians abroad. This eloquent book provides an understanding that is sorely lacking in the American community. Dr. Paul Marshall lends an insider's view into the most pressing human-rights atrocity of our times."

Nina Shea, Director
Puebla Program on Religious Freedom of Freedom House
Member, Advisory Commission to the
Secretary of State on Religious Persecution

"These horror stories of brutal persecution suffered by fellow Christians must be told. We so easily forget their suffering and courage. In this timely book, Dr. Marshall shames our complacency."

John E. Langlois, Chairman
Religious Liberty Commission of WEF, London

"Paul Marshall urges readers to abandon the wide-spread indifference to what is occurring daily to many Christians in various parts of the world. Quite properly, he also highlights other issues, including the number of Muslims in Bosnia and Chechnya murdered by so-called Christians. A profoundly moving book!"

David Kilgour
Deputy Speaker of the Canadian House of Commons

"The escalating world-wide repression of some hundreds of millions of Christians, which this landmark survey documents thoroughly, is one of the worst evils of our time. For all who care about human rights, human suffering, and helping the needy, Marshall's grim analysis is a must-read."

J. I. Packer
Regent College, Vancouver

"The plight of persecuted Christians in today's world is in desperate need of careful attention. No one is better equipped to educate us on this urgent topic than Paul Marshall. This book deserves a very wide readership!"

Richard J. Mouw, President
Fuller Theological Seminary

"This is a gripping and eloquent book. The murder, torture, and persecution of Christians in the Third World, and even prosperous countries, is one of the worst, and least-reported, of global human-rights abuses at the end of this century. From China to Saudi Arabia to Cuba, thousands of Christians have paid a terrible price for their faith. Human rights are either for *all* of us, or they are for *none* of us."

David Aikman, former senior correspondent
and Beijing Bureau Chief, *Time Magazine*

"Dr. Paul Marshall is clearly one of the leading defenders of human rights. In this volume, he gathers the data that has been growing for decades: The most oppressed and mistreated peoples of the world, in terms of human rights, are evangelical Christians. Committed believers are today more often the *victims* than the *causes* of human-rights violations."

Max L. Stackhouse
Stephen Colwell Professor of Christian Ethics
Princeton Theological Seminary

"Marshall writes with careful clarity, and passionate urgency. A superb book by a gifted Christian scholar."

Ronald J. Sider
President, Evangelicals for Social Action

"This superb book combines documentation and analysis of the persecution of Christians with deeply inspiring accounts of dignity as they witness to their faith through suffering and martyrdom. This book should be read by all concerned with religious liberty as a fundamental human right."

The Baroness Cox, President
Christian Solidarity International-UK
Deputy Speaker, House of Lords

Their Blood Cries Out

The Untold Story of Persecution Against Christians in the Modern World

by
PAUL MARSHALL
with Lela Gilbert

WORD PUBLISHING
Dallas • London • Vancouver • Melbourne

WORD PUBLISHING
Dallas, Texas

LIBRARY OF CONGRESS CATALOGING-IN-PUBLICATION DATA
Marshall, Paul A., 1948–
Their blood cries out : the untold story of persecution against Christians in the modern world / Paul Marshall; with Lela Gilbert.
p. cm.
Includes bibliographical references.
ISBN 0-8499-4020-6
1. Christian martyrs. 2. Persecution. 3. Church history.
I. Gilbert, Lela. II. Title.
BR1601.2.M37 1997 96-48119
272'.9—dc21
CIP

Printed in the United States of America
7 8 9 0 1 2 3 4 QKP 9 8 7 6 5 4 3 2 1

To those who asked that
their names not be used.

CONTENTS

Part Two: American Apathy

There was one in particular the soldiers talked about that evening (she is mentioned in the Tutela Legal report as well): a girl on La Cruz whom they had raped many times during the course of the afternoon, and through it all, while the other women of El Mozote had screamed and cried as if they had never had a man, this girl had sung hymns, strange evangelical songs, and she had kept right on singing, too, even after they had done what had to be done, and shot her in the chest.

*She had lain there on La Cruz with the blood flowing from her chest, and had kept on singing—a bit weaker than before, but still singing. And the soldiers, stupefied, had watched and pointed. Then they had grown tired of the game and shot her again, and she sang still, and their wonder began to turn to fear—until finally they had unsheathed their machetes and hacked through her neck, and at last the singing had stopped.**

* Mark Danner, reporting for *The New Yorker*, December 6, 1993, page 87, describing the army's reaction to a Christian girl from El Mozote.

And the LORD said unto Cain, Where *is* Abel thy brother?
And he said, I know not: *Am* I my brother's keeper? And he said,
What hast thou done? the voice of thy brother's blood
crieth unto me from the ground.
—Genesis 4:9–10 (KJV)

Some fifteen years ago, shortly after finishing my doctorate, I took up the subject of human rights. My interest was largely philosophical, since this was my training. But, while I have never been impressed with Hegel's idea that the philosopher is one who first of all knows everything anybody else knows, I knew at least enough to realize that you can't theorize about a subject unless you also know something a little more practical about it. Consequently, I sought to learn something about the actual practice of human rights in the world.

While I could not claim to be an expert, after a couple of years I knew more about this subject than most. Then, in the early 1990s, I was asked by some Christians to look at the persecution of Christians around the world. I gladly agreed. At the time, I didn't think it would take much additional effort. In actual fact, I found myself entering waters whose depths I have not even begun to plumb.

At first it meant entering a world of small newsletters and brief reports from, to me, strangely named organizations such as "Open Doors" or "Voice of the Martyrs." As I gradually learned to correlate these reports with the surveys produced by organizations such as Human Rights Watch or the Puebla Institute, I began to realize that there were sufferings which were all but totally ignored by the world at large. I was able to travel to some of these countries—not most but, still, about twenty of them. I began to write analyses and work with professional reports for *News Network International* of events around the world that were barely touched by other news media.

I wondered then why so few others knew these things. There were many people involved in the issue, but most of them were consumed by the day-to-day and hour-to-hour demands of addressing it. I thought about writing on it, but knew that there were many people far more qualified than I.

However, since most of them have to attend to shorter-term practical steps to relieve the immediate plight of those who are suffering, I have written this book.

I have not written it, however, without the help of hundreds of women and men. A book whose preparation has taken many years in many countries incurs many debts, and I cannot hope to thank all those who have helped me. In no particular order, some of them are Brian Stiller, Bruce Clemenger, Janet Epp Buckingham, Reg Reimer, Harold Fuller, Bill Samarin, Bill McKellin, Mat Anderson, Tom and Leslie Johnson, Bill Saunders, Hans Stukelberger, John Eibner, Mike Morris, Christopher Catherwood, John Langlois, Brian O'Connell, Danny Smith, Wilfrid Wong, Michael Bourdeaux, Vinay Samuel, Willi Fautré, Faith Mlay, Johan Candelin, Paul Negrut, Phaedon and Stelios Kaloterakis, Yoshiaki Yui, Elizabeth Doxat-Purser, Soter Fernandez, Chris Woehr Burow and Dick Burow, Alan Wisdom, Bryant Myers, Faith McDonald, George Lister, Lauren Homer, Ann Buwalda, Sam Ericcson, David Little, George Weigel, Terry Mattingly, Mike Cromartie, Joseph Cotton, Karen Lord, John Hanford, Richard Cizik, Willie Inboden, Herb Schlossberg, Stan De Boe, John Finnerty, Bob Zachritz, Larry Arnn, Dudley Woodberry, David Bentley, Jane Pratt, Rita Cartright, Sam Abraham, Belay Guta Ola, Shieffera Sedi, Liz Mellen, Miroslav Volf, Milly Lugo, Chris Dorres, Clara Payne, Keith Pavlischek, Mike Woodruff, Jacqueline Brown, Lynn Buzzard, Pedro Moreno, Patrick Neal, Max Stackhouse, Natan Lerner, Abdullah Ahmed An Na'im, John Witte, Johan van der Vyver, and Steve Ferguson.

There are many others in countries where, in most cases, it would do them no favor to publish their names. I would like to thank interviewees and correspondents in Egypt, Sudan, Ethiopia, Morocco, Algeria, Iran, Pakistan, Laos, Vietnam, Malaysia, Indonesia, and China, not only for their words, but for their example.

There are many organizations which have been very helpful, including Amnesty International, Human Rights Watch, Christian Solidarity International, the Keston Institute, the U.S. Institute of Peace, Catholic University, Droits de l'hommes sans frontières, the Rutherford Institute, Open Doors, and the Commission on Security and Cooperation in Europe.

Various stages of the research have also been aided by grants from the Free University of Amsterdam, the Centre for Christian Studies (Toronto) and, especially, the Social Sciences and Humanities Research Council of Canada, both for a three-year grant in applied ethics for work on the ontology of pluralism and a two-year grant to work on differing conceptions of human rights.

I would like to single out some people and organizations for their generous assistance, support, and encouragement, particularly in the later stages of this work. My own institution, the Institute for Christian Studies, has been generous in allowing me to travel (even suppressing the view that it had something to do with my love for scuba diving). The Institute on Religion and Democracy provided a home and advice in Washington. *News Network International* provided me with an education in these matters, and a chance to write on them regularly. The Puebla Program of Freedom House has given every aid I could ask. The Claremont Institute and the Fieldstead Company provided a supportive environment for my later work. The World Evangelical Fellowship has supported and encouraged me throughout. Caroline Cox, Nina Shea, David Aikman, Diane Knippers, Kim Lawton, Michael Horowitz, and Howard and Roberta Ahmanson have been sources of good advice, criticism, strength, and support. Nelson Keener of Word Publishing has also been a source of both encouragement and good advice.

Lastly, but not leastly, I wrote this book with Lela Gilbert. Usually a byline "with" designates someone who labored to make the author say things with some clarity. That is true in this case, but more is also true. As someone who has written on this subject herself, Lela contributed to the substance of what is here. And Dylan and Colin Gilbert graciously put up with frequent invasions of their house by an obsessed author.

None of the above, except possibly Lela Gilbert, bears any responsibility for the contents of this book, especially for any errors or misjudgements. Some of them would disagree with some of what is written here. But I owe them all my thanks and can quite simply say that it could not have been written without them.

Paul Marshall
Toronto 1997

INTRODUCTION

The mounting persecution of Christians eerily parallels the persecution of Jews, my people, during much of Europe's history. Today, minority Christian communities have become chosen scapegoats in radical Islamic and remnant Communist regimes, where they are demonized and caricatured through populist campaigns of hate and terror. As ever, shrewd tyrants understand that their survival depends on extinguishing the freedoms of communities that live beyond the reach of the bribes and threats on which their power rests. Modern-day tyrants further understand that terrorizing the most vulnerable and innocent best helps them achieve power over all.

The silence and indifference of Western elites to the beatings, looting, torture, jailing, enslavement, murder, and even crucifixion of increasingly vulnerable Christian communities further engages my every bone and instinct as a Jew. My grandparents and those who lived with them in the ghettos of Poland would well understand the meaning, and the certain effects, of such patronizing hostility.

The ignorance and silence displayed by Western Christian communities toward the suffering of fellow believers completes the litany of parallels to earlier, sordid chapters of the world's history. This history warns us that evangelical and Catholic communities in the Third World are acutely vulnerable, are profoundly worthy of our actions and prayers, are the people whose present fates can easily become ours if we remain indifferent to their fates.

Despite all, there is a powerful reason why today's anti-Christian persecutions might continue to be denied, appeased, and silently endured by the world at large—why "but I never knew" excuses will be permitted to serve "civilized" men and women well after the Sudanese holocaust has completed its course, well after Pakistani "blasphemy" and "apostasy" witch hunts have cut far-deeper swaths, well after the last Saudi Bible study group has been caught and tortured, well after the last Iranian evangelical bishop has been assassinated, well after tens or hundreds of thousands, perhaps even millions of House Church worshipers in China have been beaten, jailed, and murdered.

The reason is *ignorance*, and it is fostered by preconceptions and conventional wisdoms that lead many in the West to dismiss the fact of anti-Christian persecution as improbable, untrue, impossible. Here, as so often is the case, truth can become a victim of expectation, reality a casualty of prior beliefs.

For Western Christians, whose faith may at most cause them to be patronized and discriminated against by an agnostic culture, the notion of church attendance as a life-imperiling act may seem far-fetched. Having for so many centuries been the West's majority religionists, today's Western Christians are more likely to regard threats to their faith as coming from impolite hostility, not outright oppression. Tales of Christian martyrdom may in the comfortable worlds of Western Christians seem more suited to biblical texts and ancient Roman history than to evening newscasts, more a product of mission-board puffery than hard fact.

Government and media elites—twentieth-century products of an Age of Politics—are even more conditioned to dismiss allegations of widespread anti-Christian persecution. To them, the notion of Christians as victims simply doesn't compute. Armed with knowledge of sins committed in the name of Christianity and horridly unaware of Christianity's affirmative role in Western history, modern-day elites are conditioned to think of Christian believers as the ones who do the persecuting, not its victims.

Contrary to the February 1993 *Washington Post* description of Evangelicals as "poor, uneducated, and easily led," Christians are great forces for *modernity* in countries where the call of the twenty-first century struggles to be heard against shrill demands for an illiberal, unfree, and anti-intellectual new Dark Age. Christians are the heroes of such struggles, as well as the deliberately chosen victims of their Dark Age forces. An elite culture that speaks caringly about Buddhists in Tibet, Jews in the former Soviet Union, and Muslims in Bosnia finds it easy to dismiss the thought of Christians as equivalent victims.

It's also hard for many elites to believe that thug regimes with a shrewd sense of self-preservation feel at least as threatened by communities of faith as by secular adversaries. To them, political dissidents like the brave young man who stood in front of the tank at Tiananmen Square are the credible heroes, the likely martyrs who most stand in the way of dictatorial hegemony. It's hard for them to believe that there are, in today's world, people willing to endure the same certain fate as the Tiananmen Square hero in order to quietly profess a Christian faith. *They* surely don't know anyone who would do so, and the instinctive inclination of those whose lives are rooted in our secular culture is to believe that irrationality rather than admirable conviction is at work *if* Christian believers are being martyred.

There are, of course, many who know the lot of today's Christians in Vietnam, Ethiopia, Egypt, Cuba, and like places, but choose not to acknowledge it for "base" reasons of bigotry, for the "prudential" reason that public protest might make matters worse, for the "higher" reason that the blood of martyrs is needed to maintain Christian vibrancy. But such people are in the minority in a West whose basic impulses are decent, whose abhorrence of reigns of terror against innocent believers would cause them to speak out and to demand that their governments take steps against regimes that foster or appease such conduct.

It is thus lack of information (and, until recently, the absence of non-utopian, realistic, and achievable political strategies for change) that has for so long caused Western Christian communities to be so inert and inactive about the suffering of their fellow believers.

Likewise, it is ignorance and unconscious class bias, not malevolence, that largely explains the media's failure to report the story of today's mounting anti-Christian persecutions. The same factors explain why State Department human-rights reports are often sophisticated in their treatment of political dissidents and profoundly naive when dealing with minority Christian communities. And while less benign causes may be at the root of Immigration Service policies that ignore America's founding as a haven for religious dissidents, it is also true that this quintessentially bureaucratic institution would rapidly end its shameful bias against Christian refugee and asylum applicants if the truth about Christian persecution were widely know.

Their Blood Cries Out, written by the distinguished scholar and author Paul Marshall and his gifted collaborator, the writer Lela Gilbert, is a towering exposition of the history, causes, and facts of today's anti-Christian pogroms. It is a book that again proves the pen's mighty power and, I predict, its ultimate capacity to thwart its seemingly mightier adversary. It shatters silences and shows us how careful scholarship, well told, can make truth come alive and compel us to deal with its most unpleasant implications.

Written precisely as the American Christian community begins to stir on behalf of persecuted Christians, *Their Blood Cries Out* provides needed oxygen to sustain this effort. Written with a rare combination of balance and passion, it will provoke needed debate within the American Christian community, open skeptical minds to the truth of today's persecutions, and sear the consciences of us all.

Michael Horowitz
Hudson Institute
Washington, D. C. 1997

PART ONE

An International Lament

CHAPTER ONE

A Worldwide Plague

May 25, 1996. The grim silence in the Paris cathedral remained unbroken as Archbishop Jean-Marie Lustiger blew out the seven flickering candles, one by one. The candles, since March 27, 1996, had burned at Notre Dame to symbolize the hope that seven Trappist monks, held hostage in Algeria by the GIA (Armed Islamic Group), would be released alive. That hope, like the seven candles, was now snuffed out.

Ironically, for decades the Trappists had lived in remarkable harmony with their community, even having given a part of their monastery to the Imam, who had turned it into a mosque. Now all seven Trappists, the oldest an eighty-two-year-old doctor, had their throats slit by their terrorist captors.

During the monks' captivity, an outcry arose from Muslims, Roman Catholics, and Jews, all of whom conducted dozens of prayer vigils, pleading with the captors for the release of the Trappists, the youngest of whom was fifty-nine.

The Islamic High Council in Paris reacted to the killings in "anger and profound sadness in the face of this abominable murder."

Rabah Kebir, leader of Algeria's outlawed Islamic Salvation Front, also decried the atrocity: "I strongly condemn this criminal act, which runs absolutely contrary to the principles of Islam."

Despite rebukes from a broad array of respected Islamic clerics, the renegade terrorists remain arrogantly unrepentant.

Meanwhile, the seven monks were the last Algeria-based members of their Roman Catholic order, which had survived in their monastery through three wars.[1]

This book is about a spiritual plague. It tells of massacre, rape, torture, slavery, beatings, mutilations, and imprisonment. It also tells of pervasive patterns of extortion, harassment, family division, and crippling discrimination in employment and education. This plague affects over two hundred million people, with an additional four hundred million suffering from discrimination and legal impediments.

It is about people in India and China, Pakistan and Mongolia, Mexico and Peru, Turkey and Egypt, Nigeria and Sudan, Greece and Bulgaria.

It is not about "women," though most of those suffering are women. It is not about race, though the vast majority are black and brown and yellow. It is not about political activists, though many here fight for freedom and human rights. It is not about war, though there are wars enough included. It is not about terrorism, though terrorists wreak much of the damage. It is not about indigenous people, though it involves millions of them. Nor is it about famine and disease: These merely add to the suffering described here.

This is a book about persecution—religious persecution.

It is not about the holocaust and the hideous suffering inflicted on Jews in this century. It is not about the vicious repression of the Buddhists in Vietnam. Nor is it about the massacre of the Bah'ai in Iran. It does not deal with the sufferings of Muslims in India, nor of Hindus in Bhutan.

It is about Christians.

It is a story that is all but ignored and unknown in the world at large, and little better known in the Christian world.

It is about women and men and children who daily suffer pain, misery, and death. They do not suffer only from the myriad ills that afflict all of humankind. They suffer because they are persecuted for what they believe.

When I announce the subject of persecuted Christians, I am defensive.

Is this, then, another book claiming that Christians get a raw deal in America? No, it's not. Is it a book about the "Christian right?" No, it isn't. But current American attitudes reveal something about secular attitudes toward religion in general, so they are worth exploring a little.

Many of America's opinion-makers—that is, people who have leading positions in the media, government, the academy, the arts, and foundations—are secular in outlook. By "secular," I don't mean people who reject religion *per se*, but people who regard religion solely as a private matter. However, beyond this rather bloodless formality often lies an inability or refusal simply to take religion seriously, combined with suspicion of those that do. As Richard Land puts it, "An increasingly secularized West and its leadership elites tend to be indifferent, and often uncomprehending, of a spiritual world-view which endures persecution and death for the sake of 'belief.'"[2]

Coming into these circles, especially from overseas, is like entering a closed and parochial world. Religion is something foreign, something distant, something strange, something almost reprobate. I was once in a group of thirty political theorists who, in the aftermath of the 1994 U.S. Congressional elections, were anxious about the "religious right." I asked then how many of these highly informed, well-read, and literate people had actually read any books by people in the "religious right." None had, except for one who had read Hal Lindsey's prophetic potboiler, *The Late Great Planet Earth*, in the early 1970s and therefore regarded himself as something of an authority.

The "religious right" and, indeed, to be more accurate, theologically conservative Christians, were simply a foreign world, despite the fact that these theorists were now worried that the denizens of this netherworld might take over the country. It was as if a strange horde from afar had appeared over the mountain and, altogether inscrutable, had surrounded the city. Professors with a commitment to human rights, who could do factor analysis on the results of nationwide survey data, who could discourse on Hegel and Heidegger, and who knew the intricacies of American constitutional law, didn't know a thing about the people who lived on their street, let alone across the world.

This ignorance can erupt into outright bigotry. Charles Taylor, the distinguished Oxford and Montreal political theorist, indicated mildly in his magisterial *Sources of the Self: The Making of the Modern Identity* that his somewhat unorthodox Catholic views helped shape his perspective on what a human being is. For this, he was subjected to some vitriolic criticism. In a review, Quentin Skinner of Cambridge University, widely regarded as one of the leading historians of political thought in the English-speaking world, basically described Taylor as insane. Skinner asserted, "Theism must certainly be false. . . . it must be grossly irrational to believe otherwise. To say, however, that a belief is grossly irrational is to say that anyone who continues to affirm it must be suffering from some serious form of psychological blockage or self-deceit."[3]

Skinner's diatribe cannot be explained by some fear of the "religious right." Taylor is a social democrat whose book was published by Harvard. It reflects instead a congenital inability to see beyond the borders of a cramped, secular mind. Taylor's reply is to the point:

> I think that it probably shows up a striking blind-spot of the contemporary academy, that unbelievers can propound such crudities about the sources of belief, of a level which any educated believer would be excoriated for applying, say, to members of another confession. The paradox is that the last members of the educated community in the West who have to learn some lesson of ecumenical humility are (some) unbelievers. When these come to talk about religion, they have all the breadth of comprehension and sympathy of a Jerry Falwell and significantly less even than Cardinal Ratzinger. The really astonishing thing is that they even seem proud of it.[4]

When many secular people do talk about religion, it becomes clear that if, for example, they are lapsed Catholics, their views and knowledge of Catholicism go little further than what some eccentric nun said to them in parochial school in fifth grade. Views about evangelicalism reflect little more than having, in a fit of channel-surfing, accidentally tuned into Jimmy Swaggart at his worst.

The old cliché is: "Do you have any Jewish friends?" It is less often asked of secular people whether they have any friends who are committed Catholics or evangelicals. Since these two groups comprise a high proportion of Americans, the common failure to consider such friendships is striking.

Once I raised this issue with an agnostic friend. He replied that the comparison was not really fair. He explained that you wouldn't want an evangelical friend since they are obnoxious, and lecture rather than talk. I asked him how he knew they were obnoxious if he didn't know any. It turned out that, indeed, remote in hand, he had tuned into a garish television broadcast and had simply taken for granted that the clownish antics and ignorant statements he observed were typical of Christians worldwide.

This is prejudice. It could simply be dismissed as my own whining if it weren't for the brutal fact that this prejudice is a barrier to recognizing the suffering of hundreds of millions of children, women, and men worldwide. As James Finn says, "Advocates of religious human rights must be prepared to encounter in the secular news media less outright hostility or opposition than blank incomprehension."[5]

A refusal to take religion seriously, a disdain for those for whom faith is the central fact of human existence, a blank incomprehension of those who will die rather than forsake the peaceful expression of their beliefs—all these contribute to indifference which turns a blind eye and a deaf ear to the pain and cries of suffering believers. In a world awash with attention to ethnic and racial conflict, it produces a generation that can say "I don't know" or, more chillingly, "I don't care," to one of the most pervasive problems in contemporary human existence.

THE PLACE OF CHRISTIANITY IN THE WORLD

There are other antireligious prejudices. Too many Americans dump Christians into a stereotype of dead, white, European males.

Most Christians are not white. Christianity is non-European in origin. It was in Africa before Europe, India before England, China before America. Three-fourths of world Christians live in the Third World. It may be the largest Third-World religion. Even in the United States Christianity is far more common among non-whites than it is among whites. Eighty-two percent of African Americans are church members, compared to 69 percent of the total American population.[6]

Nor are Christians male—most are women, and not only because most human beings are women. The membership of the Christian church is disproportionately female. Nor, though vast numbers have been killed, are they dead. Despite persecution, Christianity is growing rapidly in the world, perhaps undergoing its largest expansion in history.

More people take part in Christian Sunday worship in China than do people in the entirety of Western Europe. The same is true of Nigeria, and probably true of India, Brazil, and even the world's largest Muslim country, Indonesia.

The Middle East contains people of many religions. Lebanon is 40 percent Christian; Sudan, 20 percent; Egypt, about 12 percent. Other countries have lower proportions only because of recent emigration or flight—or because Christians were subjected to genocide. At the turn of the century, Turkey was about 30 percent Christian, while Syria was 40 percent.

Tradition has it that Christianity was introduced to Egypt by St. Mark in 42 A.D. Alexandria was one of Christianity's intellectual centers and the home of major church fathers such as Athanasius, Clement, and Cyril. Turkey was the site of most of the apostle Paul's ministry. The area was Christian centuries before the arrival of Islam and, despite persecution, the Christians there have not given up their faith. They have been present for up to two millennia. Similarly, the Christian Church spread through Asia in its earliest centuries, reaching to Mongolia and India.

Christians are African women who rise at dawn to greet the rising sun in a wailing chant of thanks to God. They are Indian untouchables clearing up excrement from the streets. They are slaves in Sudanese markets. They are Chinese peasants flip-flopping by rice fields or pedaling bicycles through Shanghai. They are Mexican tribal people, driven from their ancestral homes. They are Filippina maids, misused throughout the world. They are Russian Orthodox priests, hit by cars which mysteriously careen onto the sidewalk. They are Arab women who have been raped and had acid poured on them to remove distinguishing Christian marks. And, overwhelmingly, they are people who, given a moment's time, space, and freedom, live life with joy, enthusiasm, and gratitude.

THE ROLE OF CHRISTIANS IN THE MODERN WORLD

It is futile to equate Christianity with clear-cut national, political, and ethnic boundaries. Human life always presents itself, not the least in the religious field, in a complex, intertwined, pluriform, and shaded combination of factors that is at once exhilarating, frightening, and bewildering.

But one thing we can say is that the assault on Christians is a fundamental part of the assault on human freedom itself. Many Christians are leading democracy and human-rights activists. They are also in the forefront of economic development. But perhaps more important than what they *do* is who they *are*. While usually loyal citizens, they embody an attachment to "another King," a loyalty to a standard of spiritual allegiance apart from the political order. This fact *itself* denies that the state is the all-encompassing or ultimate arbiter of human life. Regardless of how the relation between God and Caesar has been expressed, it now at least means that, contra the Romans and modern totalitarians, *Caesar is not God*. This confession, however mute, sticks in the craw of every authoritarian regime and draws their angry and bloody response.

Many Christians are therefore persecuted simply because they are Christians. Their usually peaceful and quiet beliefs stand as a rebuke to those who are corrupt, to those who cannot tolerate the presence of any view but their own, and to those who want to make their own political regime the only focus of loyalty. Their very existence is a silent witness to a claim beyond human control.

Samuel Huntington maintains that the "third wave of democracy" in the 1970s and 80s encompassing Iberia, Eastern Europe, Latin America, and the Philippines stemmed in large part from the renewed commitment to democracy and human rights in the Catholic Church.[7] George Weigel has pointed out the role of the church, and especially the Pope, in the erosion of Communism in Eastern Europe.[8] In 1988, on the thousandth anniversary of the arrival of Christianity in Russia, Mikhail Gorbachev allowed churches to ring out their bells for the first time in seventy years. Russians have described the wonder and elation they felt as a new spiritual presence resounded through the streets and squares—a presence that reached beyond Communism and hastened the loosening of totalitarianism's grip on human minds and souls.

I am not making the absurd suggestion that religious renewal, apart from any other social, economic, political, or strategic factors, brought the end of these authoritarian regimes. Societies are complex. But I am saying that it is equally absurd to discuss political freedom *without* attending to the role of religion. Czech President, and former prisoner, Vaclav Havel knows this well. With his customary clarity and prescience, he described the Soviet expulsion of author and Nobel Prize winner Alexander Solzhenitsyn as:

> . . . a desperate attempt to plug up the dreadful well-spring of truth, a truth which might cause incalculable transformations in social consciousness, which in turn might one day produce political debacles unpredictable in their consequences. And so the . . . system behaved in a characteristic way: It defended the integrity of the world of appearances in order to defend itself. For the crust presented by the life of lies is made of strange stuff. As long as it seals off hermetically the entire society, it appears to be made of stone. But the moment someone breaks through in one place, when one person cries out, "The emperor is naked!"—when a single person breaks the rules of the game, thus exposing it as a game—everything suddenly appears in a another light and the whole crust seems then to be made of a tissue on the point of tearing and disintegrating uncontrollably.[9]

If this connection has not been clear to western observers afflicted with secular myopia, it has been all too clear to the Communist authorities in China and Vietnam. As brutal practitioners of power, they are perversely aware of the power of human spirituality, and so take religion with deadly seriousness. In 1992 the Chinese state-run press noted that "the church played an important role in the change" in Eastern Europe and warned, "If

China does not want such a scene to be repeated in its land, it must strangle the baby while it is still in the manger."[10]

With this evil biblical allusion, the Chinese leadership adopted Herod as its role model. On the assumption that Communists know the Bible better and therefore see its power more than many secular westerners, perhaps it is worth outlining the texts to which the Chinese authorities refer:

> Then Herod summoned the wise men to see him privately. He asked them the exact date on which the star had appeared and sent them on to Bethlehem with the words, "Go and find out all about the child, and when you have found him, let me know, so that I too may go and do him homage. . . ."
>
> But they were given a warning in a dream not to go back to Herod and returned to their own country by a different way.
>
> Herod was furious on realizing that he had been fooled by the wise men, and in Bethlehem and its surrounding district he had all the male children killed who were two years old or less, reckoning by the date he had been careful to ask the wise men. Then were fulfilled the words spoken through the prophet Jeremiah:
>
> A voice is heard in Ramah,
> lamenting and weeping bitterly:
> it is Rachel weeping for her children,
> refusing to be comforted
> because they are no more.[11]

And Rachel weeps still, in China and elsewhere.

Because Christians are spread throughout the world in many thousand different ethnic and cultural groups, their suffering provides a touchstone for how regimes treat human rights in general. In country after country, region after region, town after town, the persecution of Christians is a harbinger of the repression of other human rights—of political dissidents, of intellectuals, of unionists, of women, of children, of homosexuals.

Those who desire to control Christians desire to control everything. Just as anti-Semitism, even apart from its own inherent evil, is a reliable indicator of the growth of other forms of repression in society, so Christians now function as the canary in the mineshaft: When they collapse, other deaths are sure to follow. In the same way, those who ignore the plight of Christians throughout the world bear an awkward resemblance to those who turned a blind eye to the persecution of the Jews throughout this century. If we are concerned about human rights of any kind, we need to pay attention to Christians—who they are, how they live, why they suffer.

Cuban Poet Armando Valladares' account of his twenty-two years in Castro's prisons includes the description of one particular Christian.

All of us called Gerardo the Brother of the Faith. . . .

His sermons had a primitive beauty; he himself had an extraordinary magnetism. From a pulpit improvised from old salt-codfish boxes covered with a sheet, behind a simple cross, the thundering voice of the Brother of the Faith would preach his daily sermons. Then we would all sing hymns he wrote out on cigarette packages and passed out to those of us at the meeting. Many times the garrison broke up those minutes of prayer with blows and kicks, but they never managed to intimidate him. When they took him off to the forced-labor fields of Isla de Piños, he organized Bible readings and choirs. Having a Bible was a subversive act, but he had, we never knew how, a little one which he always carried with him.

If some exhausted or sick prisoner fell behind in the furrows or hadn't piled up the amount of rock he had been ordered to break, the Brother of the Faith would turn up. He was thin and wiry, with incredible stamina for physical labor. He would catch the other man up in his work, save him from brutal beatings. When one of the guards would walk up behind him and hit him, the Brother of the Faith would spring erect, look into the guard's eyes, and say to him, "May God pardon you."

. . . In the midst of that apocalyptic vision of the most dreadful and horrifying moments in my life, in the midst of the gray, ashy dust and the

orgy of beatings and blood, prisoners beaten to the ground, a man emerged, the skeletal figure of a man wasted by hunger, with white hair, blazing blue eyes, and a heart overflowing with love, raising his arms to the invisible heaven and pleading for mercy for his executioners.

"Forgive them, Father, for they know not what they do." And a burst of machine-gun fire ripping open his breast.[12]

The suffering of Christians, like the pain of any human being, cries out for our attention, our sympathy, and our action. As Stephen Rosenfeld wrote in the *Washington Post*, "Politically as citizens and objectively in terms of the pain of foreign brothers, the Christian community has right and reason to be heard. The effort will save lives."[13] Maybe my defensiveness is not needed. I hope not. If it is, I hope all that follows will make it superfluous.

In China, in March 1993 . . . five Protestants from Shaanxi were detained and severely tortured. . . . "without a word of explanation." They were singled out because the authorities suspected them of contact with foreigners. According to an eyewitness account. . . .

"'The officers stripped three brethren naked from the waist and forced the women to stand with them. Not only did they then beat them, moreover they forced each of the twenty-six other local people to beat each one a hundred times with bamboo rods. If they refused . . . they would in turn be beaten. The three men were beaten until they were totally covered with blood and had gaping wounds and injuries all over their bodies. As if such violent beating wasn't enough, the officers then hung them up and began to hit them with the rods on their backs. They did this until the three men were unconscious and barely breathing. We could only hear the sound of the beating and the cursing of the officers.'"[14]

In Sudan, January 2, 1995 . . . the village of Wud Arul, about two kilometers north of Sokobat, was attacked. Raiders came at dawn, storming through the whole area, looting and burning homes to ashes; kidnapping women and children (even babies); killing old men and women. About 150–200 men came, some on horseback, some on foot, and took away sixty-three women and children, as well as four hundred head of cattle. The women and children were taken via Um Ajac to either Meyram or Abu Jabra. Then they divided the captives up: Some were sent to the market; some were to be used for forced labour in agricultural work with groundnuts or sesame; young women were to become concubines; older women to become domestic slaves.

"On arrival at Sokobat, we were greeted by the chief with a warm welcome. 'We are so glad to see you here. Often people come and say they will return, but never do. It is good for us to know that people do know about us, that they care, and that we are not suffering with no one knowing about our tragedy.'"[15]

CHAPTER TWO

The Advancing Jihad

Mary, a young Egyptian girl, displays her fragile wrist, which is encircled by an ugly bracelet of scarred flesh. Her disfigurement bears mute witness to the brutal abduction, rape and nine-month captivity she endured at the hands of Islamic kidnappers. As part of their program to transform Mary into a Muslim, her captors poured sulfuric acid on her wrist to remove the tattooed cross she wore as a statement of her faith.

Mary grew up among Egypt's six million Coptic Christians, a minority community that faces increasing mistreatment from Islamic zealots. At eighteen years of age, she was visiting a friend's home when she was kidnapped by a group of radicals from the "Gamat Islamiya."

After they raped her, Mary's captors moved her from one suburban hideout to another. Along with sexual abuse, she was required to fast, pray, and memorize portions of the Qur'an.

At first, Mary tried to refuse to wear the traditional Islamic veil. "They warned me that if I removed it they would throw acid on my face," she later told reporters. Eventually, unable to resist her captors' demands, she signed official papers of conversion to Islam.

While Mary was held hostage, her father went to the Cairo police. They told him to forget Mary—she was in the safe hands of Islam. In fact, the distraught man was ordered to sign a pledge that he would cease his search for his daughter. Along with other family members, he was warned that if any of them interfered with Mary and she was harmed, they would be held responsible.

Fortunately, Mary escaped. She was given assistance by a clandestine group called "Servants of the Cross," who sheltered her. Although conversion to Christianity from Islam is considered apostasy in Egypt, and Shari'a law calls for a death sentence, the Servants aided her as she reconverted to Christianity. In Egyptian society, rape victims are often held responsible for their plight, and are sometimes killed. With this in mind, the organization also helped Mary find a Christian husband.

Servants of the Cross took Mary to a tattooist, who reapplied the cross to her wrist, just above the disfiguring scar. One of the organization's representatives explained, "I supervise between thirty and thirty-five reconversions every month. In all Egypt there are between seven thousand and ten thousand cases of forced conversion to Islam. It is our duty to save them."[1]

ISLAM: FROM TOLERATION TO TERROR

Islam is a diverse religion. It spans many continents, takes on a variety of political forms, and at times demonstrates great toleration for other faiths. Even the strict Islamic Shari'a law, dreaded in the West because of its provisions for amputations, beheadings, and other brutalities, has its own strengths. It provides, for example, protection of privacy.

Despite its apparent inflexibility, Shari'a law is still being scrutinized and reevaluated by thoughtful Muslim scholars. Acknowledged twentieth-century leaders such as India's Muhammad Iqba and Muhummad Abduh, called for reconstruction of Shari'a law on the basis of the Qur'an. Current intellectuals like the Shi'ite Abdulaziz Sachedina maintain that earlier Islamic teachings are far more open than more recent legalism.[2]

Islam is as varied as it is enigmatic. And before judging it too harshly, westerners—especially western Christians—should remember their own history. For generations, Islam provided shelter for beleaguered Christians and Jews. Even in the eighth century, at the height of Islamic expansion, Jews and Montanist Christians fled to Arab lands to escape persecution by the Orthodox Byzantine Emperor.

When Jews were expelled from Spain by the Catholic church at the end of the fifteenth century after having lived through centuries of Islamic rule, many took refuge in Turkey. During the sixteenth century European wars of religion, the Calvinists of Hungary and Transylvania preferred the rule of the Turks to that of the Catholic Hapsburgs.

There are many other examples of Islamic tolerance, and we will refer to some of these in a subsequent chapter. For now, suffice it to say that it would be a great error simply to equate all of Islam with the cruel injustices we will document in the following pages.

Nevertheless, the situations we are about to describe are real. And these circumstances exist not simply despite Islam. Unfortunately, they are expressions of a particular and increasingly powerful form of militant Islam.[3]

Militant Muslims believe that the problems in their society have been caused by departure from the strict tenets of Islam, and that this trend can only be countered by a return to Islam in its purity. This is especially prominent in the Shi'a branches of Islam. But even a cursory look at Saudi Arabia and Egypt reveals that some Sunnis have adopted a similar point of view.[4]

In this chapter, we will focus on the plight of Christians in five Islamic countries—Sudan, Iran, Saudi Arabia, Pakistan, and Egypt. Each of these countries has a singular government, a distinctive attitude toward Islamic militancy, and a unique interpretation and enactment of Islamic laws. But in all of them, Shari'a laws are used to invoke various degrees of discrimination, repression, and outright persecution against Christians and other religious minorities. No place on earth illustrates the brutal results more dramatically than the war torn nation of Sudan.

Sudan—Islamic Enslavement

In the southern Sudan, the colorful marketplace at Manyiel bustles with activity under a scorching African sun. Local Dinka people gather around

Arab stalls, chattering and bargaining for clothing, salt, and other small necessities. The pleasant little town of Manyiel rests on the banks of the river Lol, and it is here that "Neema" tells her story.

Her brown eyes look older than her almost-twenty years, and Neema seems remarkably composed as she recounts the incident in 1988 when Moslem invaders from the north swept through her Christian village and carried her off into slavery. She speaks quietly, almost in a whisper, pausing while the interpreter repeats her account in English. "When the Arab militia came, they kidnapped many people, killing anyone who resisted. They concentrated mainly on women and children."

Neema gently calms the small boy who leans against her side, tugging at her garments, trying to catch her attention.

The westerner asks, "Did you try to escape?"

Neema nods, "Oh yes. But I was badly beaten. Finally I surrendered, and I was thrown across the back of a horse and taken away."

"Where did they take you?"

"To the north. I was sold to a man who put me to work as a servant, helping his wife pound dura and collect firewood. They gave me a Moslem name and forced me to take part in their Moslem rituals, even though I am a Christian. When I refused, I was harshly beaten. And when my master's wife went to market, or left the home for any reason, he. . ." she lowers her eyes.

Neema motions toward the child. "When my master's wife found that I was pregnant with his child, she became enraged, chased me out of the house, and I was able to escape."

"How did you get back here?"

"Slave traders helped me. They brought me back and sold me to my family for five cows. My people were glad to have me back, but now I cannot marry. I have been with a man, and I have a child. I am no longer free to marry a husband."[5]

A HAVEN FOR TERRORISTS

In a world with more than enough cruelty, Sudan is probably the worst practitioner of religious persecution and the worst violator of human rights.

The Economist describes the country as "Orwellian."[6] Its many crimes cry out for attention and justice.

Certainly Sudan, unlike many other vicious human-rights violators, finds its way onto the front pages of the world's newspapers. But the reasons for this notoriety are not usually its campaign of terror carried out against large segments of its own population. Sudan gets press attention because, along with Iran, it is one of the world's centers for the sponsorship of terrorism. Islamic terrorists train outside of Khartoum, and the present government provides money and material for militant groups throughout the world.

There are clear indications that Sudan was involved in the attempt to assassinate Egyptian President Hosni Mubarak in 1995. Led by the United States, the UN Security Council has condemned Sudan and demanded the extradition of those suspected of being involved in the assassination attempt. The Sudanese government has reacted with its usual hostility, so in February of 1996 the United States warned its citizens to leave the country and withdrew its embassy staff. U.S. Ambassador Timothy Carney left on February 7.

When Louis Farrakhan, the head of the U.S.-based "Nation of Islam," made his tour of Islamic countries, he visited some of the most savage governments on the face of the earth. He arrived in Sudan's capital, Khartoum, expressing his support for the regime and denouncing its critics. When Farrakhan returned home, he met a wave of criticism and calls for congressional inquiries into his activities. But, once again, attention was focused on his association with the regimes such as Libya and Iran which sponsor terrorism. Ironically, the fact that he kowtowed to regimes which currently practice genocide and the enslavement of black Africans was virtually overlooked, except in the African-American press.[7]

WAR WITHOUT END

Since independence in 1956, Sudan—the largest country in Africa—has endured a seemingly endless civil war. The largely Arab and Muslim north has tried to impose its will on the primarily black Christian and animist south. Since 1989, the war has reached unparalleled heights of ferocity. While the nominal head of government is Omar al Bashir, the real power in the regime is Hassan Turabi, the leader of the National Islamic Front. The western-educated Turabi is leading a program of Islamization through genocide.

The word *genocide* is a harsh one, thrown around too frequently and too cheaply. In the case of Sudan, however, it is simply a factual description. The United Nations defines *genocide* as "attempting to destroy a group by killing its members, causing serious bodily harm, subjecting it to conditions which cause its physical destruction, preventing births, and forcibly transferring children." This is a systematic description of the current situation in southern and eastern Sudan.

The Sudanese war, like all wars, is complex. It is a civil war for control of the southern part of the country. It has racial elements, in that the largely Arab north is waging war on and practicing slavery on the black African southern population. The war also involves conflict between groups which share the same religion. In the Nuba region the government burns down mosques as well as churches, since the type of Islam practiced by the Nuba is far more open than that of the Khartoum regime.[8]

ISLAM'S RELENTLESS CRUSADE

Despite these qualifications, the situation in Sudan can correctly be called a situation of religious persecution. The main terror is directed against the largely black, Christian population. Although there have been protests, even from some of its Muslim population, the government of Sudan has instituted Islamic Shari'a law. This is one of the principle reasons for the alienation of the South from the North.[9]

Besides seeking to subjugate the South, the Khartoum government also has a policy of destroying any non-Islamic religious expression. *Jihad*—holy war—is preached in mosques, universities, schools, and on TV and radio. Led by Turabi, a fervent Islamicist, the government is actively pursuing a policy of Islamicizing the entire country and eradicating any non-Islamic expressions and non-Islamic people.

The government restricts the activities of outside aid groups so that it can control the supply of food to groups of refugees who have been dumped in the desert. Non-Muslims are given the choice of converting to Islam or being denied food, clothing, and shelter. The unconverted are left to die, naked in the blazing sun.

Imagine the situation of a mother who faces not only her own death, but the prospect of watching her children starve before her eyes unless she renounces her faith. And there is no turning back. Sudan applies the death penalty to anyone who tries to convert away from Islam. In other cases, even less choice is given. Many of those who are not Muslims, especially the men, are simply massacred.

The children are the most vulnerable. Some are taken to the camps of the Sudanese militia where they are trained in Turabi's form of Islam. Since they are uprooted from family and tribe, they can be easily brainwashed to become fervent warriors for the Islamic cause.

Others, especially women and children, are enslaved, either for labor or sex, or both. As the story of Neema illustrates, slave traders now traverse the southern part of the country, doing a thriving business. Dr. Kevin Vigilante reports that in 1995, it was possible to buy a human being for as little as fifteen dollars.[10] Baroness Cox, deputy speaker of the British House of Lords, reports that on an October 1995 visit to the war areas in the South, she was told of traders bringing slaves back into the southern areas so they could get better prices by offering to sell the children back to their parents. Slaves had been branded for identification, and some have had their Achilles tendons cut so they cannot run away.[11] The going rate is five head of cattle per child, sometimes ten for a boy.[12]

DEATH IN THE NUBA MOUNTAINS

No place in Sudan has seen more devastation than the Nuba Mountains in south-central Sudan. These mountains, which have had a Christian population since the sixth century, are littered with mass graves, with the remains of destroyed villages, and with camps where women and children are kept. Nuba women are systematically raped by Arab soldiers in order to produce non-Nuba offspring. There have been reports, including from Catholic bishops, of crucifixions of Christians by the army.[13] Half-a-million Nuba have been killed in the last ten years, and perhaps two million more forced into camps. This amounts to more than half of the previous population.

TURNING A BLIND EYE

Gaspar Biro, the UN special rapporteur on Sudan, has published five public reports since he began his work in April 1993. There have been four resolutions by the UN Commission on Human Rights, as well as two resolutions by the UN General Assembly, which passed with very high majorities.

The result is still only words on pieces of paper. Biro himself was threatened by the Sudanese government. They claimed he was blaspheming against Islam by complaining that the imposition of Shari'a law violated the international human-rights standards which Sudan itself had signed.

Biro was described in Khartoum newspapers as "worse than Rushdie," and his report described as "satanic." Nevertheless, he has diligently continued his work. Sadly, it remains a subject that most of the world—especially North America—continues to ignore.

> The abuses are "past proving. . . . We are beyond that stage. . . . We are reporting on facts because these are facts. The abuse covers the whole range of human-rights violations. . . . We can find abuse on any human-rights violation from the first to the last page of any United Nations instrument."[14]
>
> —Gaspar Biro, March 1996 testimony to the U.S. Congressional Human Rights Caucus

Meanwhile, the architect of these crimes, Hassan Turabi, has continued to visit western countries, and even to speak at "interreligious dialogues" with church representatives. And Louis Farrakhan attempts to hide Sudan's atrocities and to lie about the perpetrators.

The facts are these: More than half the population of southern Sudan—eight million—is now in camps. The Sudanese death toll in the last ten years is estimated at anywhere from one-and-a-half to three million. The Khartoum government, intent on Islamization, is subjecting innocent women, men, girls, and boys to:

- Islamization campaigns in schools
- Denial of basic freedoms of press, speech, and association
- Forced conversion to Islam
- Requiring Islamization for access to food
- Forced population relocation
- Systematic starvation
- Rape
- Kidnapping of children
- Enslavement
- Widespread torture
- Abandoning people in the desert without food or water

The only apt comparison to the circumstances in Sudan is the world's turning aside from Hitler's treatment of the Jews. Unless public opinion changes and steps are taken, the end result in Sudan will be hauntingly similar.

Iran—Heart and Soul of Islam

The tiny Iranian evangelical community was saddened but not surprised. The news spread quickly, house to house, Christian to Christian. "Bishop" Haik Hovsepian-Mehr, the leader of the Assemblies of God, had been brutally killed.

Because of his status in the community, the story soon reached the West. The London Times *reported, "Bishop Haik walked always in the shadow of* violent death because of his religion, but probably that fact, together with his succor of Dibaj, was enough: At least we can safely say that he was tortured and murdered because he was a Christian and for the support he was always ready to give to his brother and sister in Christ.[15]

The "Dibaj" mentioned in the Times article was beloved Iranian pastor Mehdi Dibaj. Iran's Christians had long been concerned about Dibaj, who had been imprisoned for a decade on charges of apostasy, and had been sentenced to death by execution no less than four times. Mehdi Dibaj's broad, warm-hearted smile had never left the memory of his parishioners. They worried about him. Their hearts went out to his family. They pleaded with heaven on his behalf.

Bishop Haik had led an international campaign to save Dibaj's life. And he had succeeded—on January 16, 1994, Mehdi Dibaj was unexpectedly released. He walked from prison into the welcoming embrace of Tehran's rejoicing Christians.

Unfortunately, the long-awaited celebration was short-lived. Three days after Dibaj's release, Bishop Haik dropped out of sight. A few more days and his murder was announced by the authorities. His family was never permitted to see his remains, but a photo of his corpse was identified by his son.

On June 24, 1994, Medhi Dibaj was on his way to his daughter's birthday party in suburban Tehran. He disappeared.

Presbyterian minister Tateos Michaellian succeeded Bishop Haik as the head of the Iranian Protestant Council. On June 29, 1994, he also vanished.

A sense of dread gripped the Iranian Christian community. They braced themselves for the inevitable news. In less than a week, it came.

On July 2, Bishop Michaellian's body was found with several gunshot wounds to the head.

On July 5, the body of Mehdi Dibaj was found in a Tehran park.

During his ten-year imprisonment, Dibaj wrote to his son, "I have always envied those Christians who all through the church history were martyred for Christ Jesus our Lord. What a privilege to live for our Lord and to die for Him as well."

Iran's heartbroken Christian community found only a modicum of solace in Mehdi Dibaj's prescient words.[16]

"BESIEGED AND OPPRESSED BY CHRISTIANITY . . ."

Country after country can be cited as a participant in the advancing Jihad, in which militant Islam surges across the continents, intending to overflow all other religions. But near its heart is the Islamic Republic of Iran, where the 1979 revolution culminated in the overthrow of the Shah, and brought an Islamic Holy War into full public awareness. That war continues to escalate and, despite the death of the fiery Ayatollah Khomeini and western searches for Iranian "moderates," the call to arms still resounds from Iran.

A report by the U.S. House of Representatives' Task Force on Terrorism and Unconventional Warfare stated:

> In Tehran, President Hashemi-Rafsanjani delivered a sermon on January 7, 1994 [two weeks before Bishop Haik's death] in which he, in essence, predicted a marked escalation in the Islamists' Holy War. . . .
>
> [Rafsanjani went on to explain that] there is no longer validity to other religion, and that therefore all people should have adopted Islam long ago. However, the opposite is happening. The West, in a last desperate attempt to prevent the spread of Islam and its supplanting of Christianity, is trying to suppress Islam. These attempts are exactly identical to the futile attempt of the Christian world to block the surge of Islam:
>
> At present, history is witnessing the repeat of events that unfolded at the advent of Islam. The plight that the Islamic world faces today is the same as the one that the Prophet had to endure during the early days of Islam. A glance at the conditions of Muslims in various parts of the world, such as Afghanistan, Azerbaijan, Kasmir, Bosnia, and Palestine, and the silence of the West toward their plight, testifies to this reality.
>
> "Therefore," Hashemei-Rafsanjani declared, "Iran and the entire Muslim world must adopt 'the Prophet. . . . and Jihad as a model.' The Iranian leader concluded with the observation that just as the first Muslim community in Arabia, small and fragile, was ultimately able to surge and conquer the Christian world of the day, so will the contemporary Muslim world, currently once more besieged and suppressed by Christianity, ultimately and inevitably triumph over its oppressors."[17]

It was against that ominous backdrop that the three tragic and brutal murders of Protestant clergymen took place in 1994. A UN human-rights body censured the Iranian government for rights violations. The UN Sub-Commission on Prevention of Discrimination and Protection of Minorities charged Iran with "increasing intolerance toward Christians, including the recent murders of Christian religious ministers."[18] Undaunted by such admonishments, Iranian authorities have denied any involvement in the killings.

PERSECUTION, REPRESSION, AND DISCRIMINATION

The persecution of Christians in Sudan is numerically worse than that in Iran, simply because there are far more Christians there to be persecuted. But countries like Iran practice continuous persecution, repression, and discrimination against Christians, every bit as intense as that in Sudan.

Iran manages to get into the news more than does Sudan, largely because of its nuclear ambitions and its support of terrorism. Much attention has been paid to the fervently Islamic nature of the country. The word *ayatollah* has entered the western vocabulary as a synonym for religious extremism. The introduction of Shari'a law, especially Hudud law, the "criminal code" section of Shari'a with its provision for flogging or amputation, has attracted the attention of western media.

Iran's treatment of its religious minorities makes the news less often. Some attention has been given to the terrible situation of the Bah'ai, who are not regarded by Islamicists as another religion, but as heretical Muslims, and are therefore subjected to the harshest penalties of apostasy. The situation of Iran's Christians does not usually attract much concern. Now and then, however, a story finds its way into the West, even though the individuals involved must remain anonymous.

IRAN'S RELIGIOUS APARTHEID

A glance at the Iranian Constitution reveals that some of Iran's religious minorities—Christian, Jewish, and Zoroastrian—are in theory legally protected. They are even provided with representation in the Parliament, sworn in on their own holy books.[19] But the realities of life in Iran are different. They are described by one Christian human-rights group as nothing short of "religious apartheid."[20] This apartheid manifests itself in blatant inequities.

Religious minorities cannot handle food which is to be eaten by Muslims. Therefore, stores and restaurants owned by Christians or others must post a sign stating "Religious Minority" shop. And Muslim-owned shops cannot hire non-Muslims.

In the military, Christians are not to be saluted by Muslims, and they are therefore not promoted to levels of authority which require such salutes. Furthermore, no non-Muslim is privy to confidential information. The government does not employ non-Muslims, nor does any state-owned company.

To make matters worse, the Iranian Republic believes that anything which diverts energies away from "the Revolution" is counter-revolutionary, and anyone accused of being counter-revolutionary is subject to the death penalty. As far as evangelical Christian churches are concerned, M. Jarad Zarif, an Iranian deputy foreign minister, has stated, "We consider them to be a political organization."[21] This kind of reasoning amounts to nothing short of a *de facto* death sentence on Iran's Christians.

ONE CHRISTIAN FAMILY'S ORDEAL

Because Iran's Shari'a law considers conversion to Christianity a capital crime, when "Reza Houkas" became a Christian, Islamic authorities issued a summons for his arrest and he quickly fled into hiding. After several attempts to locate him, the Revolutionary Guards paid a late-night visit to his wife and three children.

They entered the Houkas house, and physically attacked his family. During a violent interrogation, they demanded that the wife and children reveal his location. When they were unable to do so, the militants beat the family so severely that every one of them was left bloodied and unconscious.

As the Guards left, they broke all the windows in the house. They threw the family's belongings into the streets while shouting, "These people are blasphemers!" After looting the Houkas' possessions, they set the family car on fire.

Subsequently, the Houkas children were expelled from school and the parents were threatened with death. Ultimately, the Houkas family fled Iran in February 1995.[22]

The Shi'a Muslims who dominate the Iranian Republic are clearly ruthless to Christians. In other Islamic nations such as Saudi Arabia, Sunni Muslims, who have a less militant reputation in the West, control the government. Saudi is a favorite with western powers. However, Christians—particularly Third-World Christians—face grave dangers in the rigidly Islamic Kingdom of Saudi Arabia.

Saudi Arabia—100 Percent Islamic

Oswaldo Magdangal pastored a small Christian group in Riyadh, Saudi Arabia. In 1992, when he was arrested for involvement in an "illegal fellowship," he was informed by the Metowah, the Saudi Religious Police, that he was the country's most notorious "public enemy."

A Philippine national, Magdangal was taken into custody and brutally beaten with a rattan stick. He was relentlessly pounded on the palms of his hands, on the soles of his feet, and across his back. His hands were so enormously swollen and discolored, they were almost unrecognizable.

Later, Saudi authorities informed Magdangal that he would be executed on Christmas Day. In fact, the pastor heard his own execution announced on BBC radio. Only after human-rights appeals from around the world poured into Saudi Arabia was the besieged pastor released from prison and deported.[23]

It wasn't long before a similar story appeared in Manila's Today *daily newspaper. Few Philippine Christians were surprised to learn that Saudi Arabian authorities had once again arrested believers for participating in Christian worship.*

This report said, "Joel Cunanan was caught while performing prayer. . . . with an undetermined number of people in their villa in the Malaz area in the Saudi capital. . . ."

Cunanan was one of eight Philippine Baptists arrested in Riyadh in August 1995 at a private residence where fifty Christians met to worship. Of the eight arrested, four were released after three months of captivity. The fate of the others remains unclear. In the incident, Saudi police authorities also confiscated books, pamphlets, and other materials of a religious nature at the home.

During his imprisonment, Cununan continued to express his Christian beliefs with other inmates. This led to his transfer into solitary confinement. A subsequent story in Today *quoted Cunanan as saying, "I am not sorry for what happened to me, because I feel the joy and peace of one who serves the Lord."*[24]

THE PLIGHT OF EXPATRIATE CHRISTIANS

The Saudi restriction on the expression of any religion besides Islam means, quite simply, that Christian worship is banned. It is illegal to wear a cross or to utter a Christian prayer. Christians cannot even worship privately in their own homes. Worship is allowed occasionally on foreign company sites or in embassies or consulates, but even this is not secure. Foreigners from relatively powerful countries such as the United States or Britain are often left alone to pray, provided they remain very quiet about it. Meanwhile, expatriates from less influential countries such as India, Egypt, Korea, and the Philippines bear the brunt of the restrictions.

Amnesty International has documented some 350 cases from 1992–1996 of Christian expatriates being arrested by the Mutowah for taking part in private worship services.[25] But this is only the tip of the iceberg. Philippinos and Koreans, as well as Indian and Egyptian Christians, may face lengthy imprisonment without trial. They are often subjected to torture. Third-World workers fear reprisals against themselves, or against those arrested, or against their families. For this reason, the vast majority of incidents regarding Christian persecution in Saudi Arabia go unreported.

And the worst may be yet to come. In a late 1995 directive from the Saudi minister of the interior, endorsed by the Saudi Chamber of Commerce in January 1996, all businesses in the kingdom are to "reach the non-Muslim workers as their sponsors into Islam," ensuring that "all key personnel, supervisors, and managers" are Muslim. As Nina Shea of Freedom House points out, "Not only are foreign Christians barred from worshiping according to their conscience, but it appears they will now be coerced to convert to Islam."[26]

DISREGARD FOR HUMAN RIGHTS

Because of their obdurate enforcement of Shari'a law, the Saudi government pressured the allies in Operation Desert Storm about religious observances. They demanded that Christian and Jewish soldiers not be allowed to wear any symbols of their faith when they were in service in Saudi Arabia. This was mandated, even though the troops were there to defend Saudis from invasion by Iraq. Meanwhile, religious repression has increased since the Gulf War.

The severity of Shari'a law punishments has drawn comment from the West. But its legal procedures can be equally terrifying. The Saudi judicial system provides little chance of a reasonable defense against accusations, since defendants have no right to be represented by lawyers. Torture is widespread. Confessions obtained under torture can be accepted by courts as evidence—sometimes the sole evidence—for a conviction.

Saudi Arabian laws are draconian, and the government has refused to agree to or adhere to international human-rights standards. The suppression of women in Saudi Arabia occasionally attracts the attention of the media, but typically, repression of religious minorities is usually unnoticed. Ironically, the heaviest religious oppression falls on the desert kingdom's Shi'a minority in the eastern part of the country (the dominant form of Islam in Saudi Arabia is the strict "Wahabist" form of Sunni Islam). The Shi'a are regarded as a particular threat because they deviate from several tenets of the Sunni regime. They are also viewed as possible allies of Iran in its attempts to overthrow the government.

Western response to oil-rich Saudi Arabia's view of non-Islamic activities is often spineless. For example, the Saudi government demanded that a group of Christians who met to worship in the American Consulate

General in Jiddah be disbanded. At the same time, the Saudis wished to have a nightclub on the embassy grounds closed since it served liquor and held dances. According to reports, the officials at the consulate compromised. In order to keep the nightclub open, they closed the worship services.

Tim Hunter, who served at the U.S. Consulate 1993–1994, remarks, "They made the decision that the needs of American alcoholics were more important than the needs of American Christians." Since the country is officially dry, alcohol sales are tremendously profitable and officials can get up to fifty dollars for a quart of whiskey.[27]

CHRISTIANS—UNDER A DEATH SENTENCE

As harsh as life can be for expatriate Christians, the worst adversity falls upon Saudi nationals who are Christians. Saudi Arabia is understood to be exclusively Islamic. A Christian Saudi citizen is assumed to be apostate from Islam, and therefore is automatically subject to death. In fact, according to the government, "Saudi Christians" is an oxymoron: To be a Saudi is to be a Muslim, with no exceptions. It is hard to imagine a more repressive attack on religious freedom than to face a legally-sanctioned sentence of death simply for believing a non-approved religion. One close contender, however, is Pakistan's blasphemy law.

PAKISTAN—ISLAM AND BLASPHEMY

Fourteen-year-old Salamat Masih looks innocent enough. He has wide-set brown eyes, and his boyish expression is topped by an unruly shock of straight black hair. But Salamat has not spent the past three years enjoying the normal adventures of Pakistani boyhood. He has, instead, been fighting for his life.

After a quarrel over some pigeons, an eight-year-old Moslem boy from Salamat's village reported that he had seen Salamat "writing on the Mosque walls." This was clearly untrue—Salamat Masih was illiterate. However, the next day, a group of men arrived at Salamat's Christian home, carried him off to the Mosque, and beat him there until he confessed to acts of blasphemy. He, along with two adult male Christians, was charged with insulting the Prophet of God by writing anti-Islamic graffiti.

Signs suddenly appeared in the village, "Anyone who blasphemes against the Prophet should be hanged in public." Death by hanging was demanded (and legal) for all three of the accused. While the trio was being transported to court, a gunman opened fire on them, killing one of them, a poor Catholic farmer named Manzoor Masih (no relation to Salamat) and injuring Salamat and his fellow-prisoner. The gunman turned out to be the same Imam who had originally brought the charges against the Christian threesome. Nearly two years after the original "arrest," Salamat and the other surviving suspect were, in fact, sentenced to death for blasphemy against the Prophet.

By that time Salamat's story had been reported in the West. There was such an international outcry that the sentence was overturned. The boy, along with the other suspect, fled the country, convinced they would be murdered. Their families remain in hiding. Salamat has now received asylum in the West. But Islamic blasphemy laws with capital consequences remain in place in Pakistan, often enforced against Christians.[28]

PAKISTAN'S BLASPHEMY LAW

Although Salamat's experience might seem to prove otherwise, the Pakistani government itself is not the direct enemy of Christians. However, since the nation became more Islamic under General Zia-ul-Haq in the 1980s, increasingly militant Islamic forces are launching direct violent attacks on Christians. These forces are also pitted against other Islamic groups, such as the Ahamadiya, who are regarded as heretical. These attacks vary from murders to mob violence to courtroom battles to systematic discrimination. The government is often unable to control these various groups, and is sometimes unwilling to risk alienating influential Islamic factions.

Since Pakistani Christian groups are politically weak, the government finds it easier to sacrifice them in any political conflict. Occasionally, the Pakistani civil courts have shown some courage in protecting Christians and other defendants, but many of those courts are corrupt and are gradually losing power to the Shari'a courts. As in any other country, the situation becomes complicated by ethnic and political tensions. However, the specifically religious component is now undeniable.

One of the chief current instruments of oppression is the blasphemy law (section 295-C, instituted in 1986) which provides the death penalty for one who blasphemes against the Prophet Mohammad or the Qu'ran. It states:

> Whoever by words, either spoken, or written, or by visible representation, or by any imputation, innuendo, or insinuation, directly or indirectly, defiles the sacred name of the Holy Prophet (peace by upon him) shall be punished with death, or imprisonment, and shall also be liable to fine.

In a statement to the U.S. Senate Committee on Foreign Relations, law professor David F. Forte reported, "The main effect of the blasphemy law is to unleash a reign of private terror against Christians and other religious minorities, frequently without the perpetrators being brought to justice." According to the State Department's Human Rights Report, "Christian groups rarely press charges against the perpetrators of such incidents and believe the authorities are unlikely to pursue such cases."[29]

CHRISTIANS AND "COMMUNAL CLEANSING"

The increasing use of the blasphemy law is creating terror among Pakistan's Christian population. The *Frontier Post* reported the Christians' fear that "communal cleansing" has started against them.[30] Police used tear gas to disperse more than one thousand five hundred Christians demonstrating peacefully against the law and the killing of Manzoor Masih.[31]

Beyond specific attacks, the situation of Pakistan's two to three million Christians is wretched.[32] The *Frontier Post* reports, "Terrorizing Christians with the blasphemy laws is only one aspect of this cleansing. This year there have been incidents of raids on Christian villages by communally-incited armed hordes who plundered their houses and dishonored their women. Kidnapping of young girls and their forcible conversion to Islam is another aspect."

The report goes on to say that the houses of one hundred poor Christian families were raided in twelve villages of Sial Aot (in Punjab) at the dawn of May 14. The raiders were urged on by a ringleader's cry, "This is the time for Jihad to eliminate Christianity from Pakistan!" The Christians were beaten up, with no succor from the nearby police station, and women were raped. Similar instances are common in other more remote Pakistan villages.[33]

As if the violence weren't enough, the construction of churches is rigidly controlled, with only some ten built since partition from India.[34] In fact, attempts have been made for thirty years to build a church in Islamabad with no success. One bishop of the Church of Pakistan described the situation in his diocese as follows:[35]

> Christians are denied jobs and housing. In that sense, they are persecuted all the time. Ninety percent of Christians are either unemployed or have the lowest jobs such as removing human excrement from the streets. They are not allowed to do anything else. About 8 percent are employed by the church and other Christian related ministries. Only 2 percent hold what could be called a "real job."
>
> The situation of converts is more difficult. If someone changes from Islam to Christianity, two sets of things happen to them. First, they are by law disinherited. Note that this is not just a family decision, which might be defensible, but is a legal requirement. The family itself is not given the choice.
>
> Second, they are hounded by anybody who knows about the situation and are usually driven from their jobs and their homes.

There are many weapons in the Pakistani Jihad's arsenal. But the weapon of choice for abusing Christians and other religious minorities is the blasphemy law. There has been tremendous international pressure for the law to be repealed. Yet, as a *Toronto Star* editorial observed, "[Former] Prime Minister Benazir Bhutto has stood by blaming previous governments for the law. She has failed to deliver on her pledge to amend its sweeping provisions, provide protection for the accused, and curb mob rule. She lacks the courage—and the religious credibility—to declare that the blasphemy law, besides being abused, may in fact be of questionable value.

"Islam is under no danger from any minority. Nor is the good name of the Prophet Muhammad, which is invoked with reverence and love by hundreds of millions of Muslims around the globe, around the clock every day. It's hardly in need of protection from those who inflict injustice in his name."[36]

EGYPT—ISLAMIC RIDICULE AND RAPE

When Shireen Farid Mikhail's father received the phone call from his daughter's Muslim kidnappers, he was stunned. "Your responsibilities as a father are over," a tough-sounding male voice informed him. "Your daughter has converted to Islam."

Shireen was only twelve years old. And her devastated father could well imagine what had happened to her.

The Egyptian police were unwilling to step into the situation and help the distressed father, so he hired an attorney and went to court. In a Manfalut magistrates' court, a heavily veiled female was brought forward. Not a trace of her face or body could be seen; her identity was impossible to determine. Shireen's father, who is a Copt, was ordered to leave the room.

The lawyer representing Shireen's father requested proof that the veiled figure was, in fact, Shireen. The judge dismissed his request and ordered the local authorities to register Shireen as a Muslim.

The London Observer, *referring to Shireen's case, reported, "A British human-rights group investigating complaints of conversion under duress says there is disturbing evidence that some Islamic extremists are using rape to force Christian girls to convert.*

"'Conversion offers marriage to a member of the Islamic group and security for the victim,' a spokesman for the Jubilee Campaign says. 'Returning to the family after the rape would result in potentially fatal consequences, as the victim is no longer a virgin. Alarmingly, there are reports that this practice is becoming more widespread.'"[37]

THE COPTS' HISTORIC STRUGGLE

The situation in Egypt is in some ways parallel to that in Pakistan. Egypt is often regarded as a relatively democratic country and an ally of the West.

It is also the home of the Middle East's largest Christian community, numbering some five to ten million people.[38]

Egypt was predominately Christian until the seventh century. Then, in the centuries following the Arab invasion, a Muslim majority gradually developed. Some Islamic rulers were relatively tolerant of the Copts—Egypt's Christians—but they still had distinctly subordinate status. They could be required to wear special apparel, required to ride on donkeys, not horses or camels, "in the manner of women"—that is, side-saddle—have smaller houses than Muslims, stand aside for Muslims, not raise their voices to Muslims, pay special taxes, and carry visible identification marks that they were Christians. Islamic law governed Egypt until the nineteenth century.[39]

Despite their repression, the Copts maintained a strong national identity and fought alongside their Muslim fellows, defending their nation against every kind of invasion, from Crusaders to the nineteenth-century French and British armies. After the reign of Mohammed Ali (1805–1841), the plight of the Copts gradually eased. Egypt underwent a process of secularization which reached its peak under Nasser in the 1960s.

Then, during Anwar Sadat's presidency, there was a gradual process of Islamization, a process which has continued under the current President Hosni Mubarak. Some of this reflects a genuine Islamic sentiment in the government, but a large part is intended to mollify the Muslim Brotherhood. This large association of Muslims, founded in 1928, is determined that Egypt should become an explicit Islamic state which follows Islamic law. It claims that it does not itself engage in or encourage violence, but many of the more militant groups such as Shabab Mohammed, al-Takfir wa'l-Hijra, and al-Gamaat al-Islamia are splinters from the Brotherhood. They wreak suffering on the Copts and other Christians.

SHARI'A AND BLOODSHED

In 1980, the Egyptian National Assembly declared Islam "as the 'religion of state' and Shari'a as the principle source of legislation." Mubarak has resisted the complete introduction of Shari'a, but it continues to exert more influence. Not surprisingly, one consequence of these shifts has been the increased persecution of Christians. Converts to Christianity suffer particularly terrible abuse. They face death at the hands of militants and torture at the hands of the police.

Particularly in upper (southern) Egypt, militant Islamic groups are targeting Christians for murder, assault, theft, and destruction of property. The local police have stood by, sometimes out of fear and sometimes out of sympathy with the action.

One terrible incident occurred in May 1992, when thirteen Christians living in Daryut were massacred. Other atrocities continue to this day, many of them unreported. The Cairo-based Center for Human Rights/ Legal Aid says that twelve Copts were killed in 1994, nine in 1993.[40] On February 27, 1996, a mob of some ten thousand Muslim youths attacked Christian homes in Kafr, Damyan, Ezbet Ghali, and Ezbek Malak in the Nile Delta. There is currently an extortion campaign underway in upper Egypt, whereby Islamic militants threaten Christians with violence unless they pay large sums of money. On July 31, 1996, two Christian villagers were murdered in Atledem by members of the Gama'a Islamiya, reportedly for refusing to pay "protection money."[41]

FROM ABSURD TO OUTRAGEOUS

Apart from direct violence, Christians are likely to suffer pervasive and systematic discrimination. Chris George, executive director of Human Rights Watch/Middle East, says, "The state has sent a clear message that the Copts can be discriminated against. . . . they are treated as second-class citizens."[42]

In schools, some Christian girls are forced to wear the veil, and Christian students are required to memorize the Qur'an. No matter how excellent their grades, they find difficulty in getting into university and are excluded from positions as professors. Most Egyptian Christians are desperately poor, even more so than the average Egyptian. They are employed in menial positions such as street sweeping, or subsistence farming.[43]

Despite the fact that former UN Secretary General Boutras Boutras Ghali is a Copt and managed in earlier years to rise to high position in Egypt, his situation is markedly unusual. Rigaat Said, a prominent Muslim advocate of human rights, argues that discrimination is the culmination of an "intentional policy of the government in its formal dealings with the Copts, in eliminating them from high posts in the government, in the public sector, as governors, leaders of the army and police, as ambassadors, as ministers, and so on. It has also appeared in education, at the grassroots level, in mass media, in television, and in radio."[44]

Sometimes the anti-Christian discrimination borders on the absurd. Under an 1856 statute, enacted when the Ottoman Empire controlled Egypt, no church buildings can be built or repaired without the Egyptian president's "express permission." No such permission has been granted since Mubarak came to power in 1982.

This means that churches cannot repair a roof, a window, or a toilet without the president's permission. And they face penalties if they try to do so. In 1992, one church in upper Egypt, after trying without success to obtain permission for a year, repaired its toilet. As a result they were fined heavily, and the replacement toilet was demolished by the authorities.[45]

Despite this ongoing persecution, Christians in Egypt do not receive the media focus and support given to other religious minorities. For example, on April 18, 1996, seven tourists were gunned down outside the Europa Hotel on the road to the pyramids. There were repeated questions in the press about whether or not Islamic militants were renewing their attacks on tourists. Other reports suggested that the victims may have been mistaken for Israelis, who often use that same hotel.

Little attention was paid to the fact that the tourists were Christian pilgrims from Greece. In a country where Christians are under daily assault, shouldn't observers have considered the possibility that Christians also are possible objects of assassination?[46] The reality is that, in numerous places throughout the Moslem world, the lives of women and men, girls and boys are at risk every day, specifically because of their commitment to the Christian faith.

THE WORDS OF THE PROPHET

Discrimination against Christians in Sudan, Iran, Saudi Arabia, Pakistan, and Egypt is commonplace. And, in the next chapter, we will discover even more complex patterns of oppression within Islam. Persecution of Christians is rampant. Bloodshed is, lamentably, unexceptional.

All too often, westerners—even devout western Christians—remain oblivious to tragedies that embrace their sisters and brothers half-a-world away. And when confronted with the magnitude of such widespread injustice, outrage is often mediated by bewilderment and an overwhelming sense of powerlessness.

Once we have been made aware of the reality, we ponder what might be appropriate action. In later chapters, we will explore a number of possible responses. In the meantime, when faced with Islamic persecution, a glimmer of hope can be drawn from an unexpected source. It is noteworthy that the Prophet Muhammad himself promised tolerance and protection, which he specifically bestowed upon Christians:

> The Messenger of God (God bless and preserve him) wrote to the bishop of B. al-Harith b. Ka'b and the bishops of Nairan and their priests and those who followed them and their monks, that for all their churches, services, and monastic practices, few or many, they had the protection (jiwar) of God and His Messenger. No bishop will be moved from his episcopate, no monk from his monastic state, no priest from his priesthood. There will be no alteration of any right or authority or circumstances, so long as they are loyal and perform their obligations well, they not being burdened by wrong suffered and not doing wrong.[47]

CHAPTER THREE

Islam: Fear, Friction, and Fragmentation

They attacked the village and started cutting the villagers into pieces. I myself heard the screams of a man who was having his head cut off by a saw. Then we took our children and ran away. The next day we returned to the village. The scene was atrocious. People were cut into pieces, their eyes were gouged out, their ears were cut off. We then saw the man whom I had previously seen being decapitated by a saw. The saw was lying next to him and all the blood had flowed out of the body. Another man—our uncle—was tied to the back of a tank and was dragged five hundred meters away. After that we fled to Shaumyan. Ten days later the Azeri-Turks did the same things. After that I took the children and fled. We walked for forty miles. We arrived thirsty and hungry and our clothes in tatters. We couldn't take anything with us. I've seen all these atrocities with my own eyes.

—Mrs. Shoushanik, a young Armenian mother from the north of Nagorno Karabakh, describing her experience during the Azeri-Turk offensive in 1992.[1]

ISLAM'S SECOND-CLASS CITIZENS

The last chapter described five of the worst cases of the persecution of Christians in Islamic settings. But there are many other Muslim countries also fraught with suffering, terror, and discrimination. Before considering specific cases, we need to look at some of the reasons *why* the situation of Christians and other religious minorities is so often so poor in the contemporary Islamic world.[2] There are three significant factors:

- The long-standing second-class status of religious minorities in Muslim settings.
- The deadly treatment of "apostasy" in Islam.
- The growth in recent decades of militant Islam.

Historically, other religions of the book, Christians and Jews (in Iran one might add Zorastrians), were allowed to continue their religious practices within Islam provided they accepted *dhimmi* status—a protected position that was also distinctly second-class.[3]

Living as second-class citizens can certainly be better for minorities than death or exile. In fact, as we noted earlier, it was often a better status for Christians and Jews than the treatment they got from Christians in Europe. But it can in no way be understood as genuine religious freedom. Over the centuries, *dhimmis* were given less legal rights, and their testimony was worth only half that of a Muslim. They had to pay additional taxes, were excluded from important offices, and were often forbidden to wear aristocratic clothing or ride horses or camels, since these were regarded as noble animals. They could be forced to stand aside for all Muslims. In the western world, especially since the Reformation, religious freedom has made great strides. But within Islam, the subordinate status of non-Muslims has continued. The persistence of *dhimmi*-type toleration in the modern world is at variance with all international human-rights standards.[4] Bernard Lewis, a leading authority on the Islamic world, says that in Islam, "discrimination was always there, permanent, and indeed necessary, inherent in the system and institutionalized in law and practice."[5]

THE RISK OF APOSTASY

Even *dhimmi* status can be denied to anyone who chooses to *leave* Islam. Leaving Islam—better known as apostasy—is simply forbidden. Even Muslims who might be open on many other matters draw the line here. This restriction is both long-standing and widespread within the Islamic world. It is no recent trend.[6]

So, while people may be free not *to be* Muslims, even if this means second-class status, if they are *already* Muslims by birth, or if they *become* Muslims, then there is no option, no turning back. Apostates can be forcibly divorced, denied any contact with their children, and disinherited. This applies not only to people who adopt another religion, but to people believed to have heretical views. The Bah'ai in Iran and the Ahmaddiyas in Pakistan suffer severe repression because they are regarded as heretical and therefore apostate.

One instance which received publicity in 1995 was the case of Dr. Nasr Abu Zeid, a professor of Islamic Studies and Linguistics at Cairo University. Because of some of his views, a civil appeals court declared him an apostate and he was ordered separated from his wife, regardless of his and her views on the matter.[7]

People who want to leave Islam can face death. In some situations, if they refuse to return to the fold, they may be killed—by anyone—with impunity. This is true in Afghanistan and many Persian Gulf states. In Mauritania, the Comorros Islands, and Qatar, this is not only a threat from Muslim vigilantes, but part of the legal code itself. Let us be clear about this: In several Islamic countries—in the 1990s—people who seek to change from Islam face legally sanctioned execution.

MILITANT ISLAM

A third factor complicating the lives of Christians and other religious minorities in the Muslim world is the growth in recent decades of militant Islam. This is familiar enough from the headlines in places like Iran, Algeria, Egypt, Pakistan, and Sudan. Radical Islamic groups often blame their societies' problems on "foreigners" in their midst, on the effects of western colonialism and other forms of westernization, and on the betrayal of Islam by their lukewarm Muslim leaders. Christians, even those Christians whose ancestors lived in the country for six hundred years before Islam even came into existence, are castigated as the offspring of "Crusaders."

It bears repeating that the Islamic world should never be reduced to Islamic radicalism. It also needs to be noted that, despite these problems, much traditional Islam was far more tolerant than present radicals. In this sense, the word *fundamentalist* is misleading if it implies some attempt to return to a pristine past. One of the striking things about the newer form of radicalism, especially in Shi'ite circles, is the *novelty* of some of its interpretations.[8] Several of Iran's radical "clergy," including the notorious "Judge Blood," Khalkhali, were not even allowed to run for seats in the Assembly of Experts because they failed the required examination in Shi'ite jurisprudence.[9]

Whatever the origins of fervent Islamicism, its affects on the Christian community are not in doubt: They are brutal. And, although many nominally Islamic governments are bitterly opposed to the radical Islamicist movements and repress them violently, all too often they cannot control violent attacks on other religions. In other cases, the government restricts Christians in order to appease the radicals at little cost to itself.

TYPES OF ISLAMIC COUNTRIES

Some of the countries described here, such as Algeria and Turkey, could well be included in the previous chapter. They are placed here not because the intensity of the suffering is any less. It is not. They simply have smaller Christian populations, and so the number of people persecuted is less. I will call these nations the *Fear Zones*—severely restrictive of their small Christian populations.

There is a second group of countries, such as Malaysia and Indonesia, with large Christian populations. Here the situation is complex: It cannot usually be described as persecution, yet nevertheless there is day-to-day discrimination either in the country as a whole or in specific regions. These, I will call the *Friction Zones*.[10]

There are other countries, such as Nigeria and the Philippines, which are not themselves Islamic, but where there is coexistence of large Muslim, Christian, and other populations. There is increasing community conflict, usually instigated by radical Muslim groups. Because of random violence, the day-to-day situation in these areas can often be more terrifying than in Islamic societies as such.[11] These countries can be called the *Fragmented Zones*.

THE FEAR ZONES

Word traveled quickly through the convent, and the reaction among the surviving sisters was disbelief and tears. Why would anyone murder Sister Bibiane and Sister Angele-Marie? Both were nuns of the order of Our Lady of the Apostles—peaceable women in their sixties who taught embroidery and sewing in a Catholic domestic center. The nuns loved Algeria, and their hearts were committed to the Algerian people.

Yet each had been brutally shot in the head while walking home from a September vespers service in Belcourt, a known stronghold of Islamic insurgents.

Joseph Duval, president of the Bishop's Conference of France, wrote, "Present in Algeria for thirty-one years, these nuns who had chosen to remain on the spot have risked their lives to go on witnessing. Their love to this people was boundless. . . ."[12]

Algeria

Algeria is in the headlines because of the ongoing battle waged by the National Salvation Front, and other Islamicists such as the Armed Islamic Group, against the more secular rulers.[13] The present regime is the military-backed, decaying remnants of the formerly semi-Marxist independence fighters, known as the National Liberation Front.

Algeria's proximity to Europe, and its long-standing connections with France, bring it to the attention of Europeans. There is fear that, if Algeria becomes an Islamic state, its influence will spread to neighboring Tunisia and Morocco. If this happens, Europe could be faced with an armed and hostile Islamicist North Africa directly across the Mediterranean. Along with a threat of escalating terrorism, the concern is that this could also produce a mass exodus of refugees moving northward.

Algeria's Islamicist groups have targeted those whom they believe either support the present regime or otherwise violate Islamic principles. In patterns of terrorism reminiscent of the NLF's campaigns against the French, they have targeted foreign workers and diplomats, women who refuse to adopt the mores of traditional Islam, and any others who do not conform to their view of Islam.

The plight of Algeria's women, some of whom have had acid thrown in their faces for refusing to wear a veil, has drawn attention in the West. The killing of foreign diplomats and French expatriates also draws some consideration. But, with the exception of major atrocities such as the seven Trappist monks murdered in 1996, the situation of non-Muslim people in Algeria tends to be passed over.[14] Meanwhile, Algeria's Islamic groups attack both expatriate and native Algerian Christians, especially among the 150,000 Catholic population.

On December 14, 1993, twelve Croatian and Bosnian workers were murdered in the Tamezguida Region after it was determined that they were Christians and they had been separated out from among their Muslim coworkers. French nuns and priests have been attacked routinely, despite their long-standing and popularly accepted service in the country. With the bombing of the Algerian-born bishop of Oran, Pierre Claverie, on August 1, 1996, nineteen members of Roman Catholic religious orders had been murdered, as well as numerous lay people.

The situation of native Algerian Christians is like that in Qatar or Saudi Arabia. In my own talks with them, many simply do not wish to be identified. They believe, perhaps accurately, that nobody in the outside world is going to help them, and fear that any publicity would merely increase the likelihood of persecution.

When Bishop Claverie was asked in May 1996 why he did not leave Algeria, he replied,

> The church in Algeria is Algerian, not French. Our blood is mixed. We have chosen to share the fate of the Algerian people for better or for worse.

Father Christian de Chargé, the superior of the Monastery of Tibberine, was one of the monks who had their throats slit by the G.I.A. in May 1996. He left a testament "to be opened in the event of my death." In it, he said,

> I know the scorn with which Algerians as a whole can be regarded. I know also the caricature of Islam which a certain kind of Islamism encourages. It is too easy to give oneself a good conscience by identifying this religious way with the fundamentalist ideologies of the extremists.
>
> . . . My life has no more value than any other. Nor any less value. In any case, it has not the innocence of childhood. I have lived long enough to know that I share in the evil which seems, alas, to prevail in the world, even in that which would strike me blindly. I should like, when the time comes, to have a clear space which would allow me to beg forgiveness of God and of all my fellow human beings, and at the same time to forgive with all my heart the one who would strike me down. . . .[15]

Morocco

After a successful career as conductor of the San Salvador Symphony Orchestra, Gilberto Orellana was invited by Moroccan officials to teach at Tetuan's prestigious National Conservatory. Gilbert, his wife Ruth, and two daughters accepted the invitation, and moved to the colorful North African nation. The family settled down in Morocco, and after two years had passed, had made new friends and begun a new life.

Then a nightmare began.

On December 13, 1994, five policemen raided the Orellana home, confiscating Bibles and taking Gilberto into the police station for interrogation. It was believed that he had broken the Islamic penal code, which prohibits proselytism.

He endured nine days of verbal abuse and threats, then was imprisoned along with two Moroccan friends. He was thrust, handcuffed, into a small cell with seventeen other prisoners being held for drug smuggling.

Recounting his questioning, Orellana responded, "I told them that when anybody asked me about my faith, I had explained that it was based on the death and resurrection of Jesus." He tried to clarify that he had merely said what any Christian would say when asked questions in private by personal friends. That was all his captors needed to hear.

After his arraignment, Orellana was sentenced to a year in prison. A day later, he was told that he would be set free. Then, after several days of confusion, including an unexplained internment in dungeon-like quarters, he was escorted to the Spanish border, banished from Morocco for five years.

Orellana learned that the two friends who were arrested with him had been treated severely. One had suffered a broken arm, and the other had been tortured with electric shocks. Both had been forced to repeat the Muslim creed before being released.

Orellana later said, "I would like to go back if I could, but I don't think so, for awhile. . . ."[16]

In Morocco, three subjects remain taboo: "criticizing the king, or Islam, or challenging Morocco's claim to sovereignty over the Western Sahara."[17] Morocco's Constitution provides for freedom of worship, but Islam is the official religion. The penal code prohibits "proselytizing" and provides a prison sentence and fine for anyone who attempts to "shake the faith" of a Muslim. The government refuses to recognize any church made up of Moroccan nationals.

Moroccan Christians face severe treatment. In November 1993, Zmamda Mustapha, a convert to Christianity, was sentenced to three years for distributing Christian literature. In August 1995, an eighty-eight-year-old

Christian, Mehdi Ksara, was tried for proselytism. He had converted to Christianity from Islam sixty years previously. He, along with three other Moroccans held on the same charges, were acquitted, but only after international pressure, especially by British parliamentarians, was brought to bear on the case. On September 26, Ait Bakrim Jamaa was sentenced to a year's imprisonment for not observing the Ramadan fast and for "disturbing the Islamic Religion." He could not afford a lawyer for this, his fourth conviction. In his defense he said simply, "I am a Christian, but I respect the Islamic religion."[18]

> *Rachid Cohen, a Jewish Moroccan who has converted to Christianity, was arrested September 12, 1995, for being an "unauthorized guide." Cohen's questioning soon turned to his Christian faith, his association with foreigners, and reports that he serves as a Christian evangelist. During his incarceration at Al Battaille prison in Fez, Cohen was tortured as long as ten hours a day. His interrogators burned him with cigarettes, fed him nothing but scraps of bread, shocked him repeatedly in a low-voltage "electric chair," stripped him naked and forced him to "sit on a bottle," and dunked him in his own excrement. He was released September 23, told by police that British Parliamentarians had made enquiries about his situation.*[19]

Turkey

Although Turkey is now a country with relatively few Christians, this was not always the case. Less than one hundred years ago, Turkey, or rather its Ottoman predecessor, was about 30 percent Christian. This situation changed when some two million ethnic Armenian Christians were massacred between 1905 and 1918, a genocide which the Turkish government still denies. Many of the remaining Christians fled immediately. Others, facing death threats, systemic harassment, and discrimination, followed them later.

Turkey still remains the home of the Ecumenical Patriarch Bartholomew I, the leading figure in the Orthodox churches throughout the world. However, the patriarch has been rigidly controlled, consistently denied permission to develop theological education or buildings for the Orthodox minority. The historic Chalke Theological School was closed in 1971 by the government, which has resisted attempts to reopen it. Other seminaries were closed at the same time. On May 28, 1994, time bombs were thrown over the back wall of the Greek Orthodox Patriarchate in Istanbul's Fener District. They were accompanied by death threats against the patriarch. On September 29, 1996, a hand grenade exploded at the Patriarchate. Responsibility was claimed by the Great Eastern Islamic Raiders (IBDA-C).[20]

The members of the Armenian Orthodox, the Greek Orthodox, the Suryanis, and the Chaldean Catholic churches face continued discrimination. Meanwhile, Suryani and Catholic villages in Southeast Turkey are being destroyed as part of the Turkish government's campaign against Kurdish rebels. This campaign has, in turn, spilled over into northern Iraq's Assyrian Christian community. Among the three million Kurds in Northern Iraq, there are members of the Assyrian Church, the Chaldean Catholic Church, and the Syrian Catholic Church. Kurdish Muslims from across the Turkish border have come in increasing numbers to this historically Christian area and have taken land and settled into villages earlier destroyed by Saddam Hussein. In previous years, Kurdish rebels murdered Christian village chiefs.[21]

Meanwhile, persecution of the Assyro-Chaldean minority has intensified within Turkey itself. They cannot build new churches, have no schools, and are banned from public service. They are also subjected to regular violence, sometimes culminating in murder.

> *On November 18, 1993, a sixteen-year-old Assyrian boy and his father were arrested by security authorities and were tortured by officers at the Dargieit Police Station. Melted plastic crosses were burnt into the skin of their chests. The United Nations lists the names of twenty-five Assyrians killed during 1994. Since 1975, more than one hundred thousand have left the country and only ten thousand remain.*[22]

Since the elections of early 1996, the Islamic-oriented Welfare Party has become the largest party in the Turkish Parliament, so this situation is likely to get worse. But even in the present situation, anyone who attempts to leave Islam faces the real possibility of death.[23]

KUWAIT

> *Robert Hussein (formerly Hussein Qambar Ali), a forty-five-year-old citizen of Kuwait, was charged with apostasy after he had converted from Islam to Christianity while studying at Temple University in Philadelphia. Though Kuwait's Constitution affirms that the "freedom of belief is absolute," and apostasy is not listed as a crime in either the civil or criminal codes, there are also separate Shari'a courts. On May 29, 1996, such a court found Hussein to be an "apostate" under Shari'a. Kuwaiti law itself does not stipulate any sentence for apostasy, but some Islamic countries have mandated death penalties for it, and the judge in his case said he should be killed. Hussein, a businessman by profession, was unable to find a lawyer willing to represent him at the trial.*[24]

In Kuwait, Islam is the state religion. Non-Islamic religious education is officially prohibited though, in practice, it is often tolerated.[26] However, "proselytising" is illegal, as is any attempt to leave Islam. Apart from the situation of Kuwaitis themselves, one of the major problems is the treatment of foreigners, especially domestic servants. The country contains about a quarter of a million Asian maids, mainly from the Philippines, Sri Lanka, India, and Bangladesh and including a high proportion of Christians. They are expressly excluded from the protection of labor legislation and so are left at the mercy of their employers. Among many other human-rights abuses, these employers usually restrict them from non-Islamic religious observance. Hundreds of foreign maids have sought refuge in their embassies after having suffered rape, physical assault, unlawful confinement, and withholding of wages. Human Rights Watch estimates that between May 1991 and April 1992, 14–20 percent of Filippina maids fled their employers.[27]

Kuwaiti law requires that maids who complain must either stay with their employers or else be detained until the matter is settled. This severely limits their ability to correct the situation. It also has a major chilling effect on the amount of complaints offered, so the reported cases probably reflect only a small portion of the total abuse.[28]

Brunei

The Sultan of Brunei often graces the social pages of western newspapers because of his reputed status as the richest man in the world. His fiftieth birthday bash in July 1996 cost an estimated $150 million and drew his favorite pop star, Michael Jackson.

But he is also one of the world's few real monarchs, since the Brunei legislature is largely a rubber stamp. Besides his other range of controls, he also enforces strict observance of Islam. Brunei's political creed of "Malay Muslim Monarchy" defines the Sultan as "defender of the faith," something he takes more seriously than, say, Prince Charles.

The Constitution guarantees freedom of religion, but the government's goal is to mold Brunei into a pure Islamic state. As with other enthusiastic Islamicist agendas, it is relatively little concerned about the quarter to a third of the country that is non-Muslim. The Ministry of Education is demanding that all girls in government schools, Muslim and non-Muslim alike, wear traditional Malay Muslim clothing. The government has also pressured Christian schools to abandon religious-knowledge classes and to replace them with classes in Islam. Meanwhile, in cooperation with neighboring countries, it sponsors training schools for Muslim missionaries.

The church, which is primarily ethnic Chinese, has only about five thousand people. But it is under pressure, as are the indigenous tribal peoples, many of whom are also Christian. In 1993 one tribal church worker was locked into a walk-in freezer by the police for more than three hours. The police have also raided private homes to break up Christian meetings—which are officially illegal if more than five people are present.[29]

Other Exclusively Islamic States

The small states clustered around the entrance to the Persian Gulf are similar to Saudi Arabia in their treatment of Christians and, indeed, of any other dissenting groups. In the United Arab Emirates, Shari'a law is applied, any literature considered "offensive to Islam" is forbidden, and non-Muslims may not distribute any literature.[30]

> *Ray Amey, a Briton, came face-to-face with the United Arab Emirates' anti-Christian stance. Apparently he gave New Testaments to some men he stopped to talk to. Amey speaks little Arabic or Farsi, Arabic Bibles are sold in shops throughout the Emirates, and the Farsi version that Amey had was, in fact, printed in Iran. Unfortunately for him, none of this prevented his being sentenced on October 24, 1993 to six months in prison for "promoting Christianity as a superior religion to Islam."*[31]

In Qatar, as in Kuwait, foreign domestic workers are subject to gross abuse. Islam is the state religion, and followers of other faiths may only worship privately, cannot proselytize, and face discrimination in employment. The construction of churches is forbidden. Non-Muslims cannot bring suits as plaintiffs in the Shari'a court, and public criticism of Islam is not permitted.[32]

In Oman, at the southeast of the Arabian Peninsula, the sultan is an absolute monarch who enforces Islam as the official religion.[33] In Yemen, next door, Islam is also the state religion, and Christians are forbidden to preach to Muslims.[34]

Although the states of the Arabian Peninsula have long been the heartland of Islam, parts of Africa are following the same course. In Tunisia, Islam is the state religion and propagating other religions is forbidden.[35] In Mauritania, where slavery is practiced, all citizens must by law be Sunni Muslims, and attempting to leave Islam is a crime. It is forbidden even for Mauritanians to enter the homes of non-Muslims, or to possess the sacred texts of any other religion.[36]

Meanwhile, although war-torn Somalia has been conflict-ridden both before and since the United Nations relief operations there, the various competing warlords have managed to agree on one thing: an exclusive commitment to Islam. In the northwest, in the independence-seeking territory of "Somaliland," there are reports that the ruling Somali National Movement has adopted Shari'a law.[37]

Not to be outdone by Africa's Islamic states, in January 1993, Afghanistan's newly formed Grand Council of Religious Leaders ruled that only Muslims can work for the government. It also banned all non-Muslim organizations and ordered the media to conform to Islamic principles. Justice is administered according to Islamic law, and women are under pressure to submit to traditional Islamic norms. They are routinely harassed for wearing western clothes; as in other countries, some have had acid thrown in their faces for wearing makeup.[38] In September 1996, the "Taliban," a military movement of "Islamic students" invaded the capital, Kabul, and seem to have won the ongoing civil war. Their initial acts indicate that repression in the name of Islam will become even more severe.

Similar practices occur in the small Indian Ocean Islamic states. In the Comoros Islands which lie between Madagascar and the east coast of Africa, Islam is the state religion, and any open Christian witness is forbidden. There are some Catholic churches which serve the expatriate community, but any native Comoron Christians operate underground.[39] The Maldive Islands southwest of India are one of the most controlled societies in the world. By law, the president must be both male and a Sunni Muslim. The Constitution defines all citizens as Muslims, and it is in principle illegal to practice any other religion than Islam.[40] In July 1994, legislation was passed by the parliament providing for two to five years imprisonment for "giving religious advice that contravenes independence. . . . and the policy stated by the president."[41]

THE FRICTION ZONES

BANGLADESH

Sapnahar was terrified. She was facing more horrors than most thirteen-year-old girls in the world can imagine. She had been raped, her childhood suddenly ripped away from her. She was pregnant with the rapist's child, and was now on trial by salish in a Moslem village.

Like many Christians in her native Bangladesh, Sapnahar was faced with finding four Moslem adult male witnesses to testify that she had, in fact, been raped. Such witnesses could not be found. No one with the appropriate status in the community would defend her. The testimony of Christians was unacceptable, as was the testimony of women. The alleged rapist was acquitted.

Worse yet, Sapnahar's pregnancy was viewed as sufficient evidence to "convict" her of unlawful sexual intercourse. Rather than her rapist being brought to justice, she was sentenced to be flogged, which was to take place forty days after the birth of her child.

Sapnahar was more fortunate than most girls in her predicament might have been. A women's rights group heard of her case and gave her shelter.[42]

Religious repression in Bangladesh made the headlines in 1994 because of attempts to control the anti-Islamic statements of feminist author, Taslima Nasreen. But other forms of repression continue, beyond the reach of widespread western interest. In response to the Nasreen affair, members of the Bangladeshi parliament pushed Prime Minister Begum Khaleda Ziato to introduce a blasphemy law explicitly modeled on that in Pakistan.[43]

Particularly incensed by the evangelistic fervor of a group of Koreans on tourist visas, militant Islamic groups demanded in February 1995 that all Korean church workers be expelled. The "Peer of Charmoni," one especially militant group, said that if they didn't get their way with Koreans, they would campaign to deport all foreign church workers from Bangladesh. Thus far, the government has ignored their demands.

Bangladesh's Constitution grants freedom of religion but, although it was amended in 1988 to establish Islam as the state religion, militant Muslims are still unsatisfied. Groups like the "Peer of Charmoni" are demanding that the country's name be changed to the "Islamic Republic of Bangladesh," and that the Constitution be based on the Qur'an.[44]

Meanwhile, religious minorities, including Hindus, Buddhists, and Christians, have been the victims of Muslim extremists. Incidents include "murders, abductions, rape, looting, extortion, and destruction of property, and threats to make them leave the country."[45] Among scores of other abuses, a school run by Caritas, a Catholic social organization, was burned down in January 1995.[46]

Malaysia

The treatment of Christians in Malaysia is gentler than in Bangladesh. It cannot aptly be termed persecution, although there are instances of police mistreatment.[47] The general problem is one of systematic discrimination. Prime Minister Mohammed Mahathir has pursued a program of Islamicization with a specifically Malaysian face as part of his program for the rapid economic and cultural development of the country. Malaysia has become something of a role model for other developing Islamic nations.

The capital, Kuala Lumpur, is host to the International Islamic Bank, the International Islamic Missionary Movement, and the International Islamic University. Mahathir pursues Islamicization partly due to the government's own convictions on this score, partly to shore up its own electoral base among Malay Muslims, and partly to head off more militant Islamic groups, especially the Parti Islam sa Malaysia (PAS), which are pushing for more radical proposals. Of some eighteen million Malaysians, about 58 percent are Muslim. The one-and-a-half million Christians are concentrated among the 30 percent of the population who are ethnic Chinese and the 9 percent whose origins are in the Indian subcontinent.

Part of the government's program for improving the economic status of the *bumiputras*, or ethnic Malaysians (not to be confused with the indigenous tribal peoples), is low-interest loans, business incentives, educational scholarships, and lower taxation rates. Similar privileges now extend to positions in the educational system, professions, public sector, banks, and media. One problem is that a member of the Malay group is explicitly defined as Muslim.[48] This has two consequences. One is that Muslims consistently receive economic privileges denied to Christians. Second, any ethnic Malay who ceases to be a Muslim loses his or her economic status.

Another form of discrimination affects church construction. Churches must have all land and building applications approved by the government, and the government's Islamic Relations Department has a say in this process. Consequently, it is becoming increasingly difficult to start churches. It took the Catholic Church thirty years to secure land in Shah

Alam. Once building permits were issued in 1992, construction began. However, local Muslims protested and the building permit was then withdrawn. Subsequent appeals by the Catholic Church to the government have failed to have it reissued.[49]

Due to these restrictions, many Christian groups now meet in rented offices and shops. This has two interesting effects. One is that individual congregations must remain small. Hence, when they grow they divide, creating more and more congregations. The other is that many churches now meet in shopping malls on Sunday mornings, one of Malaysia's busiest shopping periods. They are placed right in the middle of people's everyday lives. As Malaysian Christians point out with some irony, this is one of the greatest strategies for church growth ever invented.[50]

As always, there is resistance toward attempts to leave Islam. While it is not illegal for Muslims to change their religion, it is illegal to try to encourage a Muslim to do so.[51]

Other concerns are that the federal government is allowing large numbers of Muslim refugees and illegal immigrants from the Philippines to settle in Borneo.[52] Since it does not extend the same privilege to Christians, the Christian presence is being diluted in areas where it has an important place.

There have also been attempts to ban the use by Christians of certain words in the Bahasa Malaysia language on the grounds that these are "Muslim" words. One major example is the use of the word "Allah" in Christian Bibles, which has led to restrictions on the sale of Bibles in Malay.[53] Christians argue that this is fundamentally unjust and correctly claim, that, in fact, "Allah" was used by Christians in the Arabian Peninsula to refer to God for six centuries before Islam came into existence.

While most Malay Christians identify with their country and are proud of its achievements, they are fearful of the future. PAS, now the government in the northeastern state of Kelantan, has passed legislation implementing the Hudud laws, the grim criminal section of Shari'a.[54] The federal constitution presently blocks the application of such laws, and Prime Minister Mahathir has refused all attempts to amend it. However, his own Islamization campaign may have released darker forces which will lead to something far worse for the country's Christians, as well as for other religious minorities.[55]

Indonesia

The situation of Christians in Indonesia, like so much else in this vast country, has no real parallel anywhere else in the world. Indonesia is not officially an Islamic country, and the government struggles to head off any development of militant Islam. Islam in Indonesia is usually more gentle and open, having been propagated originally by more mystical Sufi missionaries. It also found its major footing in a country which had previously been Hindu, tending to absorb rather than resist new currents. The Nahdlatul Ulama, with some thirty-five million members, is probably the world's largest Islamic organization, and it has warned the government about the dangers of intolerant forms of Islam. Its leader, Abdurrahman Wahid, has supported secular rather than Islamic political figures.[56]

The official ideology of Indonesia is the Panca Sila (the five pillars) which gives the principles to be held by all Indonesians. One principle is belief in One God, and people can be Muslim, Christian, Hindu, Buddhist, or Confucian (though this is probably not much comfort to an atheist or polytheist).[57]

The majority of the population is at least nominally Muslim, making it easily the largest Islamic country in the world. Christians may operate universities, schools, newspapers, and social organizations with the same freedom and the same restrictions from the authoritarian government as anybody else. In day-to-day life throughout most of the archipelago, Christians, Muslims, and other groups live alongside and among one another in peace. Thus, Indonesians provide an example of coexistence which could be a model for many other countries.

Nevertheless, there are still problems facing Christians in Indonesia. One is that, given the Muslim majority, there is a *de facto* requirement that the majority of the leading political, educational, and military offices, as well as the presidency, be held by Muslims. (Since Indonesia has only had two presidents, this is not presently the most significant problem.) The perpetually dominant Golkar Party remains an effectively Muslim preserve.

Meanwhile, Christians tend to be concentrated in one of the relatively powerless opposition parties.

Problems can be more severe in particular regions. Some of the greatest concern is expressed by Christians in the remoter parts of Indonesia's fourteen thousand islands, where they often constitute a majority. About one hundred and ten million of Indonesia's one hundred and eighty million people live on the crowded island of Java. Hence, the government has a major program to help Javanese migrate to less populated areas. One practical effect of this policy is massive migration of Muslims into hitherto predominately Christian areas.

While sympathetic to government programs to relieve overcrowding, many Christians believe that more is involved. They feel that the resulting Islamization of their areas is not only a consequence of the government's transmigration programs, but also one of its goals.[58] In addition, because Java dominates the power structure of the country, the incoming Javanese tend to take over the leading positions. Since Christians are concentrated among the tribal peoples, who are often excluded from power anyway, the result is that they are increasingly marginalized. There were outbreaks of sabotage and violence in early 1996 in Irian Jaya, on the Island of New Guinea, which included protests by indigenous Christians against domination by the central government and foreign corporations.

In other areas, there is increasing friction between Christians and Muslims sparked by the growth of the churches, especially the Pentecostal churches. This friction is encouraged by more militant Islamic preachers. In some parts of the country, including Java, churches have been attacked and burned. On June 9, 1996, ten Protestant churches were attacked and destroyed in Muslim riots in Surabaya, eastern Java. On October 10, 1996, a further twenty-five churches were burned down, as well as two Christian schools (in use at the time) and an orphanage. Pentecostal Pastor Ishah Christian and his wife, daughter, and niece, as well as a clerical worker, were burned to death.[59]

There have also been violent conflicts in Indonesia's largest church, the two- to three-million-member Huria Kristen Batak Protestan, after the Indonesian government appointed a bishop whose authority many church members refused to accept. One man, Herbert Hutasoit, who opposed the new bishop was found murdered and mutilated in a northern Sumatra village on June 1, 1994. Indonesian security forces have arrested church members, and church leaders assert that several pastors were tortured.[60]

Meanwhile, Indonesia has been strengthening its Islamic links with other countries. It cooperates with Malaysia, Singapore, and Brunei on projects including schools to train Islamic missionaries for remoter areas.[61] One result is that ICMI, the association of Muslim intellectuals led by influential Cabinet Minister B. J. Habibie, is becoming more Islamic in outlook. It is also growing in power, and relations with the military are increasingly tense.

THE FRAGMENTED ZONES[62]

East Asia: East Timor

On June 28, 1994, during the anniversary of the Catholic Church of Santo Joseph, two Muslim members of the Indonesian armed forces asked to receive communion. It was given to them, but they then threw down the host and trampled on it. At once, Catholic worshipers attacked them.

The military claimed that the soldiers were merely curious and ignorant. But some eyewitnesses claim that the two, Bakhrul Alum and Nurcahyo, said that they were there under orders from their superiors.

Demonstrations followed. On July 11 several hundred students holding banners with pictures of the Virgin Mary, and carrying large crucifixes, scuffled with security forces.

Then, on July 13, four Muslim Indonesians were accused of harassing two nuns who were taking their university entrance examinations at East Timor University in Dili, the capital.

Students demonstrated again the following day. The violence escalated, and security forces used bayonets to disperse them.[63]

In 1975, after a brief period of independence, the former Portuguese colony of East Timor was taken over by Indonesia. There is continuing resistance to the Indonesian presence, including guerrilla warfare and demonstrations. Some one hundred thousand people, about one-sixth of the population, have died as a result of the occupation.[64] Indonesian President Suharto has referred to East Timor as "a pimple on Indonesia's face."[65]

The struggle is largely political in the sense of focusing on land and independence, rather than being overtly religious. Nevertheless, the result is that a largely Christian territory (about 80 percent of the population is Catholic) is in major opposition to a largely Muslim government. The most public figure is Bishop Felipe Ximenes Belo, the head of the Catholic Church, which is the only institution capable of rallying internal opposition. There have been at least two attempts to kill him.[66] In November, along with fellow Timorese Jose Ramos-Horta, he was awarded the 1996 Nobel Peace Prize.

The demography has in recent years given the situation the elements of a religious dispute. Consequently, while it would be misleading to describe the situation in East Timor purely as a Christian/Muslim conflict, it is a factor which needs to be addressed.[67]

One of the most publicized incidents took place in 1991, when troops fired on hundreds of people in Dili. The government claims that some fifty people died. Foreign observers put the number at two to three hundred and claim that even more people were killed in the following days in order to eradicate witnesses.

These public incidents take place against a backdrop of continuing violence and killings in remoter areas. In recent months, dissidents' houses have been attacked at night by "Ninja" gangs thought to be agents of government security forces.[68] Meanwhile, the Catholic Church and the military engage in a "war of the monuments." The church puts up crucifixes, statues of Mary, and grottoes. The military removes or defaces them, then replaces them with signs celebrating unification with Indonesia. George Aditjondro, one of Indonesia's foremost experts on East Timor, reports, "The military have been in growing confrontation with the Catholic church since the church is the only institution in Timor that it cannot control."[69] Aditjondro has since been expelled from the country.[70]

East Asia: Philippines

In June of 1994, Abu Sayyaf guerrillas stopped a bus and asked the frightened passengers which of them were Muslims. Once they were identified, the Muslims were asked to stand to one side. The remaining fifteen non-Muslim passengers were massacred on the spot by automatic rifle fire.[71]

The southern Philippines has a significant Muslim population, and for decades there has been guerrilla warfare to establish an Islamic state there. While in 1996 the Moro National Liberation Front reached agreement with the government for an autonomous region in the south, two splinter groups—the Moro Islamic Liberation Front and the Abu Sayyaf group—have continued to engage in violence.[72]

One aspect of this conflict has been the targeting of Christian groups. This is not merely because most non-Moslem Philippinos are Christians, but due to a focused attack on the Christian presence. The head of the Roman Catholic Church in the Philippines, Cardinal Jaime Sin, warned that Islamic groups posed a threat to Pope John II during his January 1995 visit. Church leaders and missionaries have been assassinated. Abu Sayyaf bombs churches and kidnaps and assassinates church personnel as well as non-Muslim government workers.

Both Christians and the broader Muslim population have protested against the radicals' activities. A demonstration by ten thousand Christians and Muslims took place on the Island of Basilan on December 13, 1994, to protest against the extremists. But the violence has continued.[73]

On April 5, 1995, two hundred Muslim guerrillas attacked the Catholic town of Ipil. They killed fifty-three people, wounding at least fifty others. The Islamists took thirty-five hostages. On April 15, they killed fourteen of these, some by mutilating and beheading.[74]

West Africa

Nigeria's one hundred million people are about evenly divided between Christians and Muslim. Muslims predominate in the north, Christians in the south, and they are mixed in the central area. Since the 1980s the northern and central sectors have been terror-ridden, and over six thousand people have been killed, most of them Christians.[75] Nigeria is one of the few areas where Christians have engaged in communal violence themselves, though most of this seems to be in reaction to the activity of Islamic radicals.

In late December 1994, a Nigerian Christian named Gideon Akaluka was accused of desecrating the Qur'an by using its pages as toilet paper. Although the local court found no evidence to convict him, they detained him anyway—"for security purposes." He was imprisoned in Bompai, in the northern city of Kano.

On December 26, the guards at the prison were overpowered by Muslim fanatics, seeking vengeance for Akaluka's alleged blasphemy. The mob forced its way into the prison and dragged Akaluka out of his cell. As the prison guards watched helplessly, the terrorists beheaded him.

After hoisting his severed head on a spike, they paraded it around the town, ending their march at the residence of the emir, the local Islamic spiritual leader. When a representative of the emir condemned the militants' action, the angry crowd then attacked him, beating him brutally.

Just weeks later, in the northern town of Lokoto, two men were involved in a brawl. One claimed that the other, a Christian named Azubike, had insulted Mohammad. Again, a mob of militants surged after the alleged blasphemer. The frightened man ran into a local police post for refuge, but the police who tried to protect him were overpowered. Azubike was more fortunate than Akaluka—he was only beaten unconscious.[76]

The violence is widespread. In September 1994, nine churches were burned in Potiskum in Nigeria's northern Yobe State. In May and June 1995, a pastor was murdered in Kano and two churches were burned.[77] The Christian Alliance says it believes that this is part of a radical Muslim design to "wipe out any traces of Christianity in the northern states."[78]

Ghana, another tense African country, has a population of about sixteen million: 60 percent are Christian and 15 percent are Muslim. As has often been the case in much of Africa, the two religions have coexisted amicably for generations. However, this amiable relation is unacceptable to radical Muslim groups.

According to Catholic Bishop Lucas Abadamloora, on January 30, 1995, in the town of Walewale, youths attacked the Catholic mission, smashed the statue of the Virgin Mary, and destroyed the surrounding trees. The mob crossed the road and then destroyed a Seventh Day Adventist church under construction. They then moved on to a nearby Baptist church, which they dismantled.[79] Clashes took place again near the end of 1995, prompting Christian and Muslim leaders to engage in joint efforts to condemn violent interfaith clashes and call for tolerance of one another.[80]

Strife-torn Liberia is about 38 percent Christian and 13 percent Muslim. However, militant "Islamic Warriors" have closed Christian places of worship and threatened to kill anyone who walks in the streets with a Bible. In Lofa County, Islamic extremists are reported to have burned hundreds of villages and killed numerous people. Christians, along with the rest of the Liberian people, have suffered grievously during the ongoing civil war. But even beyond that, they have been specifically targeted in a Jihad.

> *The Islamic Warriors "murdered three pastors and one minister of the Jehovah's Witnesses sect. One of them, Thomas Korfeh, was said to have been thrown into a tank filled with oil and had boiling water poured over his head. The Muslim extremists then reportedly lit a fire and boiled him in public, in order to inspire terror. The other two pastors, John Fallah and David Saah, were disembowled."*[81]

Some reports suggest that the situation has improved in recent months, but improvement is a relative term. Reginald Goodrich, a senior aide to Liberian faction leader Charles Taylor, says, "What the journalists have failed to point out is that this time, unlike previous fighting in Monrovia, the civilians have not really suffered. . . . In the past, fighters would rip out people's intestines and use them to string up roadblocks, or cut off people's heads. This time there has been none of that."[82]

Christians have begun to respond to these attacks violently. David Larson, who has tried to carry out reconciliation work, observes,

> It takes great courage for a pastor to go to his congregation and encourage people whose mothers' heads have been chopped off and whose daughters have been gang-raped to forgive.[83]

East Africa

In sharply decentralized Ethiopia, the situation varies from region to region. But in areas where Islam is strong, Christians are under increasing pressure, especially in the Oromo region. Leaders in the evangelical church have been targeted for assassination by extremist Muslims.[84]

In Kenya, there is growing tension between Muslims and Christians, as well as increasing hostility toward western humanitarian organizations. Some Islamic leaders from Wajir in the northeast have declared a Jihad against the Africa Inland Church and the international Christian relief organization World Vision, which they accused of desecrating two hundred copies of the Qur'an. In parts of the country there is "interreligious tension, a certain amount of insecurity, the destruction of places of worship, and threats to the life and physical integrity of priests and pastors."[85]

Bordering Kenya, Tanzania is populated by twenty-four million people; about one-third are Muslim and most of the rest are Christian. While Tanzania has long been an area of amicable coexistence, there has been increasing tension in the 1990s because of growing militancy among some Muslims. For a time, in May 1992, the government banned all religious preaching outside a place of worship and all tapes and printed matter that "preach against other religions."[86]

Central Asia

The Republics of Central Asia usually have Muslim majorities, and have only this decade been released from control by the Soviet Union. Most of them are in tremendous flux.[87] Much of the population is relatively irreligious, regardless of their formal affiliation. The governments tend to include large numbers of ex-Communists who now seem to be driven less by ideology than by maintaining some semblance of their former power. Often this means that they do not discriminate on the basis of religion: Instead, they repress any religious group that challenges them. It also means that they are resisting radical Islamic movements in the area, some of which are encouraged by Iran and Turkey. As an alternative, they seek to buy off these movements by concessions which undercut the Christian population. Consequently, both radical Islamic groups and Christian groups have come under government pressure.

President Saparmurad Niyazov of Turkmenistan has developed his own personality cult and has appointed the republic's leading Muslim cleric, Nasrullo Ibadullaev, to chair the Committee for Religious Affairs, overseeing both Christians and Muslims. But Ibadullaev, in turn, has appointed the leading Russian Orthodox cleric, Andrei Sapunov, as the deputy chairman.

Christians in both Uzbekistan and Turkmenistan have been warned that they will lose their registration if they evangelize among Muslims. A new law passed in Uzbekistan in 1995 (but kept secret) restricted all religious literature, but these restrictions were not equally applied and concentrated on anything deemed offensive to Islam. Any literature printed inside the country requires permission from the Central Asia Spiritual Muslim Union.[88]

In an ironic display of solidarity, Muslim and Russian Orthodox leaders in Kyrgystan have cooperatively opposed Protestant missionary work. Chief Mufti Kimsanbai Abdrakhmanov and Russian Orthodox priest Vladimir Savitsky wrote a joint article in *Slovo Kyrgyzstana* in October 1994, which condemned "the countless Protestant and other sects which have mushroomed." They called for a law which would ban "non-traditional" denominations from preaching.

Similarly, in July 1995, in a debate on Kazakhstan's new constitution, Manash Kozybaev wrote in *Kazakhstanskaya Pravda* that "the activity of foreign religious associations on the territory of Kazakhstan must be banned."[89] The deputy Mufti (Islamic leader) of the Tashkent-based Central Asia Spiritual Muslim Union called for Christians to be forbidden to enter "Muslim homes and speak about Christ." Meanwhile, the Constitution officially affirms the "right of religious freedom and of the choice of religion."[90]

There are also local frictions. There are some reports of harassments of Catholics and Baptists by local authorities in Kazakhstan, while in 1991, Christians in Osh, Kyrgzstan, were assaulted. These tensions are overlain by the fact that many Christians are ethnic Russians and Germans who are disliked because of their association with the former Soviet Empire.

Nagorno Karabakh

The haunted expressions on their faces were as telling as the evidence of torture on their emaciated bodies. Their story was not an unusual one among Armenian Christians, except that they had managed to survive their ordeal.

Eleanor Bugakov's son Dmitri was only four years old when the two were taken captive in Baku during the horrible winter of 1992. They were passed from one group to another—from the Azerbaijani Popular Front, to a military unit, to a tank regiment, to an "investigative prison." They had gone without food for eight days, and when water was finally given to the boy, a rat was floating in it.

When they eventually found their way into the care of friends, the thirty-eight-year-old mother was found to have been raped repeatedly, once by an entire platoon. She was still bleeding from a mauling suffered days before—she had been beaten with a chain while trying to protect her son's fur hat. The boy had been hit on the head with a hammer, and his hands were covered in cigarette burns. The hat had been given him to protect his battered head.

Like so many others who were taken into Azeri custody during the war in Nagorno Karabakh, Eleanor and Dmitri had been starved, beaten, and tortured.[91]

The entire region of the Caucasus, like many other areas along the boundaries of Islam, is in turmoil and conflict. The region has undergone ethnic and territorial conflict for centuries, and these tensions were exacerbated by the Soviet takeover after the 1917 Revolution. Stalin deported whole peoples from the area and shifted the boundaries of traditional territories in order to divide the population and weaken opposition. Recently, with the collapse of Soviet domination, the area has become a nightmare of war and massacre.

The media have reported the brutal attacks by the Russian army on the Muslims of Chechneya. Other cruelly repressed Muslim people of the area, such the Abkhazians and the Ingush, are less well-known.[92] Among the least-noticed and most severely persecuted peoples are the Armenian Christians in Nagorno Karabakh.

Nagorno Karabakh is an enclave of largely Armenian Christians in Western Azerbaijan. This enclave was transferred from Armenia to Azerbaijan by Stalin. Then, with the weakening of Soviet control, the Karabakh people sought to be reunited with Armenia. The result was fierce opposition from Azerbaijan and the Russians, which has led to ongoing war.

The dynamics of the war are complex and involve interwoven ethnic and territorial claims. Karekin I, the newly-elected Catholicos of All Armenians, and the Azeri Muslim Sheik-ul-Islam Allakhshukur Pasha Zade, declared jointly at a meeting on June 13, 1995, that they did not regard this as a religious war.[93] However, the war, like so many others, has introduced and exacerbated religious tensions so that the Armenian population has been subject to specifically anti-Christian acts. While there have also been brutalities on the Armenian side, the larger part of the violence inflicted on the civilian population is at the hands of the Azeris. And this tragedy befalls a people who have already suffered genocide at Turkish hands. The Armenians have long had to fight for their lives and, in this century, the majority of them have either been killed or brutally displaced.

After Nagorno-Karabakh sought to join Armenia, the enclave was attacked by Azeri soldiers and Soviet Interior Ministry troops in April 1990. In April 1991 these were joined by forces of the Twenty-third Division of the Soviet Fourth Army. The conduct of the war was similar to the Bosnian Serb attacks on Bosnian Muslims. Civilian areas have been attacked with artillery GRAD rockets and surface-to-air (sic) missiles which cause grave shrapnel wounds.[94] "Men were assaulted and killed, women were raped, children maltreated, civilians abducted and taken as hostages. Azeri citizens from nearby villages would come with pickup trucks and cars, looting, pillaging, and stealing everything from household goods to livestock."[95]

Since 1996, there has been a tenuous cease-fire, but the population of Nagorno-Karabakh fears the continuation of a long-term threat of exile or death. Andre Sakharov, Russian Nobel Peace Prize winner, made this the first issue that he addressed when he was allowed to speak on television after his release from house arrest. He declared, "For the Azeris, Karabakh is a question of ambition. For the Armenians, it is a matter of survival."

Despite Sakharov's appeal to the world, this conflict is all but ignored in the West. It is, unfortunately, not the first time that Armenia's Christians have been forgotten.

On August 22, 1939, Adolf Hitler informed his generals that he would send units to kill civilians in the East.

With words referring to the genocide of Armenians of 1915, he reassured them that they need not worry about any outcry.

"Who speaks today about the Armenians?"

CHAPTER FOUR

Communism's Continuing Grip

Hundreds of crimson flags flutter atop the majestic buildings that line Beijing's Chang-An Avenue, proudly proclaiming China's strength and glory. Overlooking everything still reigns the portrait of Mao Zedong.

Not many miles away, within a prison, a very different picture of Communism is painted. Outside the building, the cries are muffled; the blows falling against already bruised flesh cannot be heard. But every day, believers are "encouraged" to change their way of thinking. And they pay for their uncompromising faith in blood and breathtaking pain.

Stories of China's persecuted Christians are not usually told to visitors. Some, however, make their way to the West, and are reported by enough reliable sources to be known as facts.

There was Pastor Wang-Mingdao, who spent twenty-two years and ten months in Chinese prisons for refusing to renounce his faith. Early on, concerned about his wife's health, he wrote a "confession," renouncing Christianity. He was immediately released from prison.

Pastor Wang was free, but only superficially. He paced the streets of Shanghai in agony, muttering to himself, "I am Peter. I have denied my Lord. . . ."

Unable to live with his remorse, within days he recanted his denial, and was then sentenced to life imprisonment. This took place in the 1950s. Wang was finally released from prison in 1980, blind, sick, but still firm in his faith. He died in 1992.

There is Chen Zhuman, a fifty-year-old member of New Testament Church in Fujian. After being arrested in late 1991, he was tortured and beaten by police at the Putian County Detention Center, and left hanging upside down in a window frame for hours. In 1992, he was sentenced without trial to "reeducation through labor" for joining an "illegal" church and for having contact with a "foreign co-religionist." After transfer to a prison in Quanzhou, Chen was tortured again by guards, who also encouraged other prisoners to beat the now-disabled man. Chen has suffered hearing loss and other physical destruction as a result of his mistreatment. He remains in prison.

And there is Zhang Ruiyu, a fifty-four-year-old house church member. She was assaulted and critically injured when the Public Security Bureau raided her home in 1990. After Bibles were confiscated from her house, she was sentenced for "inciting and propagating counter-revolution" and "distributing seditious propaganda." She served a four-year prison term, during which she was tortured and beaten. She has since been released, but remains under police surveillance.[1]

When Americans have taken an interest in the persecution of Christians, they have often focused on the Communist world, especially Eastern Europe and the former Soviet Union. To some degree, this reflected a cold-war mentality, when accusations of human-rights violations were more commonly directed at America's rivals. But the criticism directed at the Eastern Communist Bloc was accurate and deserved. In fact, as most records are now becoming available, it is clear that the criticism should have been far stronger.

However, this focus on the Eastern Bloc has had some unfortunate affects. It created an unspoken assumption that the persecution of Christians was really a problem only in the Communist world, and since that world is now thought to have collapsed, it reinforces the idea that the problem is gone. This belief compounds two errors. The first—the assertion that persecution is tied largely to Communism—is, I hope, refuted elsewhere in this book. The second is that Communism has somehow disappeared. This misconception can only be maintained by failing to notice the situation of between one-fifth and one-fourth of the world's population.

Communism may have collapsed in Europe, though it should be emphasized that often the old Party hacks still hold power. Some appear to have undergone a real change, as in Poland, but others seem merely to have a glutinous attraction to power and privilege, and so adopt any position that helps them maintain their grasp.

In Central Asia, there are reports that former Communist bosses have become Mullahs. In Europe, the "transformation" hasn't been quite that dramatic, but many others have dressed themselves up as fascists, as nationalists, and as fervent defenders of the Orthodox Church, the institution they once so brutally repressed. (See Appendix G on the Orthodox Church in the USSR.)

We will address some of these developments in the chapter on Christian persecutors. But, for now, we will turn our attention to the countries where Communism has not even pretended to become something else. These include Cuba, Laos, North Korea (DPRK), Vietnam and, of course, the home of one-fifth of humanity—China.

With the exception of the DPRK, which continues to slide into decrepitude and starvation, these formerly Communist nations are trying to bail themselves out by free market reforms and are lusting after foreign investments. While they put on performances for the benefit of visiting diplomats, tourists and—above all—investors, they show no sign of being willing to relinquish their stranglehold on power. Nor do they allow any room to differ from their clapped-out nostrums. The result is that, instead of the old western Marxist dream of "Socialism with a human face," we are getting "Capitalism with a bestial face."

Despite the differences between these countries, there is a sequence of remarkably consistent patterns. In each of them, the government has begun by trying to repress and destroy religious belief.

When that has turned out to be counterproductive, which it usually has, they have tried to wear down believers and to erode the place of the church by systematic discrimination, harassment, and imprisonment. The rule of thumb for this policy was, "Create apostates, not martyrs."

When that, too, failed, they moved into a phase of registration and control, creating official government bodies to supervise religious organizations and demand that churches and other religious groups register and submit to elaborate government regulation.

Christians have in turn responded in three general ways to this third phase. The first response has been to submit to government regulation. Sometimes this has simply meant buckling under, while other times it has meant a painful compromise in order to preserve some room for genuine belief. This tendency has been more common among Orthodox and mainline Protestant groups. It is usually these groups which maintain relations with western organizations such as the National Council of Churches and the World Council of Churches.

Sometimes these churches are regarded as "sell-outs" by supporters of the "underground" Christian movements. Of course, some are. And we also know that such groups are heavily infiltrated by Communist governments. However, it must be emphasized that, even in a registered church, life is difficult. Those identified with such churches face discrimination at work, at school, and in public life. They are subject to criticism and humiliation. It is very unlikely that most of the ordinary members of these bodies would remain in them under such conditions unless they have a very genuine faith. We may criticize people who have sold out, but simply to reject the members of these churches adds to the torment of people who endure harassment far beyond most of our experience. As Kent Hill has asked, "How many western Christians would pay the price registered believers routinely paid?"[2]

The second pattern is manifested largely in the Catholic Church. Because it has had more unity and greater political sense than many other Christian bodies, it has usually tried to maintain its own independence while not pushing the government too far. In doing so, it is able to draw on the fact that it is relatively cohesive and has extensive relations with other Christians throughout the world.

The third pattern is more common among evangelical Protestants. Many of these groups have refused to submit to government regulation and have formed "underground" churches. Since they are usually not allowed to meet in church buildings, they have developed a widespread pattern of "house churches." These meet in secret locations.

The house church movement is usually a very loose network. However, some local groups have several thousand members. Since their activities usually have to be kept secret, it is difficult to estimate how many people are involved. But it is clear that these churches have been growing rapidly in Communist countries in the last five years, as has the Catholic Church.

These patterns are all manifest in the mother of all repressors—the People's Republic of China.

CHINA

In January 1996, the newly appointed U.S. ambassador to China, James Sasser, met at the State Department with representatives of human-rights organizations concerned with conditions in China. People went round the room and introduced themselves. Those people concerned with the brutal repression of Buddhists in Tibet met with a concerned and knowledgeable response from Mr. Sasser, as they should have been.

But when Peter Torry, the president of Open Doors, said that his organization was particularly concerned with the "house churches" in China, he was met by the puzzled response, "What's a house church?"[3]

China contains a large percentage of the human race. And, because of its repressive regime, China's blood-stained record of control, discrimination, persecution, and death cannot be summarized either easily or clearly. In front of me is a book from Human Rights Watch/Asia which is some 630 pages long: It is simply a listing of people held in China and Tibet for political and religious reasons. This contains a thousand precisely documented cases as well as the names of hundreds of others about whom little is known—not even where these imprisoned individuals are or what is happening to them.[4]

On October 1, 1949, Mao Zedong, the chairman of the Chinese Communist Party, proclaimed the People's Republic of China. One of the Republic's first acts was to try to separate Chinese churches from "foreign influences." This is a curious turn of phrase, since the church in China goes back at least thirteen hundred years. There were Christian monasteries in the eighth century. The Italian John of Monte Corvino was the archbishop of Beijing some eight hundred years ago. The church is one of the oldest continuing institutions in China, and it has been there rather longer than the "foreign influence" represented by the Communist Party itself. Communism grew partially out of the more arcane streams of European philosophy which arrived in China at the turn of the century.

The government started by imprisoning any religious believers who refused to accept the priority of Communism over their own faith. They were labeled as "counter-revolutionaries" and sentenced to twenty years or more in prison or labor camps. Churches and other religious institutions were closed.

Even now, nearly half a century later, religious activities are tightly controlled and are officially limited to the government-sanctioned "patriotic" churches. Seminary students are examined on political conformity as well as theological knowledge. The government regulates the publication and distribution of religious material. Meanwhile, the unofficial Catholic and Protestant churches, which comprise most of China's Christians, are rendered illegal. There are tremendous variations depending on local government officials, so that in several areas, these groups are ignored as long as they maintain a low profile, but whenever the government finds it convenient, they are subject to brutal attacks.[5]

Churches are forbidden to be under the authority of any overseas body which means that, because of its worldwide association with the Vatican, Roman Catholicism is officially outlawed.

Apart from the draconian laws themselves, there is little sign that even supposed legal safeguards are respected. The government frequently flouts its own official judicial procedures and uses abuse and torture within the prison system to extract confessions. It has refused to allow the International Committee of the Red Cross to examine its prisons.

Apart from the official prisons, there exists a separate system of control. This consists of the *laojiao*, or "reeducation through labor," camps and the *laogai*, or "reform through labor," camps. These allow for detention, and the most brutal form of detention, without even a trial, without even a hearing. At the end of 1993, Chinese authorities said that one hundred and twenty thousand prisoners were undergoing "reeducation through labor," but the actual number is certainly higher.[6] The government also practices execution on a massive scale. Recent reports have shown that it schedules some of these executions in order to harvest the prisoners' organs for transplants.

According to human rights activist Harry Wu, who has experienced that of which he speaks,

> The core of the human-rights issue in China today is that there is a fundamental machinery for crushing human beings—physically, psychologically, and spiritually—called the *laogai* camp system, of which we have identified eleven hundred separate camps. It is also an integral part of the national economy. Its importance is illustrated by the fact that one-third of China's tea is produced in *laogai* camps. Sixty percent of China's rubber vulcanizing chemicals are produced in a single *laogai* camp in Shenyang. One of the largest steel pipe works in the country is a *laogai* camp. I could go on and on. The *laogai* system is: "Forced labor is the means; thought reform is the aim." . . . The *laogai* is not simply a prison system; it is a political tool for maintaining the Communist Party's totalitarian rule.[7]

"The Chinese *laogai* camp is fundamentally no different from a concentration camp, from the Gulag. I often wonder why people know so much about the concentration camps and the gulag, but so little about *laogai* camps."[8]

In the 1950s in order to increase its control over religious bodies, China established state religious organizations including the Catholic Patriotic Association (CPA) and, for Protestants, the Three-Self Patriotic Movement (TSPM). These bodies are controlled by the government's Religious

Affairs Bureau which, in turn, answers ultimately to the officially atheistic Chinese Communist Party.[9]

Especially from 1955 onward, the government attempted to purge "counter-revolutionaries" from the church. Clergy were arrested, given lengthy prison sentences, and treated viciously in the "reeducation through labor" camps. Then, in the Cultural Revolution from 1966 to 1976, probably tens of millions of people were killed and tens of millions more disgraced. In this period, the Red Guards were particularly brutal with China's believers, whether Christian, Muslim, or Buddhist. It was perhaps the largest intense persecution of Christians in history.

The level of atrocity that took place during that epoch is beyond comprehension. In one incident a mother and son were tortured, buried alive atop one another in a single grave, then dismembered and eaten by their tormentors. There were thousands of participants in mass cannibalism. The climate was gruesome madness.

> *Strolling down the street, the director of the local Bureau of Commerce [in Wuxuan] carried a human leg on his shoulder that he was taking home to boil and consume. On the leg there still hung a piece of a man's trouser. . . .*[10]

It would be comforting to dismiss such carefully documented reports as being remnants of a distant, more brutal time, unlikely to be repeated in today's world. However, although cannibalism is absent, Roman Catholic Bishop Su Zhimin's treatment by Chinese authorities reflects a chillingly savage mentality.

> *Bishop Su spent fifteen years in prison before his release in 1993, and was subjected to various forms of torture throughout his internment. During one particular beating, the board being used by the security police was reduced to splinters. Unrelenting, the police ripped apart a wooden door frame, and used it to continue the beating until it, too, disintegrated into splinters.*
>
> *The bishop was then hung by his wrists from a ceiling while being beaten around the head.*

And, in yet another encounter, he was placed in a cell filled with water at "varying levels from ankle deep to hip deep, where he was left for days, unable to sit or sleep. . . ."[11]

Bishop Su was rearrested in the spring of 1996.

The level of repression of religious organizations in China has varied over the years. But the fact of repression has never changed. When China is criticized, it replies that people are not punished for their religious beliefs but for breaking the law. However, this simply slurs over the fact that the law criminalizes peaceful religious acts that are protected in international human rights standards.

In the 1980s, as Deng Xiaoping exercised his influence in favor of liberalizing the economy, repression eased for awhile. But from 1988 onward there was a marked increase of religious repression. This was accelerated following the demonstrations in favor of democracy which began in April 1989. After the army attacked demonstrators in Tiananmen Square on June 3 and 4, killing perhaps thousands of people, any dissent was ruthlessly suppressed.

Bishop Fan Xueyan, perhaps the most influential of China's underground Catholic bishops, died in police custody on April 13, 1992, the day before his ten-year sentence would have expired.

Color photographs taken on April 16 or 17 showed large marks on his forehead and on one cheek. Both legs appeared to be dislocated below the knee. No definitive analysis as to the cause of death could be made from the photos, but the marks were consistent with violence suffered shortly before death.

First arrested in 1958, Bishop Fan was sentenced to fifteen years' hard labor. . . . for "stubbornly refusing to accept" the official Catholic Patriotic Association. He served in labor camps. . . . Released at the end of 1969, Bishop Fan returned to his home village but remained subject to supervision. He was arrested again on April 15, 1978, and held without charge in a local county jail until January 14, 1980. During the 1980s, Bishop Fan continued his underground church activities. . . . On April 13, 1982, he was arrested again.

> *The authorities have consistently denied persecuting Bishop Fan Xueyan. According to Liu Bainian, lay member of the Standing Committee of the Catholic Patriotic Association, Bishop Fan's arrest . . . was purely "for political, not religious" reasons. According to Liu, no one has been jailed in China for religious reasons since the Cultural Revolution.*[12]

Unfortunately, all evidence points to the contrary. Especially since 1994, hundreds of local house churches have been closed and their leaders fined, imprisoned, and tortured.[13] On January 31, 1994, Orders Number 144 and 145 were passed. These regulate the religious activities of foreigners in China and control the places in which religious activities can take place. These orders unleashed an extensive round of repression on the unregistered churches. The reason churches refuse to apply for registration is neither parochialism nor obtuseness.

> If religious officials reject an application [to register], the surfaced group is forced immediately to shut down. In some places, attempts to register have been denied because local cadres are fearful they will be criticized for registering churches that do not meet the state's criteria. They prefer to play it safe. Obviously such responses have a chilling effect on church groups debating their courses of action. On the other hand, if the attempt to register is successful, the congregation opens itself to constant scrutiny of its personnel choices, religious materials, forms of worship, and topics for sermons.[14]

This situation is exacerbated by the fact that since July 1995, the Religious Affairs Bureau has been headed by Ye Xiaowen, a prominent atheist and Communist hard-liner. Following his appointment, at least four prominent Roman Catholic bishops were arrested and detained. His leadership also introduced an intensified crackdown on evangelical Protestants. Protestant house-church leaders and China observers report that this is now the most repressive period since the pre-Deng period of the late 1970s. The *Far Eastern Economic Review* reports that between February and June 1996, "police have destroyed at least fifteen thousand unregistered temples, churches, and tombs."[15] In Shanghai alone more than three hundred house churches were closed down in April 1996.

The problems of registration are illustrated in this letter to a Chinese magazine:

> Since the religious policy came down to us, we have had a meeting point in our township. Each Sunday everyone met together to pray, study the Bible, and worship the Lord. However, last October [1992] the meeting-point was closed down and a sister was detained for twenty days and fined.... The excuse given was that it was an illegal meeting-point which had not received government permission. We had applied several times [for registration] but nobody responded positively. This left more than one hundred believers here with no other alternative than to go to the city church which is fifteen kilometers away.... Those who are elderly need to leave home at 3 A.M.... I am very concerned about this situation, as there are some elderly people who are crippled and want to hear God's Word but have nowhere to go. All they can do is stay at home and weep quietly....[16]

Another problem, especially for China's Catholics, is the government's population program. Newly married couples have to be sterilized or take long-lasting contraceptives if one or both are diagnosed as having a hereditary disease making them "unsuitable for reproduction:" This includes "relevant mental disorders." It also forces women to have abortions even in the later stages of pregnancy. The result of this draconian policy can be shown in the following report:

> *Using the slogan, "It is better to have more graves than more than one child," local authorities repeatedly raid the Catholics' homes, confiscate their property, and indiscriminately beat those unable to escape into the surrounding fields. Forced abortions have been performed on women in the last weeks of pregnancy, and several nonpregnant women have been sterilized against their will. . . .*

> *. . . the reported methods of torture include hanging men and women upside down, squeezing them under a chair, exposing them to extreme weather conditions for extended periods, and burning their tongues with electric batons to prevent them from invoking aloud God's help.*[17]

Nobody knows how many practicing Christians there are in China. In his 1995 report, the UN special rapporteur summarizes the figures given to him by the Chinese government's Office of Religious Affairs. For Catholicism, 3.5 million in 1993 and 4 million in 1994. For Protestantism, 4.5 million in 1993 and 6.5 million in 1994. He also lists the figure given by the Chinese People's Consultative Conference, 7 million Protestants in 1994. However, as Tony Lambert notes, the totals do not reflect even the government's own figures for its provincial bodies, which together produce a total of some 9.2 million Protestants. By August 1996 there were indications that the government estimated that there were 25 million Christians. In contrast, some mission groups give estimates of over a hundred million.

The best estimate, one based on an extensive province-by-province and city-by-city breakdown, and which outlines its methodology, is by Tony Lambert. Lambert, who formerly worked as a diplomat in China, concluded that in September 1994, there were some nineteen to thirty million Protestant believers in China. He cautions that this represents only those Protestants who attended registered and unregistered churches and adds, "No doubt there are several million Communist Party members, intellectuals, and professionals who keep their faith secret and rarely, if ever, attend meetings."

The number has certainly grown since then. Now the Province of Henan officially has 3.5 million Protestants, compared to eight hundred thousand a few years ago. Anhui officially has two to three million, compared to five to six hundred thousand a few years ago. Guangxi officially has ninety thousand compared to thirty thousand a few years ago, and only seven thousand in 1950. In short, the government figures themselves point to explosive growth in the churches. And these are only the figures for Protestants.[18]

Lambert tends to describe his numbers in diminutives—that there are "only" this many Christians. However, if his figures are correct, the result is stunning. These would indicate that the Protestant Church has grown by a factor of twenty to thirty times since the TSPM churches were officially opened for worship in 1979.

In particular, as I noted earlier, it means that there are more Christians attending regular church worship services in China than there are in all of Western Europe combined.

The point about the number of Communist Party members becoming Christians is not an idle one. On January 18, 1995, the Chinese Communist Party's Central Committee's Organization Department and Discipline Inspection Committee released a report saying that between 7 and 9 percent of Party members in the cities and coastal regions of China have joined religious organizations or take part in religious activity. If family members are included, this figure rises to over 18 percent.[19]

Although there are officially fifty million Communist Party members, few seemed interested or willing to propagate the Party's ideology. Of course, since nowadays that ideology boils down to a combination of making a quick buck, hanging on to power at all costs, and locking up one's opponents, it is not surprising that while many people are inclined to follow it, not too many are inclined to admit that they do. Nor publicly commend others to "go and do likewise."

The Communist Party has tried to respond to this challenge. On January 26, 1995, the Discipline Inspection Committee produced a document entitled, "Suggestions About Dealing with Party Members and Party Cadres Who Take Part in Religious Organizations and Activities." This document basically says that those who take part in religious activities willingly should be expelled, and those so stupid as not to realize what they are doing should be put on probation.[20]

Meanwhile, China is suffering from a spate of Christmas celebrations. The *South China Morning Post* reported in 1994 that at Christmas, the streets of Beijing were decorated in red and green. Many ordinary shops had "Merry Christmas" signs written in their windows, which were also full of Christmas decorations. Meanwhile, local Chinese went on a buying spree for Christmas presents.[21]

> Beijing fears Christianity because it is by nature uncontrollable. Dictatorship may have the power to mold minds, but the spirit is something it can never subjugate. For China's leaders, that is a truly terrifying thought.[22]

This quotation probably gets close to the heart of why China's Communists strive to repress the Christian faith. For, as I outlined in Chapter One, whatever else they may do or fail to do, Christians have usually been reluctant to locate the ultimate source of power in the state. They have always claimed some loyalty to "Another King." Christians may indeed be confused about the relation between God and Caesar, or about the boundary between God and Caesar, but they have usually believed that there must be such a boundary. The Communist principle is simply that Caesar *is* God. In the face of that confession, all genuine religion has to be seen as a threat. This is also manifested in the fact that a good many of China's political dissidents and labor activists, such as Xiao Biguang, sentenced to three years "education through labor" in July 1996, are also Christians.

Meanwhile, despite fluctuations in economy, politics, and culture, the courage of China's Christians continues to shine.

> *In Qing Hong parish, ninety-year-old Jing Xing Zheng braves the chilly autumn rain to attend Mass every Sunday. She wears five layers of clothing to help ward off the cold inside the church and carries an old canvas umbrella to keep dry on the long walk home.*
>
> *"I started coming to this church six years ago. Before that, I wasn't a Christian," Jing says. "Since I started believing in God, I became much healthier. It was God that helped me reach ninety."*[23]

VIETNAM[24]

The pastors courageously continue their work, knowing full well that there may soon be a knock at the door. An interrogation over trumped-up charges. A prison sentence. Perhaps even worse. Yet, almost without fear, they continue. And for some, before long, the authorities arrive and the grueling legal process begins.

Reverend Dinh Thien Tu is a well-known house-church leader in Ho Chi Minh City, with over two thousand parishioners. In 1991, he was arrested and held for over two years. Dinh's "crimes" were absurdly described: "propagation of religion under the guise of social work, abusing religious duties, being involved with social work without permission, and political ambition." Clearly, the most dangerous aspect of Dinh Thien Tu, in the government's view, was his commitment to the poor and his immense popularity.

Pastor Tran Mai is the leader of a large evangelical Christian house church. He, too, was arrested in 1991, accused of "abusing religious powers, [and] pursuing religious activities to fight the government." Tran was detained for a year-and-a-half. Observers commented that his release may have been part of a Hanoi effort to engender good will with the United States.

Ngugen Lap Ma, head pastor of the Southwestern Region for the Evangelical Church in Vietnam, was placed under house arrest on April 21, 1992. His conviction included the dubious description, "Number one person against Communism." He was sentenced to internal exile, along with his wife and ten children, without a hearing, a trial, or a court appearance.[25]

In 1976, after the U.S. withdrawal, Communist-led North Vietnam took over the south and reunited the country. They followed traditional Communist patterns. It quickly became apparent, especially considering the experiences of similar countries around the world, that economically, collectivism was not going to work. In 1986, the Sixth Party Congress of the Vietnamese Communist Party began to institute a program of economic changes. Following in the path of its traditional enemy, China, it started to encourage small-scale private enterprise and to dismantle its agricultural collectives.

In 1992, it approved a new Constitution which emphasized further economic reform and, since that point, has instituted an increasingly free market economy. In 1993, it made strenuous efforts to reestablish diplomatic relations with its neighbors and institute better relations with major countries, including the United States, in order to encourage foreign investment.

Throughout this period of economic reform, it has, also like China, steadfastly resisted any political reform. The Communist Party is Vietnam's sole legal party. "People's Committees" control daily life at the local and village level. It is forbidden to question the one-party system or the government's commitment to "socialism." It is a criminal act to oppose the government or to advocate a multi-party system. Thousands of people continue to be sent to "reeducation camps." Any attempt by Vietnamese to maintain a form of life and community independent of state power is regarded as a threat to national security, and is quashed.

This means that any religious expression which is not a puppet or an echo of the Party is slated for extermination.[26] The main objects of this religious repression have been the Buddhists, who comprise the majority of this, one of the most religious societies in Asia. The Unified Buddhist Church, the Cao Dai, and the Hoa Hao have been systematically repressed, the latter two quashed by tactics including the murder of their leaders.

This suffering also extends to Vietnam's large and active Christian community. Christianity took root under French control and has grown rapidly since independence so that now Catholics constitute some 10 percent of the seventy million population. There is also a one-half million strong Protestant community, most of whose growth has come since independence, and especially since 1990. Indeed, so strong is this growth that the Vietnamese government has taken to calling Christianity a "religion from America," something which must appear particularly galling to the French.

The government controls all the media, keeps religious believers under surveillance, and frequently detains religious leaders. It has also tried to control Catholics by placing them under the control of the official Catholic Patriotic Association. This association must approve all seminary students and church appointments and tries to exercise a veto power over the Vatican appointment of bishops. The main seat of Catholicism in Vietnam, the Episcopal director of Ho Chi Minh City, has been vacant since 1975 because the government has vetoed all appointments. The Party strategy is to "decapitate the Catholic Church by suppressing the hierarchy."[27]

Protestantism is prominent, and growing rapidly among the Hmong, Koho, Jeh, Rhade, and Jerai tribal minorities of the Central Highlands. They are subject to brutal repression if they do not join government-supervised religious associations. Most Protestants are members of "house churches," and many of their leaders are imprisoned on charges of "illegal preaching." Other forms of repression include beatings, forced labor, interference with harvests, forced emigration, property confiscation, and death threats.

A more recent strategy, implemented in order to avoid the show of direct religious imprisonment, is to impose fines for "illegal religious activity." House church leaders are fined up to one month's salary. Since many of them are not even paid, they cannot afford the fine and so are then assigned to labor camps to work off the debt.

Priests and pastors are assaulted, harassed, fined, sentenced to reeducation camps (where all religious activity is forbidden), and imprisoned. Many die in prison, some of them after torture.[28]

In 1952, a Roman Catholic priest, Father Dominic Tran Dinh Thu, founded an order in North Vietnam. This entirely indigenous body, the Congregation of the Mother Coredemptrix, relocated to the South of Vietnam when Ho Chi Minh began to consolidate his Communist government in the North.

Saigon fell in 1975, and nearly all of the congregation's properties, including monasteries, a print shop, a retirement home for priests, schools, and a nursing home, were seized by the Communists.

On May 15, 1987, Vietnamese police took possession of the congregation's only remaining compound. Not only did they confiscate food and literature, they also arrested sixty people including Father Dominic, who by now was eighty-two years old. After a trial in October, Father Dominic was sentenced to life imprisonment on charges of "propagandizing against the socialist system, sabotaging the solidarity policy, disturbing public security, and terrorism." Twenty-two others from the order were also imprisoned. Nearly a year later, Father Dominic's sentence was commuted to twenty years—which means that instead of life, he could get out when he was a hundred and two.

Only after he had served six years, some in Con Son Island Prison Camp, known for its harsh climate and inhumane conditions, and only after a relentless international campaign on his behalf, was the elderly priest released in May 1993.[29]

Father Dominic is only one of hundreds of church and lay leaders who have suffered in this way. Indeed, so great is the amount of repression that the Vietnamese government seems to have difficulty keeping track of it. On August 10, 1992, the United Nations special rapporteur wrote to the government of Vietnam, inquiring about some thirty Protestants and ten Catholics in prison for their beliefs. He wrote again in December 1993, reiterating his request and asking about an additional ten. On November 22, 1994, the government replied, "Concerning specific 'cases' you mention in your letter. . . . Answering these communications really constitutes an unnecessary heavy administrative burden for the government."[30]

The Vietnamese response also insisted "that in Vietnam no person is arrested, tried, or detained for his or her religious affiliation or activities. If anyone has been so, it was for his or her violation of the law."[31] However, as Human Rights Watch notes, this contention "rang hollow, given that Vietnam's legal system criminalized acts that are unambiguously protected by international guarantees of civil and political rights."[32]

Some restrictions were lifted during 1993 as Vietnam sought to expand its diplomatic and trade contacts, and so present a more benign face to the world. It released many long-term Protestant prisoners, allowed some five thousand Bibles to be imported, and invited Mother Teresa to begin programs in Hanoi.

But especially since early 1995, a more brutal form of repression has returned. This is particularly so after the United States normalized diplomatic relations with Vietnam in July 1995, a process in which Vietnam's religious repression was ignored. Since Vietnam got what it wanted, it seems to feel little need to keep up pretenses. On October 5, 1996, it detained an American, Man Thi Jones, for the "crime" of distributing pens (to orphans) since the pens had crosses on them. The government still allows some larger measure of freedom in areas more frequently visited by foreigners, but outside the major cities the situation is considerably worse.[33] Particularly prominent in 1995 were attacks on the churches among the Hre Tribe, prompted by the fact that the church is growing rapidly there.

Pastor Dinh Thien Tu, senior minister of the largest House Church Movement in Vietnam, was in prison between 1991 and 1993. During this period his church grew from three thousand to twelve thousand regular members with some thirteen thousand others awaiting training and baptism. Tu remarks, "Persecution is not a major issue for most Vietnamese pastors. It comes with the territory. It's part of our normal church life."[34]

CUBA

Cuban Pastor Orson Vila Santoyo, a Pentecostal minister in Camaguey, refused to refrain from holding religious services in his home. He was arrested on May 24, 1995, and charged with holding "illegal meetings." When state security police visited his house church, he defied orders to close it down, saying, "The doors of my house are open. If you want them shut, do it yourself."

Authorities confiscated the church equipment and, in blatant disregard for due process, Vila was tried on the day of his arrest, receiving a sentence that was reduced on appeal to eighteen months. Despite the fact that the trial took place within a matter of hours, more than one thousand people stood outside the court, shouting, "Cristo Vive!"

Following Vila's arrest, the Cuban Ministry of Justice sent letters ordering the closure of all house churches on the island. Hundreds of the churches complied; thousands of others did not. It is estimated that there are between three thousand and ten thousand Christian house churches in Cuba.

Vila was conditionally released from prison on March 2, 1996, and immediately placed under house arrest. His release took place only after an extensive international prayer campaign on his behalf.[35]

When Fidel Castro came to power with the overthrow of Fulgencio Batista in 1959, there were hopes that after a long-running dictatorship, he would institute a more open democratic society. Many Christians looked forward to his new regime with anticipation. However, Castro began and has consistently maintained a rigid authoritarian system, combining Leninism with personal dictatorship, buttressed by placing members of his family in key positions.

Castro is the head of state, president of the Council of Ministers, chairman of the Council of State, commander-in-chief of the Revolutionary Armed Forces, and the first secretary of the Cuban Communist Party. The Communist Party is the only legal party: Indeed, it is the only legal political and civic organization. Political dissent is legally punishable, and in elections for the National Assembly in the 1990s, only those candidates who supported the regime were allowed to run.[36]

Cuba has held more political prisoners for longer periods than any other country in the western hemisphere. It has restricted access to the country by human-rights monitors and refused to cooperate with the United Nations special rapporteur on human rights in Cuba.

Within three months of the takeover, Castro's regime began to interfere with the Catholic Church. Following the attempted invasion of the Bay of Pigs by U.S.-backed Cuban exiles, the crackdown on religious bodies became more severe. All religious activities except worship services inside church buildings were prohibited, and sermons were monitored to ensure they remained harmless. Government spies infiltrated congregations, evangelism was forbidden, the Cuban Bible Society was closed, and a twenty-year ban on importing Bibles and religious literature was instituted. Believers suffered discrimination in education and employment and were systematically harassed. Parents who kept their children home from school on religious holidays were subject to imprisonment. By the end of 1961, 3,400 nuns and priests had fled from the island in fear.[37]

In the mid-1960s, the anti-religious campaign intensified. Catholics and Protestants, both lay and clergy, including the current archbishop of Havana, Jaime Ortega, were labeled "social scum" and sent to forced labor camps where many were beaten and tortured. Even those not directly subject to assault in prison were, like other Cuban prisoners of conscience, subjected to inhumane conditions. These conditions continue. Human

Rights Watch reports that "minimal infractions or nonviolent protests such as hunger strikes spawned retaliation in the form of beatings, confinement in harsh isolation cells, violent and arbitrary searches, confiscation of belongings, denial of medical attention, suspension of visits, and transfer to prisons far from their relatives. Besides serious shortages of food and other supplies, Cuban prisons were plagued with overcrowding, poor hygiene, and vermin. Prisoners typically lost weight while in confinement due to the insufficient diet provided them."[38] After the early 1970s, the number of executions diminished, but patterns of discrimination, harassment, and marginalization still continued.

Subsequent years saw shifting tactics of repression and relaxation as Castro's government sought to maneuver in its international relations and domestic control. In 1985, the government, in imitation of other Communist powers, created a Religious Affairs Office and demanded the registration of religious groups. As the Puebla Institute put it, "Since efforts to eradicate religion had failed, the Castro regime had apparently decided the next best option was to bring it under official control."[39]

In 1987, some thirty thousand Bibles were allowed to enter and, for the first time since Castro's takeover of Cuba, a Catholic girl was admitted to the psychology department of the University of Havana.[40] In 1988, many religious prisoners were released, and there was greater freedom for religious instruction, meetings, and travel. As one church member remarked, "Church members are still tied to a choke chain, but the leash is just a little longer." Then, after 1988, things again began to get worse. The Catholic Church had used its limited freedom in order to question the regime, and Castro countered by giving support to Protestants so as to undercut Catholicism.[41]

This shifting continued. By 1992, believers were, in a gesture of questionable magnanimity, allowed to join the Communist Party. However, the government still refuses building permits for the rapidly growing churches and then imprisons pastors who minister to "house churches." Since May 1995, the pressure on such churches has increased.

Currently, churches cannot run schools or use television, radio, or other mass media. Missionary activity is forbidden, and the distribution of religious literature is tightly controlled. Adventists and Jehovah's Witnesses are entirely forbidden. All the other adjuncts of religious freedom—freedom of expression, freedom of association, freedom of movement, freedom of the press, and due process of law are denied.

Despite this, Cuba's church has grown in recent years, with several hundred thousand Catholics and with estimates of Protestants, including the hard-to-identify house church groups, ranging from two hundred thousand to one million.[42]

One of the Cuban government's other major efforts to suppress religious growth is a regulation enacted in December 1995 that "prohibits the sale of paper, ink, typewriters, computers, and spare parts for printing presses and photocopy machines to religious organizations. Technicians who repair office machines for churches face dismissal from their jobs."[43]

On the other hand, at Christmas 1995, Cubans were allowed to put up Christmas trees in their homes.

In his eagerness for investment, Castro now tries to portray a mellower image, even putting on a business suit to impress David Rockefeller and company at a luncheon after visiting the UN in October 1995. Later the same day, accompanied by U.S. Representative Charles B. Rangel, he redonned his designer combat gear for a gig at a church in Harlem. There, he declared, "his voice rising and his arms flying . . . 'we will never change because we are right.'"[44]

NORTH KOREA

> *Pastor Lee, please shake hands with as many Christians as you can and bring them to us. We want to feel the warmth of believers in the free world.*[45]

Christianity began to flourish in Korea in the latter part of the nineteenth century.[46] At this point Korea was in spiritual disarray and the church grew rapidly. Since Japan had been the principle colonizer, Christians were not associated with western imperialism. As they were also prominent in their opposition to the Japanese, they quickly became accepted as authentic representatives of the Korean people. Despite the fact that they accounted for only 2–3 percent of the population, 50 percent of the country's leaders who signed a Declaration of Independence from the Japanese in 1919 were Christians.[47]

For most of the twentieth century, Korea has suffered in one way or another—under Japanese occupation, Russian occupation, the Korean War, and the subsequent division of the country into North and South. The suffering inflicted by some of its own rulers has hardly been less.

In September 1948, Kim Il Sung, with Russian backing, declared the founding of the Democratic People's Republic of Korea, and set about instituting his own form of Communism in the north. For the next forty-six years, Kim ruled one of the most restricted regimes in the world. Korea has long been known as the "hermit kingdom," but, under Kim's thrall, the North became more so, and travel in or out was severely restricted. Consequently, reliable information—especially on the religious situation—is scarce.

The North Korean government denies each and every type of human right. Opposition parties are illegal, and the population is subjected to a steady barrage of government propaganda through loudspeakers. Radios and televisions are set to receive only government channels. Citizens have been punished for listening to foreign radio broadcasts. Authorities conduct monthly checks of houses, children are encouraged at school to report on their parents, and people are given a security rating which affects their access to education, employment, and healthcare. Any criticism of the government, and especially of the Kim family, is met with imprisonment or summary execution. Sometimes entire families are imprisoned, and prison conditions are brutal. The U.S. State Department estimates that between one hundred and one hundred fifty thousand people are currently held in "reeducation through labor" camps.[48]

Despite reports that his mother was a Christian, Kim Il Sung tried to exterminate both Christianity and Buddhism. At the time of the DPRK's founding, there were some two thousand churches and hundreds of thousands of Christians in the northern part of the peninsula. The capital, Pyongyang, was nicknamed "Asia's Jerusalem." But in the late 1940s, the government closed, confiscated, and destroyed churches, and imprisoned and killed Christians.

A study by the Minnesota Lawyers International Human Rights Committee and Asia Watch (Now Human Rights Watch/Asia) says that one hundred and fifty Catholic priests were murdered in 1950. "Incarcerated Christians were kept in cells so crowded that there was no room to sleep, underfed so severely that some starved to death, denied medical care, enslaved, forced to perform harsh physical labor, and physically abused."[49] Later, in the Korean War, North Korean troops routinely killed Christian prisoners.

Children of believers were removed from their homes and no public worship was allowed. All Bibles were destroyed and religious believers were sent for ideological reindoctrination. Possession of an overseas-printed Bible could produce a lengthy prison sentence. The only Bibles allowed were government-edited versions which, by a strange coincidence, bore a remarkable resemblance to the thoughts of Great Leader Kim Il Sung.

Even the children of religious believers were classified as "hostile elements" and were often allocated dangerous work assignments. Home Bible study was forbidden, as was the religious education of children. There were no church marriages, nor baptisms, and no displays of religious symbols.

Not only were Christians prevented from practicing their own faith, they were forced, along with other North Koreans, to practice what was, in effect, another faith. Kim established a personality cult beyond the dreams of even megalomaniacs such as Stalin or Mao. The country is littered with his statues. Every adult was required to wear his likeness on lapel pins; children were compelled to sing and, essentially, to pray to him. The newspapers told stories attributing supernatural origins and powers to the Kim family. This bizarre hagiography went beyond even attempted beatification and sanctification. It became a divinization wherein the relation of Kim, the Communist Party, and the people were described in terms appropriated from Christian trinitarian theology.

When it became clear that, notwithstanding the intense controls, vestiges of Christianity would still remain, the regime switched to the other Communist tack of seeking to regulate and control it. It founded the Korean Christian Federation and the Korean Catholic Association (along with the Buddhist Federation). These were to be the only channels through which Christianity would find expression.

There are now two official Protestant and one official Catholic congregation in Pyongyang. These are widely believed to be frauds. Indeed, the deception seems to be so transparent as to be incapable of fooling anybody except for the World Council of Churches.[50]

The mass is never said at the Catholic church because there is no priest in the country to say it, and there has not been one since 1946.[51] One *Washington Post* correspondent said that none of the four "worshipers" he asked to name the first book of the Bible could do so. A British journalist met with a leader of the Korean Christian Federation, who couldn't name the first three books of the Bible. The Federation itself was headed by Kim's cousin. Other correspondents have said that visiting these churches seemed like visiting Madame Tussaud's Wax Museum.[52]

Professor Suk Ryul Yu of Seoul's Institute of Foreign Affairs and National Security says that these churches are only activated when a foreigner requests to attend a church service, and that visitors may notice that many members of the Bong-Su Protestant Church can also be seen among the Chang-Chung Catholic Church congregation.[53]

The government claims about ten thousand Protestants and three thousand Catholics in North Korea. These figures are almost certainly too low. More accurate figures, like almost everything else in this country, are extremely hard to determine. Nevertheless, from accounts by defectors and ethnic Koreans living along the China/North Korean border, some analysts now claim that there are four hundred thousand North Korean Christians.[54] These Christians meet secretly in homes, rarely in groups of more than six, and have little contact between groups.

In contrast, the church in South Korea has experienced one of the most rapid expansions in human history. With about ten to fifteen million practicing Christians, it has become one of the most "Christian" countries in the world. Its political history has also been troubled with a succession of dictators who promoted rapid economic growth but, citing the threat of invasions from North Korea, repressed political freedoms. Now, however, it shows signs of having become a full-fledged democracy.

In July 1994, Kim Il Sung demonstrated, by dying and by doing nothing interesting on the third day, that his claims to divinity had been somewhat exaggerated. As Amnesty International delicately put it, his death led to "widespread public manifestations of mourning."[55] Kim was succeeded by his son, the "Dear Leader," Kim Jong-Il, but it is not yet clear whether the chosen son has been effectively able to assume the reins of power. If he does, the severe situation of the DPRK's Christians is likely to continue since Kim is as dogmatic as his father, though apparently rather less shrewd.

An overseas Korean pastor met secretly with Christians in North Korea, encouraging them that they were not forgotten by people in the West. Once the believers learned that he was a minister, they pleaded with him to baptize some converts.

"Are you willing to die for Jesus?" the pastor asked each person before he baptized them.

Every one nodded affirmatively.

Later the people asked him to serve the Eucharist, which he gladly did. Some of the elderly Christians had not received communion in forty years.

A few days later, a group of Christians from a nearby town arrived, excitedly responding to a word-of-mouth of the pastor's visit. When they were told he had already departed, they "fell to their knees and began pounding the ground with their fists."[56]

CHAPTER FIVE

Forgotten Outcastes

Sarmali Mahilari grabbed her daughter Sion's hand, and together they ran frantically away from the angry mob. A group of forty youths had broken into the house where they, along with eight others, were attending a Christian worship service.

Sarmali and Sion hid briefly in a neighbor's house, but the men spotted them. They broke into the house and dragged the two terrified woman out. They stripped them and repeatedly beat and molested them.

Bloodied and bruised, mother and daughter were locked up in the home of one of their attackers, who abused them over the next four days.

In the meantime, a group of church members filed documents with the local police and managed to get the two released. When they were examined by a physician, thirty-five-year-old Sarmali had "multiple bruise marks on the buttocks and thighs." Her daughter had abrasion marks "on the thighs and multiple scars on the right breast."

Christian Association [of India] General Secretary Allen Brooks said "attacks on Christian converts . . . had been mounting in the Bodoland area. . . ."[1]

The popular imagination still thinks of Christianity as a western religion. Yet, throughout Asia, there are tens of millions of people whose Christian roots go back further than in most of Europe.

The same imagination also envisions religions such as Buddhism and Hinduism as particularly tolerant, at least more so than their western counterparts. This image is sustained by selective quotations from their scriptures and from rosy pictures painted by some of their adherents.[2] This is not to imply for a second that *all* of their adherents are intolerant. Many are people of great integrity and great toleration. We only have to recall the name of Gandhi to remember one of the greatest examples of this century, and of most other centuries.

However, simply to think that these religions are, in practice, tolerant would be like assuming, after reading the Sermon on the Mount, that the Christian church has always been tolerant, or that Islam is always tolerant simply because the Qur'an says that "there is no compulsion in religion."

In terms of actual practice, Hinduism and Buddhism can be some of the most violence-prone systems in the world. Gandhi was himself assassinated by an extremist for alleged betrayal of Hinduism. In fact, according to one knowledgeable observer, Mark Juergensmeyer, the "number of political assassinations in the name of religion in South Asia rivals or exceeds that in the Middle East."[3] Minority religious voices are frequently subject to discrimination and persecution.

INDIA

Sister Rani Maria had the kind of compassionate heart that endeared her to the poverty-stricken women, men, and children to whom she devoted herself. She was described as "beloved" in the Dewas district of India where, in thirty-two villages, she had organized self-help groups, credit co-ops, health classes, and leadership programs.

On February 25, 1995, Sister Rani was making one of her rare visits to her family home in Kerala when three men boarded the bus on which she was riding, searched for her, and dragged her outside.

In the bright Indian sun, before the eyes of onlookers, the three men stabbed her more than forty times. The forty-one-year-old sister died beside the road, her body mutilated by her assailants' knives.

The killers were later identified as BJP (Bharatiya Janata Party) supporters. One of them had been angered by Sister's Rani's efforts to help individuals who had clashed with the BJP's agenda.

Indra Iyengar, president of the state Christian Association, said that she believes the BJP wants to liquidate Christians, and that Sister Rani's murder was part of this plan. "Former BJP chief minister Sunderial Patwa had once described Christian missionaries as 'stray dogs,' showing the intense hatred of the BJP toward the Christians."[4]

Hinduism is so varied that it is difficult to describe it simply as one religion. In many ways, it refers not to a specific belief system but to the range of traditional belief systems in India as a whole. The words *India* and *Hindu* have a common root. Both terms were first used by outsiders to refer to the people and the religion, or culture, of the Indus Valley.[5] The question of whether the term refers to culture or to religion has even become a matter for court cases. The Indian Supreme Court held that "'Hindu' is derived from the River Sindhu. . . . no precise meaning can be ascribed to the terms 'Hindu' . . . and 'Hinduism'"[6]

This strong association has led many Hindus to believe that to be an authentic Indian necessarily means being Hindu. In the twentieth century several radical movements have been formed in order to promote and enforce this view. In 1925, the Rashtriya Swayamsevak Sangh (RSS) was founded and it developed rapidly into a paramilitary organization with combined lessons in religious ideology and martial arts. Gandhi's assassin sprang from this movement.

The RSS was once regarded by other Hindus as a fringe movement but, by the 1980s, it had become strongly associated with the BJP, the largest Hindu political party. The RSS supplies thousands of the most committed full-time activists in the BJP. In the conflict with Muslims over the Babri

Mosque in Ayodhya, the RSS and the BJP formed a potent combination, and the ensuing clashes resulted in hundreds of deaths. The BJP has continued to grow and, in the elections of May 1996, it became the largest party in the Indian Parliament and the core of a new, albeit brief, Indian government.[7] Its growing power threatens all of India's religious minorities, particularly the large Muslim community. It is also a threat to India's twenty-five million Christians. However, Christians in India have already experienced oppression for decades. This takes three major forms:

- discrimination, especially against lower caste Christians
- restrictions on changing one's religion or talking to people about changing one's religion
- persecution and communal violence directed against Christians, who are often accused of undermining Hinduism

One of the dark sides of Hindu culture is the caste system, wherein people are regarded at birth as belonging to a particular social stratum due to their cycle of reincarnation. Those in lower castes are thought to be paying the cost of wrongs they committed earlier, and are usually consigned to menial tasks and to poverty. The lowest of all are the *dalit*, or "untouchables." Untouchables, as their name suggests, are literal outcastes in the society, and face pervasive, humiliating, and intense discrimination.

Especially since independence, Indian governments have sought to alleviate the plight of the untouchables. One method is a type of "affirmative action," wherein certain university admissions and government loans and jobs are reserved for the *dalit* in proportion to their numbers in the population. This was enshrined in Article 15 of the Constitution.

Since untouchables face a bitter existence under Hinduism, many of them have found Christianity to be a liberation and over half the Christians in India are untouchables. However, this has usually not freed them from external discrimination. As Gandhi said in 1936,

> Whether the Harijan (untouchable) is nominally a Christian, Muslim, or Hindu and now Sikh, he is still a Harijan. He cannot change his spots inherited from Hinduism so-called. He may change his garb and call himself a Catholic Harijan or a Muslim Harijan or a neo-Muslim or neo-Sikh, [but] his untouchability will haunt him during his lifetime.[8]

Christians face additional problems since the Indian government explicitly excludes them from the places reserved for other untouchables. While the Supreme Court has ruled that converts should still receive their benefits, a governmental order from 1950 continues to provide that "no person who professes a religion different from the Hindu or Sikh religion shall be deemed to be a member of the Scheduled Caste."[9]

Gradually, untouchables who have embraced other faiths have been allowed to use the legal remedies for untouchable status. In 1990, the Buddhists were included. The current situation is that all religious groups are included, *with one exception*: Christians. The Indian Parliament was scheduled to review the situation in November 1996, but many Indian groups have mobilized against any change.[10] Christian *dalit* carry a double burden. They are subject to all the stigma and pain of untouchable status, yet they alone are excluded from the help offered for those pains.[11]

Christians, and especially Christians who seek to propagate their faith, increasingly come under intense criticism. Respected Hindu journalist Arun Schourie accused Christian missionaries of destroying Indians' self-respect. In doing so, he cited mainly preindependence (1947) writings, seemingly unaware that the vast majority of Christian work in India is conducted by Indians. The number of Indian Christians outnumbers the number of foreign missionaries by a factor of over twelve thousand to one.

Christians are sometimes viewed as "foreigners." However, Christianity has been in India for over a millennium. Legend has it that Jesus' disciple Thomas traveled to India: Hence, the oldest Indian church is called the "Mar Thomas" Church. We need not accept this legend, however, in order to realize that Christianity has been in India longer than in its most recent imperial conqueror, Britain.[12]

There is also opposition to people who attempt to leave Hinduism and to people who try to convince them to do so. The Indian Supreme Court has asserted that constitutional freedom of religion does not safeguard the right to try to convince others. This violates international human-rights guarantees and, in the Indian case, adds its own particular form of injustice. Since Hinduism is so pervasive, many people are regarded by law as Hindus, whether they want to be or not. This includes the untouchables, who are not even allowed to enter Hindu temples. It also affects tribal peoples who may be very distant from Hinduism.

The power of the law also comes down on religious workers. On January 22, 1996, Father L. Bridget and Sister Vridhi Ekka were sentenced to six months of "rigorous imprisonment" after having been convicted by a district court in Ambikapur of "forcibly converting" ninety-four members of the Uraon tribe in 1988.

It is not immediately clear how two people can "forcibly convert" ninety-four people. Nor were the witnesses in the trial much help in that regard. They told the court that "they were neither lured nor coerced by the accused to convert," merely that "the accused were present during the conversion." Other aspects of the "force" applied were that "the accused with the help of local people built a church at Maheshpur village. . . . [and] had also taught converted Christians about the method of offering prayers in the church."[13] Clearly, if this constitutes "force," then no conversation with anybody about religion can be exempt from state repression in the name of "freedom of religion."[14]

Beyond criticism and discrimination, Christians also face violence and murder. In September 1994, a Catholic church was bombed and three priests in the Gumla District of the South Chotanagpur Region were brutally murdered. This was only one of a series of incidents in the area.[15]

Much of this violence is related to Christian attempts to help untouchables. When Christian workers have attempted to assist *dalits*, women, and unorganized laborers, some Hindu fanatics have reacted violently.

In Sardhana, at the famous shrine of Our Lady of Grace, an Italian priest was strangled in late 1994.

Another priest, Father Paul Rebello, disappeared on a nearby road on December 27.

Father Devasia was called to the window of his room, and his eye was shot out.

Sister Rani Maria was stabbed forty times, murdered in Indore on February 25, 1995.

Five Franciscan nuns near the Ghaziabad-Delhi border were viciously attacked on April 2, 1995. One of the nuns, Sister Effy, whispered, "They didn't hit me too hard. God held their hands. . . ."

Bishop Vincent Concessao, auxiliary in the Delhi Catholic Diocese, comments that, "The more we get involved in work relating to social justice, we have to expect opposition and attacks like this. . . ."[16]

Apart from the issue of the untouchables, violence is often related to political competition. Since many of India's parties draw on communal identities, people who change religion are often also changing political support. The BJP resents the fact that, in reaction to its fervent Hinduism, many Christians and other minorities support the Congress Party or the left-wing parties. In Kerala state, the six million Catholics have formed the electoral backbone of the Congress Party since the state was formed.[17]

In November 1995, a man named John Kerketta was lynched by a mob alleging that he had damaged a temple. The only witness was an eight-year-old boy who reportedly saw Kerketta with a spear in his hand. The mob descended on his village, Latbhora, and destroyed its eighteen Christian homes. The district magistrate, D. P. Tiwari, commented, "Usually, such feelings are exploited on the eve of elections."[18] In the face of such ever-growing violence, particularly against Catholic priests and sisters, forty-four nuns of St. Anne's Convent at Madhavan, Madras, began a course in self-defense and earned brown belts in karate.[19]

India's tribal peoples face their own set of problems. Living mainly in the mountainous areas of the south and the northeast, they are quite distinct from the major ethnic and linguistic groups. Despite this, the equation of Indian equals Hindu means that increasingly they are being externally confined to a Hindu identity. The Christians among them often suffer particular harassment and murder. News of such events is scattered and sporadic, but the violence is widespread. The Kuki tribe, which contains large numbers of Christians, has been under major attack. In August 1993, eighty-seven were killed by Naga militants, while on May 15 the following year, another sixteen were beheaded.

NEPAL

On November 12, 1989, the Christian church service had just ended in Bhaktapur. Families were beginning to leave the church, when two police vans pulled up outside.

Those who could escape, did so. The forty who remained were arrested and shoved roughly into the vans. When they arrived at the local jail, they were forced to watch their seventy-six-year-old pastor, Tir Bahadur Dewan, being violently beaten.

Then it was their turn. The deputy superintendent of police threatened them with the same fate. Their only escape, he explained, was to bow to a Hindu statue and have the sign of the Tika smeared on their foreheads.

Still trembling from the sight of their pastor's ordeal, many chose to bow to the statue—an act that Nepalese authorities often tried to force upon Christians. The ones who refused were imprisoned for ten days, until bail was finally posted.

Their pastor was not so fortunate. Despite his injuries and advanced age, he was held captive for several months.

This particular effort to force Christians to bow to Hindu figures was, unfortunately, unexceptional except for one fact: It took place less than ten miles from Katmandu. Most such brutalities take place in outlying areas, well-hidden from western observers.[20]

Since the 1960s, Nepal has been imagined by Americans to be a laid-back and tolerant place. For years, Katmandu was a destination for hippies who wished to inhale and bask in the exotic and apparently open atmosphere. It remains a stunningly beautiful kingdom, resting in the shadow of Mount Everest. However, while westerners cavorted in their make-believe mountain paradise, underlying religious intolerance carried on unnoticed.

Despite its many religious fanaticisms, India's Constitution still describes it as a secular state. However, neighboring Nepal's Constitution describes it as a Hindu nation. The king, Birendra Bir Bikram Shah Dev, is revered by many Nepali Hindus as a reincarnation of the god Vishnu.

Prior to 1990, the country was ruled under an autocratic system of Hindu *Panchayat*. Those guilty of talking to Hindus about other faiths could be given a three- or six-year prison term, depending on whether their efforts met with any success. Hindus who changed their religion received one-year terms and were forced to recant. When a convert was released from prison, adherence to the new religion was regarded as ended; hence, if he or she then went to church, the person was liable to be jailed for another year. This process could continue indefinitely. In 1990, about one hundred eighty Christians were in prison for their dissent from the dominant religion.[21]

In 1990, the Nepalese king demanded democratic reforms and more freedom for the 10 percent of the country's twenty million people who were not Hindus. Every religious prisoner was then released. Since that time, the atmosphere has been much freer. In 1992, a new law even allowed Nepalis to change their religion. Although the old law which states, "No person shall be entitled to convert another person" remained on the books, there were hopeful signs that there would continue to be greater freedom in the country.

However, in February 1994, two Christians were arrested and detained for three days near Katmandu and were warned not to violate conversion laws.[22] Six months later, hopes for greater freedom among the country's two hundred thousand Christians were further damaged. In the eastern town of Danabari, a group of eleven men and women, mostly younger than twenty-five and including four teenagers, were arrested and charged with attempts at conversion.[23]

Most of those charged were refugees from nearby Bhutan, from which thousands of refugees have fled to Nepal in recent years. The police accused the group of preaching inside a Hindu temple, but other sources say that they were arrested while on their way to a private prayer meeting at a

Christian home. Simon Pandi, general secretary of the National Churches Fellowship of Nepal, says that "even the girls were beaten very badly."[24]

It is not clear whether these arrests indicated a return to a more repressive climate or whether they showed the difference between the more open atmosphere of the capital and the more closed countryside, where democratic reforms have had far less influence. As it was, many Christians welcomed the election of a Communist government in November 1994.[25]

The eleven Christians were sentenced in August 1995 to two years' imprisonment.[26] However, the king, who seems to be far more open about these matters than many of his subjects, pardoned them. But despite the fact that trends in Nepal seem to be improving, Christians and other minorities still face the threat of imprisonment if they should be thought to be trying "to convert another person."[27]

SRI LANKA

Just before Christmas in 1994, more than one hundred Christians gathered in Galewala, Sri Lanka, to celebrate the birth of Christ.

An angry mob of around thirty young men descended on the house, armed with poles and rocks, shouting, "This is a Buddhist village!" The mob's threats and taunts continued while the pastor called the police.

When authorities arrived later that evening, their inquiries showed that the instigators of the attack were Buddhist monks, one of whom was the local leader of Jayagrahaniya (SUCCESS). He declared that they had personally dedicated themselves to opposing Christian conversion. "It is an island-wide problem," the monk explained.

The local authorities eventually closed the case by stating that Christians could freely practice their faith, but only in church buildings, not in houses.

Nevertheless, the local Buddhists were unrelenting—they continued to demand that the Christians move their worship someplace else.

"This," they continued to insist, "is a Buddhist village."[28]

Like Hinduism, Buddhism has a reputation for tolerance. One pervasive image is of a type of Zen, and popular culture is replete with images of peaceful Buddhist monks deep in meditation, filled with inner harmony. Like many popular images, this one also has some basis in truth. And like the other religions we describe, Buddhism contains outstanding patient, loving, and wise people.

Also like other religions or rather, like all things which involve human beings, realities can be quite different from ideals. In practice, Buddhism can manifest great intolerance and chauvinism.

On June 10, 1995, when Sri Lanka's President Chandrika Kumaratunga addressed the tenth assembly of the Christian Conference of Asia in Sri Lanka's capital, Colombo, she maintained that Buddhism is a religion "unique in its unstained record of tolerance." She urged the churches to help dispel "the lie" that religious bigotry is at the heart of the violent struggles presently wracking Sri Lanka.[29]

If President Kumaratunga is referring only to the vicious conflict between the Sinhalese majority and the separatist Tamil guerrillas in the north, she may well be correct. The struggle is at heart a political one over the control of territory, with the Tamils fighting for either independence or a very large measure of self-government. However, since religion does shape people's culture, then different religious histories find their reflection in the conflict. The Sinhalese are predominately Buddhist and the Tamils are predominately Hindu. The Tamils also contain a higher proportion of Christians than the 8 percent present in the rest of the country.

In one major incident in the ongoing civil war, government forces bombed a Catholic church in the northern town of Navali, killing at least sixty-five people and injuring another one hundred fifty. The Catholic bishop of Jaffna, Thomas Savundaranayagam, called on President Kumaratunga to tell the military to cease targeting civilian buildings such as churches.[30]

One major problem facing most Christians in Sri Lanka is living their lives among the majority of Sinhalese Buddhists who inhabit most of the island. Sri Lanka, off the southeast coast of India, was reputedly settled by Theravada Buddhists in the third century B.C. It has since been ruled by a succession of Buddhist dynasties. This particular form of Buddhism, and the Sinhalese language itself, are unique to Sri Lanka.

Modern Sri Lankan nationalism has emphasized this unique heritage and has stressed that it is a fragile treasure that must be preserved and defended.[31] This is reflected in the Sri Lankan Constitution, where Article 9 assigns preeminence to Buddhism and obliges the state to protect and foster it. Buddhist temples are maintained and Buddhist "clergy" are paid by the government.

This defensiveness about Buddhism came to a head just before Pope John Paul II's January 1995 visit. In his book, *Crossing the Threshold of Faith*, the Pope described Buddhism as having "an almost exclusive negative soteriology [teaching on salvation]" and suggested that the Buddhist concept of enlightenment could produce "an indifference to what is in the world." In mid-December, five leading Buddhist prelates demanded an apology from the Pope for what they termed these "insults" and said that his visit would be "an act of aggression."[32] Sri Lankan Catholic bishops immediately conveyed their "deepest regrets" to Buddhist leaders for the Pope's remarks.

Despite the bishops' regrets, it is difficult not to agree with the observations of Malcom Ranjith, the auxiliary bishop in charge of the papal visit, when he said the Pope should not apologize:

> There is a difference between insult and opinion. . . . If I differ with what you believe and understand, I need not apologize. You can ask for an explanation, but you cannot demand an apology.[33]

Whether or not we agree with the Pope, he was offering a defensible and not uncommon analysis of Buddhist soteriology. Unless we say that we should never disagree with any religion, which simply implies that no religion believes anything worth disagreeing with, then it's difficult to see what else he, as a Catholic teacher, could or should do.

The Buddhist leaders seemed to be demanding that nobody should ever criticize or disagree with their views. However, this is not a demand for religious toleration. It is a demand for immunity from any disagreement or criticism whatsoever. It should also be added that some Buddhist leaders in Sri Lanka have never been reticent about making criticisms of Christianity, as is their right. In fact, compared to the vehemence of some of these criticisms, the Pope's remarks are almost friendly.

Sri Lanka's Sinhalese Buddhist nationalism took an extreme and violent form in the Deshapremi Janatha Viyaparaya (JVP) which, in the 1980s, killed hundreds, perhaps thousands, of people in its attempts to take over rural areas and undercut a government which it regarded as too secular. In 1989 and 1990, the army brutally repressed it, killing many thousands of its followers. The military left their bodies along the main roads *pour encourager les autres*.

As in many other situations we have covered, the Sri Lankan government has combined resistance to militant religious groups with attempts to buy them off by concessions, and by espousing a milder form of religious nationalism. One result has been opposition to conversions away from, not to, Buddhism and increasing harassment of Christians.

The Constitution of Sri Lanka, in Articles 10 and 14, recognizes a person's right to adopt and practice the religion of his or her choice. Yet cases where people, especially Buddhists, have sought to adopt another religion are met frequently with open hostility and occasional harassment, especially from Buddhist monks in rural areas.[34] There are continuing efforts to introduce a legal ban on converts. The newspaper *Lankadipa* published a resolution by the major Buddhist organization SUCCESS calling on the government to pass anti-conversion laws. The parliament of Sri Lanka planned to introduce a bill in 1995 which would do this and also ban missionaries and all forms of "proselytizing." However, the introduction of legislation was delayed by an escalation in the war with the Tamil separatists.[35]

The Christian Consultation of Sri Lanka has expressed its concerns about "misguided people who have been incited to attack Christian ministers and destroy places of worship. We have documented cases of intimidation, threats of violence and arson; all this in the cause of religious intolerance."[36] The UN special rapporteur on religious intolerance has received reports that evangelical Christians "are often subjected to manifestations of hostility and sometimes to violence by the local Buddhist clergy." He recounts instances where an evangelist had his house stoned and local Christian villagers were threatened with denial of burial rights in their village.[37]

In July 1995, the Colombo office of the National Christian Council (NCC) was raided by forty armed police, allegedly searching for subversive literature. An American intern, Kenneth Mulder, was detained, transported back to Colombo, questioned, and deported five days later. The homes of ten young Tamil women who worked in the NCC office were also searched.[38]

Anyone can sympathize with desires to preserve religious traditions. However, like every other country in the world, Sri Lanka does not have just one culture or religious tradition. It contains a multitude of diverse people with both deeply entrenched and shifting allegiances. The attempt to preserve religions should be pursued by religious means, not by violence or state enforcement.

MONGOLIA

Mongolia is another country which has recently sought to maintain and renew its Buddhist tradition, though also often at the cost of discrimination against minorities. For most of this century, Mongolia has been controlled by the Soviet Union and shaped by its very own clone of Stalin, Tholbalsan. In the late 1980s, as conditions eased in the Soviet Union under Gorbachev, there were even more rapid changes in Mongolia. In the aftermath of perestroika there has been a striking resurgence of Buddhism.

Buddhism has deep roots in Mongolian society. As recently as 1911, Mongolia's hereditary Buddhist leader, Bogda Gegeen Javzandamba Hutagt, was proclaimed as the Khan of Mongolia, exercising both secular and spiritual authority. The drafting committee of the new 1992 Constitution gave serious consideration to including a clause which would have proclaimed Buddhism as the state religion, but settled instead on support for "the traditions of [Mongolia's] history and culture."[39]

However, this reticence concerning state support of Buddhism receded in 1993. The November 30, 1993 "Law Concerning Relations with Churches and Monasteries, Number 196 (696)" included the following provisions:

- Article 4.2—". . . The state will respect the predominant position of the Buddhist religion in Mongolia."
- Article 4.7—". . . The organized propagation of religion from outside [is] forbidden."
- Article 4.8—"The absolute number of lamas and clergy and the location of churches are controlled and regulated by [the] State."
- Article 7.5—"It is forbidden to introduce activities which are. . . . alien to the traditions and customs of the Mongolian people. . . ."[40]

The law also forbade religious activities from state-owned halls and restricted all Christian activity to the confines of church buildings.[41] Since few churches can afford to own buildings, and most other possible rental spaces are owned by the state, this is a crushing restriction—one which does not apply to Buddhism, Islam, or Shamanism.[42]

In January 1994, the Mongolian Constitutional Court struck down three articles of the 1993 law. However, in hearings which excluded the churches' legal counsel, the Court let stand the provisions guaranteeing the predominance of Buddhism and the prohibitions on religions "against Mongolian customs."[43]

This concern to maintain Mongolian traditions even by repression has its ironic side, since Mongolian Buddhism has its roots in Tibet. Tibetan is its canonical language, and every major temple has a throne for Tibet's exiled leader, the Dalai Lama. In the 1990s, one of the leading spiritual authorities has been the Indian ambassador, who was given diplomatic status by India when the previous Communist authorities in Mongolia had refused to give him a visa to visit.[44]

Churches have faced difficulties with registration, without which they cannot function legally, and there is a proliferation of anti-Christian articles in state-run newspapers. On April 11, 1995, the Mongolian state newspaper *Ardyn Erh* urged that Buddhism should replace western idealism. It claimed that Christianity promotes the ideals of "freedom, equality, and the brotherhood of man," but that such concepts are "unreal" and "can never be fulfilled." "Pressing all to this ideology is the cruel feature of Christianity."

There is also violence. On April 23, 1996 a Christian, Amgalan-Baatar, was beaten and stabbed. The same month, Bible Society executive secretary Altan-Chimeg and her husband had their home vandalized twice. There are other reports of harassment since the passage of the new law.[45]

On a more positive note, on May 26, 1996, the Catholic Church was able to leave its rented property, which had once belonged to the Soviet Army, and inaugurate its first permanent place of worship. More democratic forces won the elections in June 1996 and it is as yet unknown whether this signals better things for the future.[46]

BHUTAN

If Bhutan is known at all in the popular mind in the West, it is likely through some travelogues written by Shirley MacLaine at her dopiest. She portrayed the country as a Himalayan Shangri-La—a haven of peace, having everything, except possibly Ronald Coleman.[47]

Of course, people in Bhutan are like people in Tibet or India or any of the countries we have described. They are some of the most delightful on the face of the earth. But they do not inhabit a Hollywood sound stage.

The population in the south of the country is largely ethnic Nepalese and Hindu. The government has portrayed them as a threat to the cultural survival of Buddhism and, in the 1990s, has "forcibly evicted some one hundred thousand. . . . through rape, torture, and burning of homes, giving the kingdom the distinction of having the highest per capita refugee population in the world."[48]

In Bhutan, Buddhism is the state religion, with Hinduism as another recognized religion. The government, with a powerful monarch, subsidizes monasteries and shrines, and supports many of the kingdom's monks. The monks also have official positions on major government bodies. People of other beliefs are allowed freedom of worship but are not allowed to spread their faith. In fact, conversion to a non-approved religion is illegal.[49]

There are also repeated calls in Bhutan's National Assembly for Christianity to be banned. However, the government has been content to maintain the present restrictions. The UN special rapporteur on religious intolerance described these incidents in his 1995 report:

> *Dal Jit Rai, assistant to the head of the village of Kikhorthang in Cirang District, was allegedly dismissed on the orders of the Dzongda (District Commissioner) because he is a Christian.*
>
> *On December 25, 1992, when Mr. Dal Jit Rai was celebrating Christmas with other Christian families, a former policeman is said to have photographed them at prayer. After this incident, the worshipers were summoned by the village head who said there was a ban on practicing Christianity and took them to the Dzongda.*
>
> *The Dzongda is reported to have reaffirmed the strict ban. Shortly afterwards, three Christians, Harka Bahadur Chimery, Raju Lama, and Bhin Thapa, were allegedly beaten during interrogation. All Christian families were allegedly forced to sign an appeal for permission to leave the country.*
>
> *On February 5, 1993, the Christians are reported to have been expelled and to have sought refuge on February 13, 1993, in a camp in Nepal.*[50]

In response to these charges, the government of Bhutan replied that Christianity is not banned in Bhutan, and that "a person can practice any religion privately in his home." It also said that "attempts to convert others" are "strictly forbidden" and claimed that "there are two religions practiced" by the people of the area, which seems to imply that Christians do not exist, even in private. It thought the question was settled, since the people involved had now "emigrated."

BURMA

> *In a Karen village, Pastor Timothy found two children, six and eight years old, weeping inconsolably. They told him that their parents had been killed.*
>
> *Invading Burmese troops (SLORC) had invaded the Salween area of North Kwatholei, ransacking homes and slaughtering animals. Then, while the local people hid in the forest, soldiers laid mines on the steps of the houses.*

> *The children's mother returned to the house for rice for her family. As she went up the stairs, she stepped on a mine and was blown apart before her children's eyes. The father, who was walking close to his wife, lost his leg. Because there was no medical care, he soon bled to death.*[51]

Burma (called Myanmar by the current dictatorship) is one of the most repressive governments in the world. After a long period of torpid dictatorship, there were parliamentary elections in July 1990 in which the National League for Democracy (NLD) won 392 out of 485 contested seats. This victory came despite the fact that its leaders had been imprisoned since July 1989.

The military refused to abide by the results and imprisoned nearly a third of those elected, in addition to those already in prison. Since then, the State Law and Order Restoration Council (SLORC) has continued a brutal policy of crushing all opposition. Meanwhile, the courageous resistance of Aung San Suu Kyi, the head of the NLD, has continued to draw the attention of the world.

The military's campaign has involved repression of opposition political leaders, violent restraint of the country's minorities, and merciless war on the independence-seeking tribes at the country's perimeter. It has abused all of its citizens, regardless of color or creed. There is no freedom of speech, of assembly, or of the press. Teachers are required to teach government propaganda, and any criticism provokes an instant crackdown.

SLORC represses religious groups along with the rest of the population. While it allows freedom of worship, it cracks down immediately on any activity which could make religious adherence a center of loyalty competing with the government. Nevertheless, like many repressive governments which lack support, it tries to acquire a mantle of legitimacy by drawing on the people's deeper-rooted attachments. Consequently in recent years it has tried to link itself to Buddhism. There are reports that non-Buddhists have worked as forced labor on Buddhist construction projects.

The U.S. State Department says there are "credible reports. . . . of Buddhist missionaries dispatched by the central government, and local military personnel actively working to expand Buddhism, sometimes through compulsion, in minority areas. Religious publications are rigorously controlled, as are secular ones. Bibles in the indigenous languages cannot be imported and it is extremely difficult for Christian and Muslim groups to obtain permission to build new centers of worship."[52]

SLORC's most brutal acts take place in its campaigns against the country's ethnic and religious minorities. The worst is probably its merciless assault on the Rohingya Muslims in northern Arakan, along the border with Bangladesh. There it has engaged in a little-noticed campaign of "ethnic cleansing" involving murder, systematic rape, and forced labor, which makes even the Serb attacks on Bosnian Muslims seem comparatively mild.[53]

Similar campaigns have taken place against the better-armed people on the eastern frontier, especially the Mon, the Kachin, and the Karen tribes. A large percentage of these latter people are Protestant Christians and their Christian faith dates back centuries. They are also ethnically distinct from rest of Burma's population.[54]

Since the end of World War II, where they were distinguished by their refusal to submit to Japanese rule, the four-million-strong Karen have waged a campaign for independence. There are reports that SLORC forces have used chemical and biological warfare against them, as well as their usual tactics of forced labor, rape, massacre, and the use of human beings as mine-sweepers.[55]

> SLORC representatives . . . have . . . intensified their attacks on Karen border villages using the same terror tactics. . . . burning crops and homes, systematic rape and abuse of women, and forcing them then to act as both porters and prostitutes for the SLORC soldiers. The children as young as four or five years old are forced to act as human mine-sweepers, walking in front of the Burmese soldiers so that they are either maimed or killed rather that the SLORC militiamen.[56]

In January 1995, the government renewed its war effort and sought to create a split between the Karen's Christian and Buddhist members. While Buddhist and Christian leaders throughout the country have sought peaceful and cooperative relations between their communities, the government is trying to marginalize the people in the border regions by stressing its ties to Buddhism, the majority religion. There are reports that, in SLORC offensives, when Karen villagers were captured, "Buddhist villagers were interrogated and released, whereas Christians were tortured, given the opportunity of converting to Buddhism, and if they refused to do so, executed."[57]

According to November 1995 testimony before the Australian Joint Standing Committee on Foreign Affairs, Defense, and Trade, SLORC has recently begun explicitly anti-Christian propaganda to "point out the weak points of Christianity through the spread of Buddhism." According to government documents: "Christianity must be destroyed by peaceful means as well as violent means."[58]

SLORC officials have sent a letter to Buddhist leaders in refugee camps on the border saying that Karen Buddhist families would be permitted to return to Burma but that "no Christian will be given safe passage." The rules in the camps for those returning to Burma state "no religion apart from Buddhism is allowed to be discussed in the compound."[59]

Karen refugees have come under attack from a breakaway faction called the Democratic Karen Buddhist Army, which is now allied to SLORC.[60] The Karen had been the sole surviving holdout against the central government, but now thousands of additional refugees have fled into neighboring Thailand, fearing the collapse of what the *Economist* calls, "The last center of democracy in Myanmar."[61]

KAMPUCHEA/CAMBODIA[62]

In recent decades the people of Kampuchea have suffered as much as any on earth. In the late sixties they were drawn into the Vietnam War. In April 1975, the Khmer Rouge seized power, launched a policy of autogenocide and inflicted a regimen of suffering on the population as only Paris-educated intellectuals could envision and enact. By conservative estimates, over one million people out of the approximately seven million population died of torture and starvation.[63]

In December 1978, Cambodians went from this fire into the frying pan when they were invaded by Vietnam, who installed a puppet government largely staffed by ex-Khmer Rouge cadres. A decade of repressive rule and incipient civil war ended with the expulsion of the Vietnamese in September 1989. More turmoil was followed by an uneasy truce, and then United Nations-supervised elections in May 1993. These introduced an increasingly authoritarian and corrupt government that has gradually repressed its opposition. Today, much of the country remains chaotic, and continuing conflicts with the Khmer Rouge still afflict areas outside the capital, Phnom Penh. Looting, rape, forced conscription, and extortion are common.[64]

Given such a history, it seems gratuitous to focus on the suffering of any one part of the population. However, if it is possible, the suffering of Cambodia's Christians may have been even worse than that of the population at large. Under the Khmer Rouge, religion was branded as "Enemy Number Three to the Revolution" and was to be exterminated. Some 90 percent of the Protestants and one-third of the Catholics were killed, many by torture. Sometimes Christians were suspected of having been contaminated by contact with foreign influences, but often they were attacked simply because their beliefs themselves were regarded as antithetical to the revolutionary program. It was a Catholic missionary, Father Francois Ponchard, who first brought news of the Cambodian genocide to the world's attention.

Under Vietnamese control, which for many of the inhabitants was in some ways a partial liberation, Christianity remained illegal. The remaining Christians were forced to meet in secret under the threat of arrest and imprisonment.

The ban was officially lifted in 1990, under the leadership of "Second Prime Minister" Hun Sen. While the current Constitution provides for freedom of religion, Buddhism is now the state religion. There is much more freedom than ever before, but the government reaction is varied and sporadic. Local government officials can either be open or repressive.[65] On October 12, 1994, the Ministry of Religious Affairs directed all church groups to register with the government, to unite under a national church council, and to use only one version of the Bible. Many observers think that these steps would be good ones for the Cambodian church, but it is hardly the government's business to make it so.

In March of 1994, American and Cambodian Christian relief workers were abducted in the southwest by the Khmer Rouge.[66] There are reports that Christian converts have been threatened and church buildings destroyed. At present the church is growing, but the future remains uncertain.[67]

Mr. Mom Barnabas' personal history mirrors Cambodia's bloodstained past. At seventeen, in 1970, he became a spy for the Khmer Rouge. Then, after becoming a Christian two years later, he was thrust into a decades-long struggle for life and freedom.

By the time the Khmer Rouge won their war against Lon Nol in 1975, Barnabas had become a church leader. Fleeing Phnom Penh for his life, he wandered for three months in search of his family and was arrested as he crossed the Mekong River. Only eight of eighteen prisoners interned with him in the "reeducation" camp survived.

Three labor camps followed, each one more cruel than the last. In search of warmth, he would crawl into the rice fields at night, seeking shelter among the embankments.

For years he was released, rearrested, threatened and, miraculously, spared. When Pol Pot was driven from power, Barnabas discovered that his father, six brothers, and twenty-nine family members had been slaughtered by the Khmer Rouge. Somehow, his mother had survived too.

In 1985 Barnabas was married, but soon had to flee yet another warrant for his arrest, this time from the Vietnamese occupiers. Finally in 1992, he returned to Cambodia with his family. Today, he is rebuilding his country's mutilated church in the face of ongoing uncertainties and hostility from the current Buddhist regime.[68]

CHAPTER SIX

Christian vs. Christian

Christians suffer oppression and discrimination not only from political ideologues, power-hungry tyrants, and other religious groups; they also suffer at the hands of other Christians. Except in Ethiopia and parts of Mexico, the scale of suffering is now usually much less than in other situations around the world. It is more usually a type of discrimination and harassment rather than outright persecution. Nevertheless, it needs to be exposed, not the least in order to show that problems don't occur just with "other" religions. In doing so, we need to give some history, especially of Orthodoxy, since this is little known in the West. (A more complete outline is given in Appendix F.)

THE HISTORY OF ORTHODOXY

Much of the old Eastern Bloc has been molded by the view that government control of religion is simply the normal state of affairs. Communist domination schooled generations to believe that the state had to impose basic religious doctrines. Even many who opposed Communism, and suffered for it, still yearned not for an open society, but merely for state enforcement of different beliefs.

This Communist repression in turn built on the pattern of the czars and drew on some long traditions within Orthodoxy itself. Byzantium, the eastern branch of the Roman Empire centered in Constantinople (Istanbul), always maintained strong links between the emperor and the church. While they had distinct tasks, they were united in a "symphony," in a joint mission. This pattern of the "second Rome" was dominant in the eastern Mediterranean, the Middle East, and North Africa. On its home ground, it lasted until the Ottoman Turks conquered Constantinople in 1453.

Russian rulers then married into the family of the last Byzantine emperor and Ivan III appropriated the title of "caesar," rendered as *czar*. Philotheus of Pskov, in a famous and well-remembered prophecy, proclaimed to Czar Basil III that: "Two Romes have fallen. A third stands fast. A fourth there cannot be."

These roots made the Orthodox more likely to become intertwined with state power. Other branches of Christendom have also shown these tendencies; however, Orthodoxy's subsequent and often tragic history has reinforced these practices.

Since these churches existed in the original heartland of Christianity, they were those most affected by the early spread of Islam. Most lived under Islamic rule for centuries. The name "Slav" itself comes from the fact that many were sold as slaves to Muslim countries. Under the Islamic *dhimmi* or *millet* system, Christians could govern many of their internal affairs. This, in turn, meant that the church became the expression of peoplehood, and church leaders became a type of political authority within the Christian community.

The history of the Orthodox Church was, and is, often a brave one. Many have survived under a situation of oppression and occupation for up to thirteen hundred years, largely forgotten by the outside world. But this has often led them to identify themselves with the nation and the nation with themselves. It is doubtful whether they could have survived otherwise. Nevertheless, it has reinforced Orthodox claims to have exclusive religious jurisdiction over the people in its territory. Other religious bodies are often cast as "interlopers." And in this century, they have suffered perhaps their greatest persecution.

THE RUSSIAN ORTHODOX CHURCH UNDER COMMUNISM

The Russian Communists tested, developed, and perfected the techniques of repression described in the previous chapter on Communism. Church leaders struggled with great courage to resist this control. The first patriarch under Communism, Tikhon, was imprisoned for his resistance. His acting successor, Metropolitan Peter, refused to register the church, and he too was imprisoned. His replacement, Sergei, felt that he had to seek registration, but resisted enough that in December 1926, he too was arrested, along with one hundred seventeen other bishops. The authorities tried to persuade Metropolitan Kirill to succeed him, but he too resisted.

> *When one official tried to impress on the churchman the necessity of removing a bishop from his See, if the Soviets demanded it, Kirill responded, "If the bishop is guilty of an ecclesiastic offense, I shall do so. But otherwise I would call him and tell him: "Brother, I've nothing against you, but the civil authorities want to retire you, and I am forced to do so."*
>
> *But the Communist bureaucrat was not satisfied. "No, you must pretend the initiative is yours, and find some accusation." Metropolitan Kirill would not budge. "You are not a cannon, and I am not a shell with which you want to destroy the Church from within." On the same day this confrontation occurred, Kirill was sent back into Arctic exile, where he died seventeen years later.*[1]

In the 1920s and 1930s approximately two hundred thousand Russian Orthodox priests, monks, and nuns were slaughtered. A further half million were imprisoned or deported to Siberia. According to the Russian State Commission headed by Alexander Yakovlev, investigating the NKVD and KGB archives,

> Most priests were shot or hanged, although other methods used by Communist death squads included crucifying pastors on their church doors [or] leaving them to freeze to death after being stripped and soaked in water during winter.[2]

This early history is worth recounting, both for its own sake, and to reinforce the point that the history of the Orthodox Church under Communism was never one of simple subservience. Many who cooperated with the regime believed that it was preferable to the likely alternative of the complete eradication of the church. Even then, they often did so only after imprisonment. People who have never faced such a situation should not easily judge those who have. In the same situation, our performance would likely be far worse. Dmitri Dudko, who before his imprisonment in 1980 was one of the most outspoken Orthodox priests, was asked why he continued to defend the church authorities. He replied,

> Who has fewer civil rights than the patriarch? They say he's surrounded by thousands of informers. He so much as sighs and it's heard in every government department. Everything he does against his conscience he does under pressure and, of course, out of weakness, like any man. But you don't want to be compassionate. You sit in the judge's seat and pronounce sentence.[3]

In Gorbachev's first years, he mouthed slogans about the dangers of religion. But, when faced with declining Communist authority and the fragmentation of the Soviet Union, he moved quickly in the direction of religious freedom. The one thousandth anniversary of Russian Christianity was approaching and the church was the only other organization which provided a link between the Soviet territories.

In the weeks before the 1988 anniversary, the churches were granted public meetings and access to the mass media. Church bells, forbidden for decades, rang out over the cities and villages—an experience whose effect we can hardly begin to imagine. These events probably hastened rather than stopped the breakup the Soviet Empire. It is, at the least, ironic that the breakdown of Communism coincided with the millennial celebrations of Christianity in Russia.

The Orthodox churches have risen from a nightmare which few of us can imagine. They are emerging into a world where ideas and movements are spreading rapidly in areas they had previously regarded as their own. And they are emerging—shaped by a history which has given them little experience for dealing with it. This does not justify all current Orthodox attempts to reassert religious hegemony. But it should give us a greater ability to understand it, and greater patience as we observe it.

RUSSIA SINCE THE FALL OF COMMUNISM

The Orthodox Church is now the most respected institution in Russia. Consequently, many groups struggling for power are trying to use Orthodoxy to bolster their own image. These groups range from conservative nationalists to fascists and anti-Semites to not-so-reformed Communists. Many have united in a "red-brown" (Communist-extreme nationalist) alliance, some of whom want to restore a Soviet Empire based on Orthodox nationalism. Even the 1996 Communist presidential candidate, Gennady Zyuganov, is talking this way. In addition, there are indications that the old state apparatus, including the KGB, has become tied to these circles. Meanwhile, Boris Yeltsin has also courted the Orthodox hierarchy, giving the patriarch a suite of offices in the Kremlin.

The Union of Orthodox Brotherhoods and anti-Semitic factions such as those around Metropolitan Ioann of Petersburg and Ladoga (who commended *The Protocols of the Elders of Zion*, a forgery purporting to outline Jewish plans for world domination) have engaged in propaganda against the non-Orthodox as undercutting the Russian people. The Union also attacked many Russian Orthodox clergy, including Alexander Men, as "Judaizers."[4]

Men, though little-known in the West, was of deserved and towering reputation in Russia.[5] He resisted the authorities, carried out an extensive pastoral ministry, especially among intellectuals, and sought conciliatory relations with others, both Christian and non-Christian. Men was Jewish by birth and a strong opponent of anti-Semitism, both under the Communists and among the newer nationalist movements. On September 9, 1990, on his way to church, he was killed with an ax, the traditional Russian weapon for revenge. Shortly thereafter, two other prominent Moscow priests were also brutally murdered.

> *Christmas 1990 had barely passed when Father Lazar's flat was broken into and he was murdered with "a heavy metallic object." He had been entrusted by Metropolitan Iuvenalii with an investigation—there was said to be corruption surrounding the late Patriarch Pimen that involved the KGB. All his electronic aids as well as his briefcase disappeared.*
>
> *In March 1991, a third murder occurred. This time, Father Seraphim, a thirty-three-year-old priest-monk, was assassinated, mutilated while he was still alive.*
>
> *Father Seraphim had just returned from the Russian Orthodox Mission in Israel. He had many baptized Jews in his parish and clearly preferred them to the group of anti-Semitic Pamyat activists who made up the rest of his congregation.*
>
> *The three murders have never been solved*[6]

The Russian Orthodox Church hierarchy has reacted in varied and contradictory ways to the "red-brown" alliance. Patriarch Alexei II was, for a time, the official patron of the Brotherhoods and tolerated the ravings of Metropolitan Ioann. However, in 1994, he condemned them both. Members of the hierarchy were also prominent in, and hosted, the All-World Russian Assembly conference of May 26–28, 1993, which defined a Russian (*Russkii*) as one from the traditional Russian areas, plus those "aliens" who had been baptized into the Orthodox faith. This made religion one of the criteria of Russian identity.[7] At the same time, Alexei has condemned extreme nationalism and affirmed that he wishes to have a separation of church and state.[8] In the 1996 Russian presidential election, he gave support to Yeltsin.

The neo-fascist Vladimir Zhirinovsky, who has never shown much sign of genuine piety, also stresses the role the Russian Orthodox Church could play in fulfilling his imperial ambitions. During a January 1994 visit to the Bosnian Serbs, he claimed to champion the Orthodox cause and was greeted as "Zhirinovsky, Orthodox Savior."[9]

Many strong nationalists also claim a common cause with Muslim groups. Ruslan Kasbulatov, the former speaker of the Russian Parliament, who strenuously opposed Yeltsin and sought to resurrect the Soviet Union, was Muslim by background. He maintains that he performed the Hajj to Mecca in 1992 at the invitation of the king of Saudi Arabia.[10]

Into these swirling currents came a deluge of foreigners. Domestic non-Orthodox bodies also expanded. Many Orthodox regarded them all as intruders, even including the Catholic Church and other bodies, such as Baptists, who have deep roots in Russia. But there were also many newer evangelical missions which offended not only the Orthodox but also Russian evangelicals and, indeed, other more responsible evangelical missions.[11]

Dimitry Pospielovsky, borrowing from Patriarch Alexei, describes them as "churches competing with each other, trying to outdo each other, taking advantage of the economic bankruptcy of the Orthodox Church and, as it were, buying converts by offering free English-language classes, credits to businessmen, and food parcels for converts, in which American fundamentalists are actively engaged, makes religions in the eyes of the average Russian no better than traders in the marketplace."[12] This picture is exaggerated, being based largely on Alexei's description of an American group who tried to rent Red Square for a religious pageant at Easter 1991.

But there are other, more sober descriptions which, nevertheless, convey something of the tensions. Michael Bourdeaux says there were "innumerable people who humbly and genuinely wanted to help Russia reestablish the roots of its faith. Their quiet dedication was often swamped by the insensitivity of others. Cohorts of disparate foreign preachers were to be found roaming the streets of the major cities, employing brash evangelistic methods and backed by what to Russians seemed limitless reserves of capital . . . foreign agencies bought not just air time, but sometimes even whole radio stations. Foreigners who had never learned a word of Russian, who did not know the history, the classics of literature, or the particular richness of the Russian Orthodox tradition, suddenly launched themselves at an unsuspecting public genuinely eager for something spiritual to fill the void left by Communism. . . ."[13]

Foreign evangelicals are often accused of being agents of western imperialism. Metropolitan Filaret of Minsk said that ". . . this rush of missionaries is not really a religious phenomenon but more a political phenomenon. . . . In Russia, the Ukraine, Belarus, our strength was the Orthodox faith. The religious idea was our strength, our political strength. The politicians understand this very well, also those overseas. It is not so simple to conquer Russia, by force especially, so they act, they prepare a special plan for how to stop or hinder the growth of Russia. The armed threat is senseless . . . so they have to undermine Russia spiritually."[14]

Worry over the fragmentation of the church and the influx of groups has crystallized around attempts to formulate a new religious freedom law. Beginning in 1988, Gorbachev instituted laws providing for genuine religious freedom but, by the early 1990s, many people were wondering whether this had been such a good idea.

In November 1992, Khasbulatov signed a decree establishing an "Experts' Consultative Council." To many, this looked suspiciously like a resurrection of the old Communist Council on Religious Affairs, especially as it included some of the same people.[15] This council set about drafting a new, more restrictive religion law. In April 1993, the patriarch called for a "joint commission . . . [with] powers for a period of five to seven years to veto the licensing and activities of foreign religious organizations."[16] In August, the Union of Orthodox Brotherhoods called for a law defining "crimes on religious grounds." The Russian Parliament also considered making certain religious activities by foreigners illegal. These proposals were at first welcomed by the patriarch, the chief mufti of Russia, and the chief rabbi of Moscow. But they were criticized by Russian Protestants, Roman Catholics, the press, and many junior members of the Orthodox Church.

The law went through revisions and drew both domestic and international criticism. Nevertheless, a restrictive version was sent to President

Yeltsin that summer. He sent it back. Parliament then submitted a revised version which on September 17, Yeltsin again returned unsigned.

Alexander Torshin, who actually delivered the law to Yeltsin, also carried a recommendation that he should sign it. When Yeltsin demurred, Torshin asked, "The Moscow Patriarchate approved, so what more do you want?"

Yeltsin said, "That's just the problem."[17]

Four days later, Yeltsin dissolved the parliament. Since the parliament declined to be dissolved, he sent troops and tanks the following month in a successful attempt to change its mind.

Since the elections of December 1993, the fights have continued. In 1995 a more liberal law pushed by religious-freedom activist Gleb Yakunin (see Chapter Seven on the churches) was blocked after intervention by the patriarch. In 1996, the Patriarchate itself introduced amendments that would ban all independent activities by foreigners. The Duma (parliament) gave preliminary approval on July 10, 1996. In November 1996, from his sickbed, Yeltsin submitted proposals for a more liberal law. Now about one quarter of Russia's provinces have laws restricting religious freedom.[18]

Meanwhile, there is sporadic violence against non-Orthodox churches. Moscow's largest Pentecostal church, for example, has received bomb threats and its worship services have been disrupted. Alexander Purshova, the pastor, says he receives about five death threats a day. His office was burned, and a car belonging to the church was sprayed with bullets.[19]

On December 12, 1995, Vitaly Viktorovich Savitsky, chairman of the state Duma (lower house of parliament) Committee for Liaison with Public and Religious Organizations, was killed in a car crash. Savitsky, the third Duma member to have been killed in the last two years, was an avid supporter of equal constitutional protection for all religious faiths. Many people do not regard his death as really accidental.[20]

Despite these events, the struggles over religious freedom in Russia have usually remained nonviolent. However, they involve attempts to legally control minority groups, and illustrate a pattern occurring throughout the post-Communist world where the Orthodox Church is strong.

We can sympathize with the ecumenical patriarch, Bartholomew I of Constantinople who, in late 1995, on his first official visit to the World

Council of Churches, was "disappointed" by the "unfriendly actions of some Roman Catholic circles" and "many Protestant churches as well." After enduring "fifty to seventy years of pitiless persecutions," the Orthodox had expected "fraternal support or at least understanding" instead of being "targeted" by missionaries.[21]

However, the only effective solutions to such problems are via genuine dialogue and the revitalization of the church itself. As is shown by experiences elsewhere and by Russia's own history, legal repression is not only unjust, but is likely to make the situation much worse. This is demonstrated in other eastern European countries where Orthodoxy maintains a strong influence.

EASTERN EUROPE

The Ukraine stands at the confluence of Catholicism, Orthodoxy, and Islam, and this produces complex religious relations. In 1596, a compromise between the Vatican and the Russian Orthodox authorities led to the formation of the Ukrainian Catholic (or "Uniate") Church. This was under Vatican authority but followed Orthodox patterns, including having married priests. As a church almost unique to the western Ukraine, it became closely tied to Ukrainian identity. Elsewhere in the Ukraine, since the Ukrainian Autocephalous Orthodox Church had been wiped out by Stalin in 1930, the Russian Orthodox Church had become dominant. In 1946, Stalin then forced the Uniate members into the Russian Church.

When the Soviet Union broke up in the late 1980s, two things happened. First, the members and clergy of the Uniate Church, which under Stalin was probably the largest underground religious organization in the Soviet Union, and possibly the world, sought to recover their independent status. Second, prompted by Ukrainian nationalism and animosity toward the Russians, many Ukrainians tried to form their own independent Ukrainian Autocephalous Orthodox Church. The Moscow Patriarchate countered this by offering a not-quite-so-independent Ukrainian Autonomous Orthodox Church. Currently these three bodies, along with break-away factions, are engaged in a multi-sided struggle over ecclesiastical control and expropriated property. Ukrainian

President Leonid Kravchuk has interfered in these disputes, trying to use nationalist sentiment to consolidate his power.[22]

In July 1995, Patriarch Vlodymyr Romaniuk, head of the breakaway Ukrainian Orthodox Church-Kiev Patriarchate, died, apparently of cardiac arrest. His followers claimed that his death was suspicious. There were fifty injuries and at least thirty-three arrests when police attempted to prevent the patriarch's interment in Kiev's St. Sofia Sobor Church. The government had rejected a request for the Patriarch to be buried there, claiming that it was a state-owned building.[23]

Meanwhile, Ukrainian Protestant groups are concerned about discrimination by the government and by the Orthodox and Uniate churches.[24] In January 1994, the Ukraine added amendments to its 1991 Law on Religious Freedom to restrict activities by foreigners and require the government's specific approval before foreigners can enter religious work. Since the government, even when willing, is slow, this produces major bottlenecks.[25]

The patterns of church control and church subservience in Romania were similar to those in the Soviet Union and, in fact, they were somewhat worse. In the centuries of Ottoman Turk control and since the birth of the modern Romanian state in the mid-nineteenth century, the Romanian Orthodox Church and Romanian national identity have been closely intertwined. Orthodox leaders played a major part in struggles for independence, and even the terms "Orthodox" and "Romanian" could be used interchangeably.[26] The Communist leaders then sought to replace Orthodox identity with socialist nationalism. Nicolae Ceausescu, who came to power in 1965, developed a cult of personality rivaling that of North Korea's Kim Il Sung.

The Communist grip on Romania was even tighter than in the Soviet Union. "[To] describe Romania under Ceausescu as a police state would be a grave understatement. Romania was caught in the iron grip of one of the most effective thought-control networks ever devised."[27] Even before Ceausescu came to power, more than a million Romanians had been put in prisons or concentration camps, and at least two hundred thousand were killed. In turn, some major figures of the Romanian Orthodox Church cooperated with the government in what Walter Bacon has called a "sycophantocracy."[28] Some lower levels of the clergy were, however, far more courageous and, in an act of solidarity with their fellow Christians, dozens of them went to prison rather than take over Uniate parishes when that church was banned in 1948.

The leadership's servile nature meant that the church provided little focus for opposition to the regime. That opposition grew primarily in the Reformed Churches in the northwest, particularly around Pastor Lazlo Tokes in Timosoara in December 1989. Since these groups were, however, identified with the Hungarian minority, they could not set the pattern for the rest of the country, one reason why Romania has never made a clear break with its Communist past.

The state continues its efforts to control or suppress minority religious groups, including Catholics, ethnic Hungarian Protestants, and evangelical Protestants. It has threatened to remove churches from the Hungarian minority, while the education law makes religious study compulsory in primary schools, even if parents oppose the instruction.

There are now reports that Protestant groups and Jehovah's Witnesses are being physically attacked by Orthodox mobs and militia. In July 1996, Hillary Rodham Clinton, who was on a visit to Romania, wisely refused her scheduled visit to the Orthodox Church in Kretulescu because, according to a press attaché of the American Embassy, "Her presence on the property of a church which has shown religious intolerance contrary to democratic principles does not fit the purpose of Mrs. Clinton's visit to Romania."[29]

In Bulgaria, the government has sought to limit religious expression to Bulgaria's "traditional" religions. It follows the traditional method, demanding registration by religious groups. The Council of Ministers can refuse such registration under the 1994 Persons and Family Act, and some forty-five "non-traditional" religious groups have been denied it. They cannot enter into any contractual relations such as renting halls or publishing. In February 1995, police broke up a meeting of the "Word of Life" group in Veliko Tarnovo because, they said, the assembly was unregistered and therefore illegal.[30]

Meanwhile, the media are conducting a campaign of slander against Protestants. One newspaper claims that "sects ruin the character; they brainwash, destroy the mind, and break up the values of Bulgarians [and] make society . . . vulnerable to the political, economic, and 'cultural' expansion which spreads after the coming of missionaries."[31] But many of the one hundred thousand Protestants have had roots in Bulgaria for over a century. The Logos Bible Academy, whose registration has been blocked, traces back to 1898.

There are also increasing threats, including bomb threats, against Protestants.[32] In June 1994, a gang of skinheads attacked one Protestant service, holding three hundred worshipers captive and severely beating seven of them.[33]

In Belarus, there are tensions between the majority Russian Orthodox church and the Catholic Church, which comprises about 10 percent of the population. This is compounded by Russian/Polish tensions, since the churches are associated with different ethnic backgrounds. Catholic priests from Poland have been excluded on the grounds of their nationality. On top of this are the usual problems with registration: Some fifty Protestant organizations face major difficulties in getting legal status and the government of the authoritarian President Aleksandr Lukashenko has restricted the entry of "foreign religious groups."[34]

Problems between the Orthodox and other churches are not confined to Eastern Europe. They also occur, sometimes in a far stronger form, in Greece, the Caucasus, and Ethiopia.

GREECE

Konstantinos Kyriopoulos, a well-known dental surgeon from Patras, filed a complaint on behalf of his fifteen-year-old son, Stavros. The teenager had been ordered by his teachers to recite the daily Orthodox prayer through a microphone in the schoolyard; he refused, was expelled for two days, and received a negative behavior mark.

Kyriopoulos tried to have the punishment repealed, but neither a school investigative team nor the Ministry of Education and Religion sided with him.

Interviewed by the daily newspaper Ta Nea, *Kyriopoulos said, "In fact, I am Orthodox, but I cannot stand religious fanaticism."*[35]

Greece usually has a positive image in western minds, which associate it with the classical roots of western democracy and philosophy. Often forgotten is the long and pervasive Christian heritage dating from the earliest decades of the Church. As in other Orthodox countries, the Greek Church has been a focus of national identity, especially under Turkish occupation. At present, some 96 percent of Greeks are nominally members of the Orthodox Church, while there are smaller groups of Catholics, Protestants, and Jehovah's Witnesses, as well as Muslims.

In 1821, it was the Metropolitan Bishop of Patras, Germanos, who launched the revolt against the Turks from the Greek Orthodox monastery of Agia Lavra. The first Hellenic Constitution of 1844 gave the church prominent legal status and forbade any "proselytism" against its members. The 1975 Constitution then extended this prohibition to any officially recognized religion.[36]

Foreign members of minority religious groups are restricted by visas and residence permits. State permits are required for building non-Orthodox places of worship and Catholic churches have waited up to six years for them. In April 1993, the Greek Parliament upheld a law requiring that citizens' religious affiliations be stated on their identity cards and passports.[37]

Behind these restrictions is a widespread hostility. On August 4–5, 1993, the Greek newspaper *Eleftherotypia* published an outline of a report by the Greek National Intelligence Service, dated January 19, 1993, entitled "Contemporary Religious Heretical Sects and Para-religious Organizations in Greece." This report divided Greeks according to their religious beliefs, the Orthodox being described as "genuine, pure, incorruptible Greeks," the rest as "non-genuine, impure, corruptible Greeks." The report suggested measures to "cleanse the media and the schools and to limit the use of non-Orthodox places of worship." It listed various religious organizations as "enemies of the state."[38] The government subsequently disowned the report and there is no indication that its recommendations were carried out. However, it reveals the mindset operating in some government agencies.

In recent years, enforcement of the proselytism laws has been spotty, since local judges have declined to enforce them or have interpreted them narrowly. Often, local relations between different religious groups are good. However, the laws continue to be used, particularly against Jehovah's Witnesses, and their threat hangs over other religious minorities. From 1983–1992 there were two thousand arrests and four hundred convictions for "proselytism."[39]

Evangelist Dimitris Iliadis has been arrested ten times for conducting open-air meetings, but all his charges were later dismissed by a judge.[40] Occasionally, opposition to proselytism has erupted into something more sinister. In 1991, four evangelical air force officers were called to court to testify about their alleged proselytizing activities. On their way, they were killed in an accident. Many people, including members of the Orthodox church, express doubt as to how "accidental" these deaths actually were.[41]

In early 1993, Greece provoked the first international human-rights legal case involving "proselytism." Mr. Kokkinakis, one of thousands of Jehovah's Witnesses arrested in Greece in previous years, had been sentenced to three months for "the act of proselytism on members of another faith." On appeal, the European Court of Human Rights emphasized that Article 9 of the European Convention on Human Rights "included in principle the right to try to convince one's neighbor," and it found against Greece.

In an interview by *Human Rights without Frontiers* with Orthodox Bishop Anthimos of Alexandroupolis, the following exchange took place.

> HRWF: *What do you think of the decision taken by the European Court some months ago in the Kokkinakis case?*
>
> Bishop Anthimos: *What's the Kokkinakis case?*
>
> HRWF: *Kokkinakis is a Jehovah's Witness. Some years ago, he was going from door to door to preach and he was arrested. He was sentenced for proselytism. In Strasbourg, the European Court held that Greece has violated his right to freedom of thought, conscience, and religion, and the Greek State was ordered to pay him more than three million drachmas.*
>
> Bishop Anthimos: *I don't know of such a case. Anyway, the Orthodox Church is not interested in the decision taken in Strasbourg.*[42]

ARMENIA

Armenia officially became a "Christian country" in the year 301, reportedly the first country to do so. But even before that, from the second century there was a Christian church in the now-destroyed state of Caucasian Albania. Like other Orthodox countries, the Armenians suffered from repeated invasions and frequently had no independent state, so that the church became a "hidden state." After the collapse of the Soviet Union, and in the war with Azerbaijan, the identification of Armenia with the Orthodox Church has returned.[43]

This has led to increased controls on non-Orthodox groups. In April 1995, paramilitary gangs attacked Pentecostals, Jehovah's Witnesses, and Hari Krishnas. The government claimed not to be involved, but the gangs put several of those attacked into a prison run by the military police.[44]

There were other attacks on religious minorities. The churches of the Protestant Armenian Missionary Association of America were subject to raids, and armed police and border guards took over its offices and harassed the staff.[45] Molotov cocktails were thrown through the kindergarten window of the Gyumri Evangelical Church and a grenade was tossed into the principal's home.[46] This attack may seem to be connected to the fact that most of these bodies are pacifist. These attacks were made at a time of military conscription.[47]

ETHIOPIA

> *In the first half of 1992, one member of the Mekane Jesus Church was reported killed and hundreds of others were wounded.*
>
> *Twenty-four Lutheran churches were burned in the Provinces of Wollega and Kefa.*
>
> *At Alamatta, in the Wallo Region, two Pentecostals had to be married under police protection and in a prison after Coptic Orthodox members attacked their wedding.*
>
> *In Northern Ethiopia, a girl who had become a Protestant and refused to recant had her eye pulled out by a Coptic mob.*[48]

In Ethiopia, events have gone beyond discrimination and harassment to full-scale persecution. After the Coptic Church itself had suffered intensely under the Marxist Mengistu regime, it used its liberation to oppress possible competitors. Evangelical Protestants, especially, have been violently attacked.

Members of the Meserete Kristos Church were assaulted in late October 1993 by a Coptic mob attacking a funeral service for a Protestant church member. Over one hundred people wielding clubs demanded that the already-buried corpse be dug up and moved. One member said, "If we didn't take out the dead body, they would have killed us."[49] Similar events took place in June 1994, when the funeral of a fifteen-year-old girl was attacked by five hundred people led by a Coptic priest, and her body had to be dug up and reburied.

Also in 1994, Protestants around the town of Tilili were "separated from their families, chained and beaten like criminals, forbidden to go to towns, forbidden to sell and purchase goods from markets. . . ." Protestants have been singled out by name from Coptic pulpits, and their homes have subsequently been ransacked. These events continue. The newspaper *Muged* reports that in July 1995 Coptic mobs in Wolechi, East Shoa, burned Protestant houses and properties, including a gas station.[50]

Real religious freedom will require the Orthodox churches to renounce their imperial pretensions. This doesn't mean that they should adopt some pallid imitation of Western liberalism or Protestant individualism, but it does mean openly facing a world where different religions will coexist in the same lands for the foreseeable future. Such a renunciation will not itself rein in dominating politicians, manipulative bureaucrats, or ambitious bishops, nor would it quickly overcome the deep-seated prejudices of ordinary citizens. Nevertheless, its effects could be profound.

PROTESTANTS IN EASTERN EUROPE

Estonia, Latvia, and Lithuania had a quite different religious history from the other European countries absorbed into the Soviet Union.[51] Lithuania has traditionally had a Catholic majority, while the others were primarily

Lutheran. But, as elsewhere, the churches provided focus for national feeling, even when in practice, many of the inhabitants were quite secular in outlook.

Under Soviet control many at least nominally Orthodox, ethnic Russians migrated into the Baltics. Since independence, this has produced a complex brew of interwoven political, ethnic, lingual, and religious loyalties. Ethnic Russians are often regarded as foreigners, leftovers from the imperialist Soviet State, and are denied civil and political rights in the hope that they might go back to Russia. This is paralleled by discrimination against the Russian Orthodox Church. Russia has, in turn, supported its ethnic fellows in the "near abroad" and, so, has also defended the Orthodox Church.[52]

Facing both Russian pressure and the influence of western culture, the Baltic States have tended to defend their "traditional faiths" by means of legislation and government discrimination. In Estonia, there are complaints that a disproportionate amount of state funds go to the Lutheran Church, the nominal ecclesial home of 70 percent of the population. Religious groups must have their centers within Estonia in order to have legal status, something which creates great problems for Roman Catholics and Russian Orthodox. The Russian Orthodox Church has been denied official registration by the government.[53] Meanwhile, in Latvia, Archbishop Gailitis has declared that foreign missionaries "import spiritual chaos," and the government is delaying the registration of "non-traditional" religions.[54]

ROMAN CATHOLICISM

The changes in the Roman Catholic church since the Second Vatican Council have shaken much of the world. *Pacem in Terris* (1963) called for "democratic and participatory" forms of government while the *Declaration on Religious Liberty* (1965) emphasized rights of conscience. Since the 1970s, Catholics have shaped what Samuel Huntington calls the "third wave of democracy." They provoked and strengthened demands for democracy in Portugal, Spain, Czechoslovakia, Poland, Hungary, the Philippines, and throughout Latin America. Catholic international relations scholar

George Weigel argues that this shift was a major factor in the downfall of Communism.

However, in several parts of the world, more traditional Catholics continue to use the power of the state to maintain Church privileges. For example, in Malta the small evangelical community faces discrimination and social ostracism. Charles Scicluna, a canon lawyer at the bishops' organizational headquarters, says, "In Malta, you can't be Maltese and not be a Roman Catholic. It's almost unthinkable."[55] Problems also occur in Eastern Europe and Latin America.

EASTERN EUROPE

At times the Catholic Church's relation to nationalism has been similar to Orthodox churches. In Lithuania, it opposed the creation of a Christian college by western Protestants. The Pope made the dangers of evangelicals one of his themes on his visit there.[56]

Similar dynamics have occurred in Poland, another country often under the thumb of its neighbors. The commitment of the population to Catholicism has given the church a central place in the Polish nation, especially under Communism. The Communist authorities responded by playing on the long tension between Catholics and Protestants by giving favors to the latter, not out of any great love of Protestantism, but simply to undercut Catholics.[57] After liberation, these tensions remain. Three-fifths of the population feel that being a Catholic is essential to being a Pole.[58] In 1993 and 1994, other religious groups were concerned about a Concordat proposed between the government and the Vatican to establish the position of the Catholic Church in Poland. Since a Concordat is an international treaty, it could shape the country's constitutional future, including the place of all the churches. But other groups were given little input on the matter.[59]

LATIN AMERICA

In Latin America, there are frequently close relations between the Catholic Church and the state. While a state church necessarily infringes on religious equality, it need not be much of a problem depending on how many privileges it has. Such churches exist in Western Europe, including the United Kingdom, and have not produced any major outcry, since they are combined with effective guarantees of freedom for other religious groups. This is one reason why international human-rights documents do not condemn state churches *per se* as violations of religious freedom.

However, in some Latin American countries, the state churches are not the rather *pro forma* institutions that exist elsewhere. Since the Second Vatican Council, the overall movement in Latin America has been toward openness, but tensions have been exacerbated due to the explosive growth of Protestantism, especially Pentecostalism.[60]

In Argentina, although the government has recently dropped the constitutional requirement that only Catholics can be president, there are still problems. Under Argentine law, the Roman Catholic Church has "natural legal status," which means that its activities cannot be regulated by government rules. But a law passed under the military dictatorship treats other religious bodies only as associations on a par with charities or sports clubs. Their houses of worship have the same legal status as shops or dance halls. (A similar situation exists in Chile.) The government requires information about pastors and leaders, times of services, and numbers in attendance.[61] In 1993 the Catholic Episcopal Conference declared that the "dogmatic" sections of the Constitution should not be reformed, and the Argentine Constitutional Assembly reaffirmed in 1994 that "Argentina sustains . . . the . . . Roman Catholic Church." The government continues to support church budgets.[62]

The Bolivian Constitution also declares that "the State recognizes and sustains the Roman, Apostolic, Catholic Church." In November 1994, Army Commander General Renaldo Caceres issued an order banning non-Catholic ministers from military bases in the country, basing his order on the fact that the "Constitution recognizes Catholicism as the official state religion."[63] The Bolivian president countermanded this order, but General Caceres virtually ignored him.[64] The Educational Reform Law of 1994 makes Catholic instruction compulsory in public schools, while all non-Catholic churches need to register with the government, a process which requires many signatures, including the minister of foreign relations and the president of the country. This entire process can cost up to three times the average annual income.

Costa Rica still maintains Catholicism as the official religion, and recently rejected United Nations criticism of its ban on non-Catholic teachers in its schools. All teachers of religion must be certified by the Roman Catholic Episcopal Conference.[65]

In the Dominican Republic, under a Concordat signed with the Vatican in 1954, Protestants cannot serve as chaplains in the police or the armed forces. Unlike Catholic priests, they cannot perform wedding ceremonies which have legal force. The government also contributes funds toward the maintenance of Catholic practices.

In several Latin American countries which do not recognize Catholicism as the official religion, there is still a pervasive bias. Ecuador's new law requiring government-financed religious education in all schools is supported by the Catholic Church but opposed by almost all others. There have been riots, and Anglican Archbishop Walter Crespo went on a two-week hunger strike. The minister of education resigned because she opposed the law.[66] Similar laws exist in Venezuela, Peru, and Chile, while Nicaragua is debating introducing one.

Like Eastern Europe and the former Soviet Union, these conflicts have usually been confined to legal disputes. However, in Mexico, there is continuing violence against Protestants.[67]

MEXICO

For most of this century, Mexico's government has restricted the Catholic Church, and only recently has it eased its grip. However, the situation of Protestants is still precarious.

Throughout much of the country, Protestants suffer religiously motivated violence. In the central state of Oaxaca, on September 11, 1994, the Evangelical Covenant Church in San Pablo Yaganiza was raided during Sunday worship and church members were driven out and beaten. The evangelical pastors in the area have all received death threats, church members have had their water and drainage services cut off and farm animals taken. On May 28, 1995, two Protestants in the town of Pueblo were jailed and denied food and water. Another was tied to a tree all night for trying to defend them.[68]

Several incidents have taken place in towns such as Cancun and Acapulco, towns well-known to Americans. However, away from the beaches and "Love Boat" voyages, Protestants have been brutally attacked, some on their wedding day.

> *On October 9, 1994, an evangelical church was destroyed in Acapulco by a mob wielding clubs and pickaxes. The attackers tore down the roof and walls and threw the contents into the streets. They did the same to the parsonage, despite the presence of the pastor, his wife, and children.*
>
> *On November 18, 1995, the Shalom Presbyterian Church in Cancun was attacked by twenty people during a wedding. Fifteen of those attending the church were wounded. Local police did little to stop the attack.*[69]

The greatest assaults have taken place in Chiapas. This, the most southerly of Mexico's states, has made news because of the Zapatista rebellion that broke out in early 1994, after the signing of the North America Free Trade Agreement. Even movie director Oliver Stone has gone there searching for more revisionist history. However, since the Zapatista leader, Sub-Commandante Marcos, always has his face covered, we are unlikely to see Kevin Costner portraying him on film anytime soon.

Despite this attention, the persecution of the evangelicals in Chiapas by both sides in the conflict, as well as by local landowners, has scarcely rated a mention. The story bears some telling since it is happening, ignored, right next door to the United States.

There are some one hundred and ten thousand evangelicals among the indigenous tribes in Chiapas, particularly among the Tzotzil, Tzeltal, Ch'ol, and Tojolabal. They represent 20 percent of the population. From 1967 onward, some thirty-five thousand have been driven from their homes and lands. Their "crime" is that they refuse to participate in ceremonies which, while nominally Catholic, incorporate parts of tribal religions. As preparation for these ceremonies, tribespeople are required to purchase candles, flowers, tobacco, food, and alcohol from the village authorities at inflated prices, and many have been bankrupted in the process. The ceremonies are a form of extortion by the local leaders, known as *caciques*, and lead to debt and servitude that can last for decades.

> *Attorney Abdias Tovilla Jaime recalls the first day he arrived in the Chiapas town of San Cristobal de las Casas in February 1981. On that day, traditionalists destroyed the Presbyterian church. The following months, they killed evangelist Miguel Hernandez after they had kidnapped him, cut out his tongue, and set him on fire. All around, other evangelicals, the poorest tribespeople, were being driven from their lands and beaten. Tovilla was then a young graduate from theological seminary. He decided to enroll in law school.*[70]

The chief instigator of these atrocities is Domingo Lopez Ruiz, mayor of San Juan Chamula, a territory covering some ninety-three settlements. He has been a key figure in the Institutional Revolutionary Party, which has held a virtual monopoly on power in Mexico for the last eighty years. As an elected government official, he is exempt from prosecution except by permission of the Mexican Congress. In February 1994, he boasted, "The expulsions are necessary. . . . and we will continue until there are no more [Protestants]." This persecution combines a desire by the authorities to maintain their control with a desire to compel adherence to a complex of Catholic and traditional practices. Local Catholics who have supported the Protestants have also been expelled.

Catholic Bishop Felipe Aguirre Franco of Tuxtla Gutierrez, the state capital, asserts, "Chamula authorities use the Catholic religion for their own economic and political interests." They are "only Catholics by baptism and are considered polytheists, since their greatest god is John the Baptist and other saints." He also maintains, "Expulsions are a violent act which cannot be based on reason, nor on faith, nor on law, and therefore they constitute a direct attack on human rights."

The persecution reached new heights in September 1993, when a further 584 villagers were driven from their homes. They took refuge near the

Mexican Indian Affairs Commission. Shortly thereafter, in January 1994, Chiapas made the world's headlines when the Zapatista guerrillas rebelled against the Mexican government. Of the twelve thousand people displaced in the rebellion and the army crackdown, about half were evangelical Protestants.

The refugees speak about houses stripped clean, animals stolen, harvests destroyed, and communities shattered. Many evangelicals sympathized with the guerrillas in their demands that the rights of all the landless peasants in Chiapas be respected. Because of their pacifist beliefs, however, few joined the Zapatista ranks. Consequently, some have also suffered at the hands of the guerrillas.

When the Mexican government replaced the state government in Chiapas with interim Governor Javier Lopez Moreno, there was renewed hope that the evangelicals' plight could be addressed and, in subsequent months, many tried to return home. However, apart from words of encouragement, the government did little. Subsequent months brought more violence, and the murder of evangelical leaders. On March 29, 1994, 228 more people were driven off their lands.

Next, the Mexican National Human Rights Commission called for judicial action against the local authorities in the area: "It is clear that the human rights of the Indians have been violated by denying them justice, by systematically affecting their liberty to profess the religious beliefs that they choose, consecrated in Article 24 of our [Constitution]."

The government did nothing, and frustration began to grow. Some of the 584 exiles kidnapped Domingo Lopez Ruiz, claiming it was the only thing they could do to call attention to their plight. Supporters of the mayor then assaulted five evangelicals who were in the area. Subsequently, two thousand armed people supporting the mayor attacked the Indian Affairs Compound where he was being held. He was released unharmed. Tovilla, the evangelicals' legal counsel, said the exiled Christians ". . . are tired, they are desperate, the laws . . . have never worked for them, the government has never fulfilled its role."

On September 29, three hundred people attacked the homes of Miguel Mendez Santiz and Miguel Lopez Perez, leaders of the 584 Christians exiled a year previously. They were murdered. Also killed were Miguel Mendez Santiz, president of the Exiles Committee, and his wife, Veronica Diaz Jimenez. Mendez' daughter was also shot and raped, but survived. Some of the bodies were mutilated, "The woman's body—her face—was all chopped [up]."

After some thirty years, Domingo Lopez Ruiz was finally charged in 1994 with some of his crimes. But in October, he resigned after having apparently cut a deal with the authorities. All the charges against him were dropped, and he then appeared before crowds in the town proclaiming that he was "still in charge." In subsequent months there have been further murders and expulsions. On July 9, 1995, two more Protestants were attacked and driven from their homes. In October 1995, masked assailants killed pastor Aurelio Gomez Ramos and his assistant. On November 19, other evangelicals were killed. Some five thousand Protestants still worship secretly in the area, not too far south of the United States. Tens of thousands remain landless, forgotten, and destitute.[71]

PART TWO

American Apathy

AUTHOR'S NOTE

The chapters that follow are not a survey of how Americans, Christian and secular, *have* responded to religious persecution elsewhere. They are a survey of the ways they *have not* responded, or have responded with silence. I have coupled this with an exploration of the reasons for this silence.

In providing this survey, I do not want to imply that nothing has been done or is being done. The Appendices, Chapter Nine, and the Notes throughout should be enough to dispel that impression. Nevertheless, despite the heroic efforts of a few, the overall situation is one of blank ignorance or studied neglect, and it is *this* situation that needs our attention.

I criticize many people and organizations for their failings, and I make no apology for that. Nor do I want to leave the impression that their failings in the area of religious persecution imply a blanket condemnation of all their actions. There are people and organizations weak in this area who do fine work in other areas. To take but four examples: I criticize the *New York Times* for its widespread neglect of religion in its general news coverage, especially in the international sphere, but, in Peter Steinfels, it has a religion editor with few, if any, equals in North America. I point out weaknesses in Amnesty International and Human Rights Watch, but they have done more than almost any other organizations to bring religious persecution to our attention. I criticize the National Council of Churches for its silence, but its former head, Leonid Kishkovski, has said similar things himself, and its former counsel on religious freedom, Dean Kelley, did sterling work for many years.

Admittedly, as diplomats well realize, it is also very difficult to know when to remain silent and when to speak, and if something must be said, what words to use and how many. These struggles may have been particularly true for the NCC, the Billy Graham Evangelistic Organization, and the U.S. State Department. But the overall American record has not been one of pugnacious words ill-spoken, but of silence ill-considered.

In any case, despite good work and good intentions, the plague continues, and little is done in America to contain it. The facts are well enough established and they need to be addressed. If we fail to examine the reasons for our silence, the ignorance will continue, the apathy will continue, and preventable human suffering will continue.

CHAPTER SEVEN

American Christians: Peace at Any Price

It is Sunday morning in Sudan, in China, in Nepal, in Iran, in Cuba. As the sun rises, millions of Christians awaken to the grim awareness that they are about to face another exhausting week—a week that will be marred by fear, hatred, and violence.

Some dress themselves quickly and make their way across their villages to attend worship services. They glance around cautiously from time to time, wondering if anyone is watching. Intent as they are on gathering together with other believers, they know full well that they may pay dearly for doing so.

Others arise with the dawn, assemble their poorly-fed children inside shabby homes, and those that have them read quietly from well-worn Bibles that remain carefully hidden during the week. They pray for their daily bread and for the courage to carry on.

Still others encounter the first day of the week in the darkness of their prison cells. Prayer is on their lips, too, as they look forward to further interrogation, torture, and perhaps eventually execution.

Meanwhile, in America, a somewhat different scene unfolds. From a glass cathedral in Southern California to a Pentecostal tabernacle in the Deep South; from a high-tech mega-church in Chicago to an Episcopal chapel on the East Coast, a glorious message is declared. Worshipers in air-conditioned buildings, at ease in upholstered pews, eagerly receive the Good News.

Encouraging words are offered in myriad sermons, dramatic presentations, and testimonials. The message is televised, recorded in countless books and on audiotapes. It is sung in anthems, cried out in rock tunes, and chanted in gospel choruses. It is expressed with tearful promises, with witty anecdotes, or with pop-psych platitudes. The promise is one of peace.

THE PAIN AND THE PUZZLE

In 1995, Michael Horowitz, a senior fellow at the Hudson Institute, wrote an editorial for the *Wall Street Journal* in which he pointed out that the "evidence of growing and large-scale persecution of evangelicals and Christian converts is overwhelming." He challenged American Jews like himself to not be silent in the face of "persecutions eerily parallel to those committed by Adolf Hitler."

Horowitz went on to say, "America's Christian community is most directly challenged. Its moral authority will be gravely tarnished if it fails to exercise its growing political influence on behalf of people now risking everything to engage in the 'simple' act of Christian worship and witness. . . ."[1]

Horowitz wasn't finished. He also wrote a letter to nearly one hundred fifty denominational mission boards. He began, "As an American Jew, I've been deeply grateful for the fellowship and support of the Christian community in recent struggles against anti-Semitism. I very much doubt, for example, that the rescue of Jews from the former Soviet Union could have taken place without the morally rooted and committed assistance of the Christian community.

"I am writing because I am pained and puzzled at the relative lack of interest shown by many within the Christian community of fellow Chris-

tians who are now increasingly persecuted—as Christians and for their beliefs alone—throughout the world."[2]

The vast body of Christians in the United States, along with their major organizations, have indeed abdicated their responsibility to deal with the persecution of Christians. Of course, there are numerous exceptions. Many people do wonderful work, and this book reflects their strenuous efforts. But the overall record of church bodies is abysmal. Despite a plethora of TV programs, radio stations, and magazines, despite the presence of the tens of thousands of workers overseas involved in missions, education, and relief and development work, despite networks of contacts worldwide and a vast array of internetted agencies, the situation of Christians overseas is passed by silently. Consequently, I will focus on what is *not* done. This will include the theologically conservative evangelical churches and the theologically liberal "mainline" churches. There are different reasons in each case, but the abdication is common to both.[3]

Seeking Inner Peace: The Evangelicals

> You have sown much and harvested little;
> You eat but never have enough,
> drink but never have your fill,
> put on clothes but feel no warmth.
> The wage-earner gets his wages only
> to put them in a bag with a hole in it. . . .
> And why?. . .
> because while my House lies in ruins,
> each of you is busy with his own house.
>
> —Haggai 1:6, 9

In response to Horowitz's letter, Reverend David Stravers, vice president of the Bible League, gave two reasons for Christians' relative lack of interest in the plight of suffering sisters and brothers worldwide:

1. "American Christians for the most part are not interested in *anything* that happens outside the boundaries of the United States, and in many cases outside the boundaries of their own little community. . . .

2. "American Christians have no experience of persecution or suffering for their faith which remotely resembles the experiences of many of our overseas brothers and sisters. It is difficult to empathize. . . . many, many, many American Christians refuse to believe what is reported because it is so far outside their experience."[4]

There are other factors which marginalize evangelical action on overseas persecution. It is difficult to describe these in any short compass, since evangelicals do not act within one overall body. Rather, they exist in a contradictory and bewildering array of denominations, churches, organizations, ministries, and mailing lists.

This is at once their strength and their weakness. It is a strength because it allows a variety of creative responses and the use of entrepreneurial skills in quickly responding to problems. It is a weakness because it produces fragmentation, scattered energies, and all-too-frequent competition. Rather than trying to summarize this fantastic array of hundreds of thousands of organizations and tens of millions of people, I will focus on some of the pervasive cultural and theological factors which so far have rendered the evangelical response to persecution negligible.

One is a popular form of success theology which stresses prosperity and inner peace as results of spiritual virtue.

A second is a nationalist form of Christianity which confuses God and America.

A third is obsession with end-times prophecy, which produces favoritism and fatalism.

A fourth is fierce competition for fund-raising dollars by emphasizing only an organization's own efforts.

A fifth is a simple lack of information. Because of an indifferent secular media, news about Christian persecution rarely reaches the West. We will look at this in the next chapter. For now, we will concentrate on the other factors.

PEACE AND COMFORT

Evangelical media offer primarily a smorgasbord of entertainment stars and uniquely western self-improvement opportunities. In books, seminars, and TV shows, star motivational writers and speakers provide steps for career achievement. Entertainers, television personalities, and Grammy Award-winning contemporary Christian music artists deliver tips for discovering inner peace and joy. Professional sports heroes and Olympic medalists contribute suggestions for accomplishing one's personal best. While worthwhile things are said in these testimonials, profound human suffering is hardly ever mentioned.

It would be dishonest to claim that *all*, or even *most*, Christians in America have simply followed a consumer gospel. A thoughtful Christianity still remains intact in the hearts of countless believers, as well as in many churches, schools, and homes. However, consumerism is widespread and increasingly combined with the shallower forms of modern psychology. The call to "seek peace and pursue it" has become, in many churches, a ceaseless quest for personal tranquillity: no stress, no guilt, no "unhealthy" emotions. A proliferation of self-help and recovery groups feeds preoccupation with emotional well-being.

There are countless books and articles on the shelves of Christian bookstores that articulate this self-absorbed world-view, covering subjects a world apart from overseas Christians whose lives are on the line for their faith. One best-selling writer, Dr. Frank Minirth, quotes Solomon, "As a man thinks in his heart, so is he," and takes this to imply, "How we think . . . is the key (to mental health)." He then provides a guide to a healthy life:

1. Memorize Scripture.

2. Be willing to love.

3. Take time to laugh.
4. Face your fears.
5. Accept yourself as you are.
6. Refuse to worry.
7. Give everyone, including yourself, a break.
8. Give problems time.
9. Watch closely how you allow yourself to be entertained.[5]

The problem is not whether some or all of this may be good advice. It is that this inward focus is *all* the advice that is given: It leaves the impression that life is about inner peace. It is difficult to imagine Christians immersed solely in this perspective being able to get their noses out of their navels long enough to consider whether their peace should be tied to the fate of suffering sisters and brothers around the world. It is equally difficult to imagine such a list giving much comfort to Christians who really *are* persecuted. (Though it is striking that persecuted Christians often laugh much more than many of their pallid western counterparts.)

Minirth has authored or coauthored best-selling books including, *The Power of Memories*, *The Freedom from Depression Workbook*, and *How to Beat Burn Out*. Perhaps the last one could be useful to Christians abroad.

As evangelical theologian David Wells puts it:

> We imagine that the great purposes of life are psychological rather than moral. We imagine that the great purposes of life are realized in the improvement of our own private inner disposition. We imagine that for those who love God and are called according to his purpose, all things work together for their satisfaction and the inner tranquillity of their lives. Modernity has secured the triumph of the therapeutic over the moral even in the church.[6]

The subject of persecuted Christians is jarring to an obsession with personal peace. It is hard to feel tranquil or serene when faced with the helpless plight of other people who are brutally abused. It is disturbing to one's peace of mind to contemplate their physical torment and emotional despair. The very existence of such pain casts a deep shadow over the promised "wholeness" that Christianity is said to offer.

A best-selling author and famous television preacher, says, "It seems as though the 'Good Fridays' are tough and real. We feel swallowed up in our personal problems and world tragedies. The ensuing days seem short in patience and long in suffering. But the Christian faith is one based on fact. The fact that 'all things work together for good.' The fact that God's ways are not our ways. The fact that Easter sunrise will come, the problem will blossom into a possibility, and the tragedy will become a triumph."[7] Other best-selling Christian authors' books include such titles as *God's Vitamin "C" for the Spirit*, *Tea Time with God*, and *God's Little Instruction Book*.

Clearly, a positive outlook can have value in dealing with most of our ordinary day-to-day frustrations. But if God is always supposed to provide relief, then suffering Christians seem to make God appear untrustworthy and the product unreliable. Why hasn't Christianity "worked" for the Sudanese the way it does in America? How can the prayers of suffering Christians in Vietnam remain unanswered?

Historically, the heart of the evangelical gospel has been "Christ died for your sins," not the modern preoccupation "Christ died for your problems." If religious teaching becomes a promise of psychological benefits, then a seemingly logical conclusion is that suffering stems from a lack of faith.

Many trends in modern Protestant teaching fly in the face of the Reformation's stress that God's gifts are not earned by good behavior. There is a *quid pro quo* in some versions of modern Christianity. We will get God's blessing if we behave properly.

But what does this mean for those who struggle against adversity, persecution, and poverty? If obedience is the key to the future, then they must somehow have failed, somehow fallen short of God's best, somehow been disobedient. What does it say of the apostle Paul, writing letters from a prison cell, not to mention Jesus, who was markedly "unsuccessful." He found himself betrayed, abandoned, and hung on a cross.[8]

These are not the only tendencies in evangelicalism. But they are the dominant ones. They are the themes that dominate the best-seller lists, the magazines, the TV shows, and all-too-many of the churches. The result is a faith that has its eyes turned resolutely inward.[9]

Self-absorption is clearly not the only reason western evangelicals remain unconcerned about their persecuted counterparts across the sea. But it certainly contributes to the apathy. So does rampant Americanism.

GOD AND AMERICA

Critics of American evangelicalism, many of them evangelicals themselves, point out the pervasive confusion between God and America. John Seel observes, "At times it has seemed that if evangelicals were to wake up as citizens of an African or Asian nation, their identity as followers of Christ would be profoundly shaken. Why? Not simply because of the differences in language, food, and culture, but because many American evangelicals have been truly more American than Christian, more dependent on historical myths than spiritual realities, more shaped by the flag than the cross."[10]

Believers should certainly love their country, but nationalism can never be the mediator and shaper of faith.[11] Whether the homeland is America or anywhere else, the nationalist focus undercuts any sense of "one holy, catholic, and apostolic church." Foreign lands become unknown realms where God works partially and mysteriously, if at all. Distant suffering is simply foreign—of no real consequence to faith and daily routines.

Although current best-selling books by conservative Christian political leaders like Ralph Reed's *After the Revolution: How the Christian Coalition Is Impacting America* [12] and Gary Bauer's *Our Hope, Our Dreams: A Vision for America* [13] address a range of issues, they do not deal with anything in the international arena. Concern with American families, American values, and American morality—eclipses a sense of a worldwide Christian presence.[14] (Bauer himself and his publisher, Focus on the Family, have, however, taken important steps to address the issue of persecuted Christians.) Clearly, an American public will be concerned first about matters at home: But is this all it should be concerned with?

There is an evangelical left, but it is often more derelict, since it lays claim to a more international focus. For all the concern about suffering in the world, writers such as Jim Wallis and Tony Campolo are wrapped up in America, albeit sometimes a type of anti-America, and center their attention on issues such as American poverty and American immigration policies. They are as silent as many of their conservative counterparts on the subject of Christian persecution abroad. Wallis has involved himself in international issues such as Nicaragua and South Africa, but he rarely strays beyond the usual concerns of the American left.[15]

Tony Campolo, a frequent White House guest, devotes an entire book to such quintessentially American themes as illegal aliens, prayer in public schools, TV talk shows, and gun control. Fair enough, perhaps. But he adds an introductory "Note to International Readers" which finds "the same forces at work and the same dangers evident in other countries. . . . that is why I believe that this book is relevant beyond the borders of the United States. The names, places, and political parties undoubtedly are different from other countries, but the issues, dangers, and concerns remain the same. . . ."[16]

I read this upon returning from Southern Sudan, where *Baltimore Sun* journalists and a TV crew had just managed, on camera, to buy Christian child slaves. It is hard to know whether to laugh or cry, or perhaps pray.

In Campolo's defense, it could be said that gun control *is* an issue in the Sudan. But so is bomb control. And food control.

IN SEARCH OF ARMAGEDDON

Those evangelicals who do talk about the international arena are often obsessed with arcane types of biblical prophecy. This trend is especially prevalent among fundamentalists and charismatics.[17]

"The evangelical predilection, when faced with a world crisis, to use the

Bible as a crystal ball instead of as a guide for sorting out the complex tangles of international morality was nowhere more evident than in response to the Gulf War. Neither . . . did evangelicals engage in significant discussions on the morality of the war, the use of the United Nations in the wake of the collapse of Communism, the significance of oil for job creation or wealth formation throughout the world, the history of western efforts at intervention in the Middle East, or other topics fairly crying out for serious Christian analysis. Instead, evangelicals gobbled up more than half-a-million copies each of several self-assured, populist explanations of how the Gulf Crisis was fulfilling the details of obscure biblical prophecies."[18]

During the Gulf War Saddam Hussein and Iraq were found prefigured in the Bible: Indeed, the juxtaposition of Baghdad and Babylon seemed to cry out for some such link. John Walvoord's book from the 1970s, *Armageddon, Oil, and the Middle East*, was reprinted with a run of some 550,000 copies. It sold very well. One of Walvoord's students, Dave Hunt, has produced best-selling books seeking to portray current events in the light of biblical prophecy. He seeks to interpret the invasion of Kuwait, and almost everything else, in terms of the imminent arrival of the Antichrist.[19]

An especially destructive pattern begins to emerge when such commentators then proceed from purported prophetic claims to purported political principles. When they believe an event is foretold in the Bible, whether an assault on Israel or the war around Iraq, they often support the policy of (usually) the U.S. or Israel, since these policies will then, presumably, bring about the fulfillment of the prophecy.

American best-selling author Hal Lindsey has said that one day the Russians will attack Israel and thus set in motion a whole set of biblically ordained events.[20] He couples this with a tendency to "cooperate" with prophecy. But can anything be defended simply because it might eventually help bring about a predicted end? By this logic, one might as well support Saddam Hussein on the grounds that he, too, is fulfilling biblical prophecy.[21]

The point is not whether Christians should support Israel. Especially given the history of Christian anti-Semitism, it is imperative that the churches defend the people of Israel from potential destruction. But this support cannot be by a blind use of prophecy that can end up portraying people on the wrong side as wholesale "enemies of God" whose hopes, fears, and dreams can be ignored, and whose destruction is awaited.

For those who take the Bible as an authority, it must be emphasized that God calls people to love their neighbors (and enemies). There are neighbors in Israel, and the U.S., and also in Russia, and in Iraq, and in Iran. There are serious Christian discussions of what this means for international law, war, and human rights. These, not any speculative view of predictive prophecy, would be seriously biblical criteria for judging international relations.[22]

In the absence of such criteria, the world becomes portrayed in Manichean and conspiratorial terms, wherein some people, organizations, and countries are portrayed as the fountains of all light and others as the pit of all darkness. Dave Hunt ruminates on the European Community as the core of a "revived Roman Empire over which the Antichrist will reign." "The scenario becomes macabre when one notices that the twelve stars representing the members of the E.C. on the Council of Europe poster are not ordinary stars, but upside-down pentagrams, the symbol of the Goat of Mendes, Satan."[23] Hunt sees Pope John Paul II as "working feverishly to merge all faiths," and draws parallels between Gorbachev and the Roman Emperor, Constantine, in their desire for a global Holy Roman Empire. This is interspersed with insinuations that the Antichrist's "stamp of approval," 666, will be manifest through worldwide electronic banking.[24]

Meanwhile, Arabs and others can be identified, without discrimination, as the obstacles to God's purposes. The result is that Arab Christians, not to mention others, receive a double blow. Christians in Egypt and Iraq suffer not only persecution at home, but are ignored or sometimes cast as enemies of God by some western members of their faith.

THE GREAT ESCAPE

Another major prophetic theme developed in the nineteenth century is a belief in "the Rapture." It has many variations, but basically maintains that before a "Great Tribulation," thought to be predicted in the Book of

Daniel in the Old Testament and in St. John's Revelation in the New Testament, the entire Christian church will be supernaturally removed from the earth. Christians will be taken up into heaven just before God's wrath is poured out on non-believers during seven years of apocalypse.

Author Hal Lindsey promoted and popularized this teaching in *The Late, Great Planet Earth* which, apart from the Bible, was perhaps the best-selling book in America in the 1970s.[25] In a recent sequel, also best-selling, he predicts an acceleration of Christian persecution worldwide, but offers this comfort:

> And for those of us living in this world today as we approach an age of growing persecution, there's something else to look forward to. For God promises that He will take His flock out of this world just before the persecution becomes most unbearable.[26]

Apparently Lindsey must mean that this will happen before *Americans* get persecuted, since in Central American jungles, Soviet Gulags, Chinese labor camps, Pakistani jails, Indian riots, and Sudanese villages countless believers have already paid the ultimate price for their faith. This teaching on the Rapture and persecution is currently a largely Western-oriented idea, and its teachers seem oblivious to the level of suffering other Christians endure.

This stress on the Rapture can have one other effect. It implies that the problem will be solved only by direct Divine intervention. While in strictly logical terms, this does not necessarily imply that Christians need do nothing about current persecution, it does in practice seem to lead to a fatalism wherein persecution is simply taken for granted. The result is a stunning passivity that calmly accepts such suffering. Perhaps this, too, could be justified if we were dealing with our own suffering. But to do this with the suffering of another amounts to theological sadism.

DUELING FOR DOLLARS

In efforts to raise funds for their international concerns, many organizations—evangelical, denominational, church, and para-church alike—

focus attention on one crisis after another, sending out urgent appeals for further help (i.e., money). A crisis per month is usually required, since many organizations send urgent appeals on a monthly basis. Sometimes a crisis is also required in time to be included in a thank-you letter for donations raised during the last crisis.

Some of these fund-raising letters exaggerate conditions in order to shock donors into making large contributions. This desensitizes westerners to an apparently endless series of emergencies. Emotional manipulation also makes it harder for the more responsible groups, such as the largest—World Vision—to establish consistent funding or to develop long-range fiduciary goals.[27]

While this spectacle can be ugly, perhaps some of it could be justified. After all, this book, too, is intended to promote a sense of crisis. I sincerely hope for an increase in monthly mailers on this issue. But further dangers arise because of the aggressive competition for dollars in the entrepreneurial evangelical culture.

One organization becomes offended with another, and subtle (or not-so-subtle) criticism is exchanged. Disagreements regarding theology, tactics, personalities, or political viewpoints are aired in magazine articles, on Christian network interviews, and in hastily published promotional books.[28] Holier-than-thou statements are often accompanied by pleas for cash to help further the "righteous" cause of the offended ministry. A "them" against "us" approach is used both to stir emotions and loosen purse-strings.

One lasting example of this, in the area of religious persecution itself, involved two ministries who were both working on behalf of Christians in the former Soviet Union. Kent Hill reports, "Richard Wurmbrand's Jesus to the Communist World and Joe Bass's Underground Evangelism were sometimes guilty of mud-slinging. . . . Wurmbrand and Bass regard the registered churches as nothing more than pawns of the state, devoid of real spirituality, and they have sometimes sensationalized the plight of the unregistered. . . . To make matters worse, the two groups were involved. . . . in suits and countersuits against each other."[29]

More recently, a conflict took place when Nelson Graham's East Gates Ministries International claimed, "The days of smuggling Bibles into China are over. . . ." This was in an appeal for funds for Bibles that would, with the permission of the Chinese government, be printed and distributed inside China. It was attacked by others whose focus has long included Bible smuggling.[30]

Inter-organizational disputes regarding strategies and political philosophies spill across borders, involving the indigenous groups for whom help is being sought. Catholics in Germany have been critical of Sudanese Catholic support of non-Catholic groups, despite the fact that the Germans have done little work there themselves.

Doubtless there are also other factors in the failures of the more conservative churches. But, whatever the reason, the conclusion is clear. As a whole, the American evangelical churches have ignored the plight of their sisters and brothers overseas.[31] Meanwhile, their counterparts in the mainline churches have problems of their own.

Seeking Outer Peace: The Mainline Churches

> They dress the wounds of my people
> as though they were not serious.
> "Peace, peace" they say,
> when there is no peace.
> Are they ashamed of their conduct?
> No, they have no shame at all;
> they do not even know how to blush.
>
> —Jeremiah 8:11–12

If the principal message of the evangelical churches is "inner peace," then the message of the mainline denominations is "outer peace." Yet the record of these denominations is probably worse than that of conservative evangelicals. One of the best ways to illustrate this is by reviewing the activities of the National Council of Churches, the umbrella group which is frequently used as a focal point for joint action among these denominations. The NCC embraces the largest Methodist, Episcopalian, and Presbyterian bodies as well as several Lutheran bodies and Orthodox groups.[32]

In earlier years, the Council firmly opposed the persecution of Christians as well as other religious groups. But this began to recede in the 1960s, after it took a strong stand against the U.S. involvement in Vietnam and became strongly affected by the radicalism of that time. There is no reason why a liberal stance *per se* should deflect from concern about Christian persecution. Congressmen such as Tony Hall and Tom Lantos have been active on this issue. In Britain, support for persecuted Christians is as strong on the left as on the right, reflecting that country's strong element of Christian socialism. However, the NCC's new orientation has had three further elements.

First, there emerged a marked attachment to professedly left-wing governments, combined with a tendency to romanticize them.

Second, in its fear of doing anything which might appear to give sustenance to right-wing positions, the NCC has glossed over religious persecution enacted by left-wing groups.

Third, the NCC became highly critical of the United States, and reemphasized that its first political duty was to be critical of its own country. This led to "balancing" any situation of persecution and suffering elsewhere with a comparable critique of tendencies within the United States. One does not need to have a rose-tinted view of America to see that such a procedure can trivialize the repression of believers in other parts of the world.

There is one other relevant trend, this one more specifically theological in nature. Many mainline church seminaries now tend to downplay any stress on the specific truths of Christianity. One of the major emphases has become openness to and dialogue with other religions and ideological movements. While dialogue and a critical openness is certainly to be welcomed, one of the results has been reluctance to raise anything which might damage peaceful relations with conversation partners. This also leads to an animus against people engaged in seeking to propagate their faith, with an implication that such troublemakers might deserve what they get. This means that the NCC doesn't seem to like evangelism (or "proselytizing"), and is not very sympathetic to those who suffer for it.

The result is that the mainline churches' treatment of religious persecution is marked by a reluctance to criticize left-wing regimes, a focus on

U.S. faults, a pattern of maintaining good relations with dialogue partners, and a suspicion of evangelicals. These patterns mark NCC actions to this day.

PEACE WITH COMMUNISM

The Council's publications demonstrate these trends. In 1972, the NCC stopped funding the research and distribution of its excellent journal, *Religion in Communist Dominated Areas*. Soon thereafter, its Friendship Press produced a series of studies which ignored or whitewashed the persecution of Christians in countries such as China, North Korea, and Cuba.

China: Search for Community contains a forward by Robert McAfee Brown which maintains that visitors to China are "almost always . . . enthusiastic," especially on "the role of the church."[33] The book describes the Cultural Revolution of the 1960s as an "outstanding campaign" for "moral renewal" which "emphasized community interest, anti-elitism, commitment to revolutionary social goals, dignity of manual labor, equality of women and men, and education for the common people." It notes that freedom of religious belief is guaranteed in the Chinese Constitution and "Christians, Moslems, and Buddhists continue to meet together for worship and fellowship. . . . Past years have seen periods of local repression and hardship for religious believers, but current reports indicate that Christians and other believers quietly but openly practice their faith." It notes the existence of "house church" groups but implies that they meet in homes because "foreign-style churches . . . carry a stigma from the former colonial days."[34]

The NCC's booklet on Korea sets up parallels between the North and the South.[35] It describes the division as providing "the ruling groups on both sides with the pretext for suppression and exploitation," and implies criticism of "those Christians who move to the South because of the Communist persecution and purge of Christians in the North" for their apparent embrace of the South, despite its "authoritarian" policies. It claims, "Apparently there was less violence and less resistance to the Soviet takeover in Northern Korea than to U.S. Control in Southern Korea." Further parts of the book concentrate on criticizing the authoritarianism of the South, while developments in the North are passed over. The book is generally silent on the persecution of Christians there.[36]

When Dorothy Ogle, NCC "associate director for education and advocacy on Korea peace and reunification," testified before the U.S. House of Representatives Asian Affairs Subcommittee, she said, "North Koreans are proud of their beautiful cities, schools, healthcare facilities, apartments, immigration projects, dams, and locks." Subcommittee Chairman Stephen Solarz (D-N.Y.) remarked that many of her claims "seemed to come straight out of Pyongyang."[37]

The NCC's book on Cuba proclaims, "The revolutionary government declares that ultimately all social services—education, healthcare, hospitalization, sports facilities, transportation, and telephones—will be free or virtually free. Later on the leaders are to call that Socialism. The poor people call it great."[38] NCC officials accompanying the Reverend Jesse Jackson on his 1984 "mission for peace" to Cuba supported "the positive role played in the revolution by Christians."[39]

> Armando Valladares, a poet who spent twenty-two years in Cuban prisons, describes the use authorities made of naive American Christian support for Castro.
>
> *"During those years, with the purpose of forcing us to abandon our religious beliefs and to demoralize us, the Cuban Communist indoctrinators repeatedly used the statements of support for Castro's revolution made by some representatives of American Christian churches. Every time that a pamphlet was published in the United States, every time a clergyman would write an article in support of Fidel Castro's dictatorship, a translation would reach us and that was worse for the Christian political prisoners than the beatings or the hunger.*[40]

The paradigm established in the early 1970s did not change. The best illustration of this was the June 1984 NCC-organized junket by 266 church leaders to the Soviet Union. According to the *New York Times*, it "ended a two week tour of fourteen cities with praise for the status of religion in the Soviet Union and condemnation of the United States' role in the arms race."[41]

Leaders of the group "voiced irritation that the harmony of their visit had been marred when two demonstrators, demanding religious freedom, held up banners during a Baptist church service." The tour's leader, Bruce Rigdon, said of the demonstrators, "They were asked to leave and they were conducted out by members of the congregation. We believe they are free. I understand that in the United States, a situation like this would have been handled by the police." Three weeks after this, one of the people with the demonstrators—Veniamin Naprienko, a Baptist—was sent to a Soviet Labor Camp.[42] The NCC ignored Naprienko's imprisonment.

Rigdon defended the group by emphasizing that its overriding goal was not human rights, but "to demonstrate that the unity which God has given the church transcends all boundaries of ideology. . . ." As Rabbi Rudin, national director of interreligious affairs for the American Jewish Committee, said, it is "unacceptable to contend that human rights are secondary to Christian unity."[43] It is also difficult to see what genuine form of Christian peace and unity can result if people are excluded from it simply because they dare to mention that they are persecuted.

The NCC has been reluctant to acknowledge this record. In 1987, Arie Brouwer, the general secretary, said, "The record in fact shows that we have frequently stood against abuses of human rights and other injustices in many countries, including the Soviet Union."[44]

It is true that the NCC has offered criticism in resolutions, in "quiet diplomacy" and by other means, of persecution in the countries we have described.[45] But, while it has devoted extensive resources to attacking apartheid in South Africa, U.S. policies and military governments in Latin America, and repression in Asian countries allied with the U.S., its efforts for those in Communist countries have been far more limited.[46]

In its concerns in Southern Africa and Latin America, the Council has hired staff, developed newsletters, started research centers, funded institutions, and given monetary and logistical support to those whose causes it has championed. But, for example, when resolutions were passed concerning China after the Tiananmen Square massacres of 1989, the result was only pieces of paper.

PRESENT PEACEMAKING

In more recent years the NCC and associated agencies have given some signs of self-criticism, particularly under the leadership of Leonid Kishkovski and, to some degree, its current general secretary, the Reverend Joan Brown Campbell. Nonetheless, the basic pattern set in the 1960s is alive and well.

In October 1995, Cuban President Fidel Castro attended the United Nations fiftieth anniversary meetings in New York. He was shunned by the Clinton administration but happily received by one hundred church leaders at a meeting convened by the Interreligious Foundation for Community Organization and General Secretary Campbell. They seemed to share Castro's own glamorous self-image of a rebel in designer combat gear facing down the U.S. colossus.

The NCC press release on this occasion highlighted its call for an end to the U.S. trade embargo against Cuba. It noted that the Council "continues to raise questions about such situations as the detention of some pastors and the closing of some preaching centers." However, the statement hastened to add that "such disagreements notwithstanding," Campbell "expressed her appreciation that Cuba has 'made a priority of caring for the poor.'" The bulk of the NCC report praised Castro, noting "great improvement in the situation of the Cuban churches." Campbell herself asserted that Cuban churches "now are able to carry out all the work of the church, that is, the training of pastors, Sunday school teaching, evangelism, and service to the society."[47]

The NCC's latest publication on China continues the patterns of previous decades.[48] In contrast to earlier claims, this work now portrays the Cultural Revolution as having "unleashed its fury against all forms of religion in China." However, the overall apologetic stance continues. The Tiananmen Square Massacre is trivialized as a "demonstration" "resulting in the tragedy of the fourth of June 1989 in which both demonstrators and soldiers were killed." China's repressions are mentioned thus: "Human rights, as perceived in the West, continued to bedevil China's international image."

It focuses on defending the government's Religious Affairs Bureau and the officially accepted church bodies, the China Christian Council, the Three-Self Patriotic Movement, and the Catholic Bishops' Conference. This is combined with a defense of the government's 1994 regulations of religious freedom. Those outside the official bodies are often spoken of in negative terms. "(T)here are many followers of itinerant, self-proclaimed evangelists who meet in unregistered places. The government regards such behavior as 'abnormal' and does not protect it. . . . some take advantage of their followers by cheating and selling miracles."

There are indeed many wonderful and committed Christians in the official church bodies, as I can testify personally. And leader Bishop K. H. Ting has at times spoken out against government policy. But, in a repressive society, they cannot be regarded as independent actors. The book records how, when Konrad Raiser, general secretary of the World Council of Churches, met in 1994 with Ting and other leaders, "none of the church leaders with whom he met complained about 'open infringement of religious liberty.'" Curiously, it doesn't seem to ponder how such an absence of complaint might be connected to a quotation further down the same page, "If the Christian churches do not have good relations. . . . with the government, then we won't be able to preach."[49]

PEACE WITH THE STATUS QUO

In early 1996, the NCC and its affiliated bodies were asked to endorse the National Association of Evangelicals' (NAE) "Statement of Conscience." This was a statement of repentance for the Association's previous neglect of Christian persecution worldwide, combined with a call to action. The NCC declined to cosign the statement on the ground that it referred only to Christians. It is certainly true, as the Council maintains, that we should be concerned about the persecution of people of any and no faith, something which the NAE statement itself emphasizes. Nevertheless, it is a poor excuse to avoid one crucial issue simply because it does not include another.

The NAE's statement is part of a growing consciousness about Christian persecution. This concern led to hearings in February 1996 before the House

Subcommittee on International Operations and Human Rights. Albert M. Pennybacker, associate general secretary of the National Council of Churches, testified before these hearings, expressly speaking for the NCC's policy-making body, the General Council.

In contrast to the NAE's self-criticism, Pennybacker was not critical of his own Council's history. He claimed, "We have been a long-standing, vigorous advocate" of religious liberty. "During the difficult years of Soviet domination of Eastern Europe, we maintained strong, affirmative, and cooperative ties with the Christian communities of long and faithful histories, who maintained their faith under conditions of painful, almost unimaginable religious persecution, even martyrdom." He stated that the Council maintains "ties of support, encouragement, advocacy, and even direct aid" with Christians in "Cuba, China, North Korea, Vietnam, Pakistan, and other nations."[50]

Then, rather than exhorting further action on these matters, Pennybacker focused on caution in dealing with them. First, he warned that such action should respect "the integrity of the resident religious communities." Clearly this is true. Nobody wants a bunch of foreigners trampling in, regardless of the wishes of those who actually suffer. But what Pennybacker does not acknowledge is that the ties the NCC maintains with these countries are frequently with the state-sponsored and state-controlled official churches who are, in turn, compromised in their relations with their own governments. In these situations, as we shall see in our discussion of the World Council of Churches, "respecting the integrity" of state-sponsored church bodies can mean giving *de facto* veto power to the governments concerned.

Pennybacker also expressed caution because what "may appear as 'persecution,' and indeed is resistance, may in fact be the wish to preserve authentic religious and cultural traditions." It may indeed be such a wish. And such wishes should normally be respected. But not if they involve the imprisonment of those held to be outside the "authentic" religious tradition. Such a stance can also open the door for repression of any religious activity held to be a violation of "cultural" traditions, something argued for by China, Burma, Sudan, and other authoritarian governments in recent international debates over human rights.[51]

Pennybacker's other major concern is "a careful assessment of the claims of religious persecution." He calls for "genuine investigation and assessment" and advises "it is premature to move quickly to the appointment of a special adviser to the president on these matters" [as has been called for by the NAE and President Clinton's political advisers]. This limited call for yet more study of the matter seems to flow from a certain skepticism about the whole enterprise, since he is content to write, "IF it is true that the persecution of believers of all faiths is pervasive, it is rightly a cause for deep concern and lament" (emphasis added).

SEEKING INTERNATIONAL PEACE: THE WORLD COUNCIL OF CHURCHES

> "It is difficult to reach you,
> So very difficult. . . .
> Much more difficult than to reach God. . . .
>
> —Russian Deacon Vladimir Rusak,
> to the WCC General Assembly, 1983[52]

The World Council of Churches has taken some good stances.[53] It condemned the Soviet invasion of Czechoslovakia. It offered public support to Baptist pastor Georgi Vins when he was imprisoned for a second term. It issued statements of support for Solzhenitsyn before his expulsion from the Soviet Union. But its overall record in relation to church persecution is not a happy one.[54]

To understand the WCC's actions in today's world, it is worth scrutinizing its conduct before the Soviet Union's demise. Since 1992, Soviet archives have been opened, so it is possible to see the deception and cynicism to which the WCC succumbed. This is doubly important since, unfortunately, there is little indication that the organization's procedures have changed.

The WCC has a policy of acting only with the agreement of its member churches in the country where the actions are to take place. As a general principle, this cannot be faulted. However, all good general principles have exceptions. Two obvious exceptions that come to mind are, what if the WCC member body from a country represents only an atypical minority of the Christians in that country? Second, what happens when the WCC representatives are effectively screened by a country engaged in persecution? By controlling their WCC church representation, authoritarian governments can exercise veto power over any WCC action. The result is that WCC policy will ultimately be controlled by those who have no interest in, or are even engaged in, persecution. In many instances, this is precisely what has happened, particularly since 1961, when the Russian Orthodox Church became a member, followed in subsequent years by several other Soviet and Eastern European bodies.

PEACE WITH THE SOVIET UNION

One of the most dramatic instances occurred in the WCC General Assembly in Nairobi in November 1975. The Assembly received an "Appeal to the Delegates" from Father Gleb Yakunin, a Russian Orthodox priest, and Lev Regelson, a lay physicist. This passionate, detailed, and precise letter brought attention to the persecution of the church in the Soviet Union and laid out careful proposals for how the WCC could respond to it.[55]

The Russian delegation reacted swiftly. It did not attack the particular claims made in the appeal, claims which have never been discredited. Instead, it followed traditional tactics by attacking the character of the letter's authors. The attack was led by Metropolitan Yuvenali, leader of the Russian Orthodox delegation and chairman of the External Church Relations Department of the Moscow Patriarchate (and revealed by 1992 investigations in the KGB archives to carry the KGB code name, "Adamant.")

The appeal created a stir and became the major issue at the Assembly, which then passed a resolution to respond actively to it. However, the matter did not end there. During the break following the vote, there were discussions among the conference organizers and the chairman, Dr. Ernest Payne, declared that the motion had been out of order and should be referred back to the resolutions committee. This committee, including its

Soviet member, worked out a substitute amendment which dropped all mention of the Soviet Union and referred to "alleged infringements of religious liberty."

The Assembly itself then partially rectified this whitewash by demanding consultations with the member churches in the areas covered by the Helsinki Agreement. Dr. Philip Potter, the new general secretary of the WCC, was to report back in 1976 to the WCC Central Committee on the subject of religious liberty.

Meanwhile, back in the USSR, Yakunin and Regelson were encouraged. They indicated in a March 1976 letter to Potter that they believed this to be the beginning of action from churches outside the country. In December 1976, they also founded the "Christian Committee for the Defense of Believers' Rights." In its first three years, this committee produced 417 documents, of which Michael Bourdeaux, one of the world's leading authorities on the topic, says, "Not one single fact in any of these 417 documents has so far been shown to be false and their tone is objective."

However, back in Geneva, the WCC Central Committee decided that "no new program or structures would be required," and called for a small consultation on the subject. Potter contacted the Moscow Patriarchate (the leading body of the Russian Orthodox Church), but not Yakunin and Regelson, about how this should be handled. At the meeting, neither Yakunin nor Regelson was present. But the Moscow Patriarchate was fully represented in the person of Alexei Buyevsky, who seemed to have gotten his way. When Potter subsequently reported on the consultation the following month, he said that it had merely confirmed the work that the WCC had already been doing. And then he immediately changed the subject.

Back in the U.S.S.R., Yakunin was arrested on November 1, 1979, and Regelson on December 25, 1979. Yakunin's appeals to the World Council of Churches were one of the items used against him at his trial. Regelson was forced to recant and Yakunin was sentenced to ten years, the first half in prison, the second half in exile. The WCC reaction, outlined in their telex to Keston College, stated, "Presently no immediate action contemplated." Apparently no non-immediate action either.

A Soviet priest listened to a speech by a western clergyman who preferred "the whole world (to become) Communist than even one bomb be dropped."

Afterward the priest remarked, "And you expect me to tell the likes of him that my church is being persecuted?"[56]

At the WCC's 1983 Assembly in Vancouver, similar dramas were replayed. The Archbishop of Canterbury, the head of the Church of England and the leader of the Anglican Communion Worldwide, was told by Deacon Rusak of the Russian Orthodox Church that Rusak was being persecuted for his efforts to write a history of the Russian church in the twentieth century. The Archbishop supported him, but a spokesman for the Russian Orthodox Church responded by claiming that Rusak should be ignored, "because he had been kicked in the head by a horse when a child! He did not explain how, if Rusak was mentally defective, he had been accepted for seminary training, and indeed had served on the editorial staff of the *Journal of the Moscow Patriarchate* for many years."[57]

In April 1986, Rusak was arrested and was sentenced to a total of twelve years' labor camp and exile.[58] The WCC responded in the way they had to Yakunin's and Regelson's plight. They did nothing. Sentencing to labor camps had become an occupational hazard for people in the East Bloc who tried to get the World Council to pay attention to their persecution.

Laszlo Tokes, a WCC member and a Reformed pastor in Romania, was one of the principle figures in stimulating the popular movements that overthrew the Ceausescu regime. He notes that when he was almost killed in struggling against the regime in 1989, the WCC (as well as the World Alliance of Reformed Churches) gave no support.[59]

PEACE WITH THE KGB

Some reasons for the WCC's dismal record can be found when we see who the Orthodox representatives actually were in its deliberations.

The then secret "Furov Report" to the Central Committee of the Communist Party by the deputy chairman of the Soviet Council on Religious

Affairs (the state body charged with overseeing religion) described the ruling bishops by the degree of their compliance to government wishes. In the most compliant category were those "not personally involved in spreading the influence of the Orthodoxy among our population." These included Patriarch Pimen Izvekov, who headed the Moscow Patriarchate from 1971 to 1990, and his successor Alexei II, the current patriarch.[60]

Pimen was claiming as late as 1987 that "there's no truth in the assertions that the church is oppressed in our country."[61] Furov described others, such as Metropolitan Nikodim Rotov, as combining pastoral work within their own church with external compliance to government wishes. Nikodim was also a president of the World Council of Churches.

In 1992, Yakunin, now a member of the Russian Parliament, and Lev Ponomarev, a physicist, announced preliminary results of their Parliamentary Investigatory Commission into the files of the KGB and the Communist Party.[62] They found that thirty bishops of the Moscow Patriarchate had official code names as "agents in cassocks" of the KGB. Alexei II carried the KGB code name "Drozdov." He served on the Central Committee of the World Council of Churches from 1961 to 1968 as well as functioning on many other church bodies. As mentioned earlier, Metropolitan Yuvenali (code name "Adamant") led the Russian Orthodox Delegation to the 1975 WCC Nairobi Assembly.

The point is not that these men were necessarily direct agents of the KGB. They may well have been engaged in a struggle of being subservient in some areas in order to maintain freedom in others. This is, at least, their own version of events. However, we can certainly say that their position was radically compromised. Given that, under WCC procedure, they exercised a *de facto* veto on any complaints about the USSR, so was the WCC.

In the 1990s, current Patriarch Alexei II has equivocated on repenting for and renouncing this past. However, when the Communists attempted to recover power in a coup in August 1991, he warned the Communist controlled troops who surrounded the parliament building where Yeltsin (and Gleb Yakunin) were resisting, that those who took "up arms against their neighbor, against unarmed people, take the gravest sin upon their souls, the sin which excommunicates them from the church and from

God."[63] Also, in his 1993 Lenten Message, he confessed, "Every one of us has sinned against God. But, my fellow-brothers, the greatest blame lies with us, archpastors and pastors. We will have to answer for our flock at the Last Judgment. . . ."[64]

PEACE WITH CHINA AND ISLAM

All this might seem like water under the bridge since there is no longer a Soviet Bloc. However, this is not merely pedantic history but a consistent pattern of activity. There is little sign that the pattern is changing.[65] This is true in relation to two of the worst areas of persecution in the world today, China and the Islamic world.

Current relations with the official church bodies in China continue to parallel the relations with the former USSR. As we noted previously, after meeting with Chinese government-approved church leaders in 1994, the general secretary of the WCC announced that "none of the church leaders with whom he met complained about 'open infringement of religious liberty.'"[66] He didn't seem to wonder how this lack of complaint might be connected to what problems such leaders might face if they said anything else. Perhaps they might even have learned that people who voice their complaints to the WCC have an unfortunate habit of ending up in labor camps.

In relations with the Islamic world, the WCC once again gives priority to dialogue and peaceful relations.[67] It sponsored a Christian-Muslim dialogue on "Religion and Human Rights" in Berlin in 1994 which announced a mutual commitment to "religious liberty" and "freedom of conscience." The resulting communiqué labeled "International Human Rights Documents," including religious freedom guarantees, as arising from "historical experience whose framework is primarily secular humanist."

It is rather curious to hear the WCC refer to "secular humanists," an expression hitherto confined to fundamentalists. (Jesse Helms, the conservative chair of the U.S. Senate Foreign Relations Committee, describes the UN in a similar way.) Its stance parallels efforts by the governments of China, Singapore, Indonesia, Syria, and others to brand human rights as

"Western ideologies," inappropriate to their countries.[68] Similar concerns have been raised by some Muslims, and the WCC seems to want to woo them, even at the cost of leaving one of its previous dancing partners—the United Nations—jilted at the doorway.

Dialogues, especially with Muslims, are necessary and should be encouraged. I have helped draft guidelines for and participated in them, and hope to carry on doing so. But there is no point in entering them naively or cravenly. Indeed, any Christian who enters such dialogues needs, rightfully, to be prepared to address, for example, the murder of Muslims by so-called Christians in Bosnia and Chechneya, not to mention Ingushetia.

However, the Christian side of such dialogues usually does not include agents for the Serbian butchers of Bosnia nor the Russian thugs in Chechneya. But in tragic reminiscence of the Council's dealings with the former Soviet Union, their dialogue partners include Muslim representatives of those who themselves perpetrate persecutions. The Berlin Conference included Ghazi Salahuddin Atabani, representing the government of Sudan. Abdullahi An-Na'im, former head of the Africa division of Human Rights Watch, depicts him as "very intolerant even with Muslims who disagree with him, let alone non-Muslims."

David Little, head of toleration studies for the U.S. Institute of Peace, adds that several of the participants resist meeting people of other religions back in their home countries, but then "travel to distant countries to talk with foreigners who are less informed and critical, and so are unable to challenge them."

A month earlier a rather worse "interreligious dialogue" took place in Khartoum, the capital of Sudan. This drew people from the World Council of Churches, the Middle East Council of Churches, the Anglican Church, and even Cardinal Arinza, the Nigerian head of the Pontifical Council for Interreligious Dialogue of the Catholic Church.

The Muslim participants included not only religious teachers but also, unlike the Christian contingent, government representatives from Sudan, Pakistan, Libya, and Yemen. The final communiqué affirmed "religious liberty," and called on Christians and Muslims jointly to offer an "alternative vision to the materialist, secularist view which dominates western society."

While nobody has totally clean hands, the notion of Sudan sponsoring a gathering on religious liberty is a sick joke. A ghoulish air was added to the proceedings when the keynote address was given by Hassan Al Turabi, head of the National Islamic Front of Sudan and widely regarded as the actual power in the Sudanese regime. An-Na'im, himself a Sudanese Muslim, laments, "How can people take this seriously? Why don't they look at what the Sudanese government is actually doing, not what it says?"[69]

The Council currently plans to hold another major Christian-Muslim Conference in Tehran, Iran, in October 1996. Tarek Mitri of the WCC's Office on Interreligious Relations says they will not meet as "two blocs facing each other, but (as) people with similar questions involved in discussion."[70]

However, real dialogue must deal not only with the conferees' theological positions, but with the concrete acts of governments, especially when there are state-sponsored Islamic participants. If this duty is shirked then the result will be "mutual trust" in people beholden to regimes which actively repress religious dissenters. For the WCC, it wouldn't be the first time.

THE CATHOLIC BISHOPS AND THE AMERICAN MUSLIM COUNCIL

The WCC's example could suggest caution to the National Conference of Catholic Bishops (NCCB). On March 13, 1996, investigative journalist Steven Emerson published an article in the *Wall Street Journal* alleging that the American Muslim Council (AMC) has links with the rulers of Sudan and that it is an apologist for the Palestinian group Hamas, for the Ayatollah Khomeini and his Iranian successors, for Sheik Abdul Rahman and the World Trade Center bombers, and for the Algerian terrorist F.I.S.

Previously, William Cardinal Keeler had received the AMC's 1995 Mahmoud Abu Saud Excellence Award. He sent a March 26 letter of support to the Council for its press conference of March 27, which conference denounced the charges. In his letter, the Cardinal referred to "a relationship of trust and goodwill" with the AMC. He, along with other Catholic bishops, stressed the need to avoid "Muslim-bashing."

A March 28 statement to the press was then endorsed by Bishop Lipscomb on behalf of the NCCB, along with the endorsement of the National Council of Churches and several other "mainline" church bodies. The statement describes the AMC as "the premier mainstream Muslim group in Washington, D.C.," and maintains that the Council denounces terrorism.

The problem with these churches' stance is that they nowhere offer any refutation of the substance of Emerson's charges. In the face of specific, detailed criticism, they have offered *ad hominem* attacks and blustery denials. NCCB staff have said they "do not intend to debate Emerson, point by point."

I claim no independent expertise on the AMC nor judgment on its status. But I have seen Mr. Emerson's supporting evidence, and it consists of specific quotations from AMC representatives, with checkable sources given, which, if accurate, substantiate the majority of his charges. In the absence of specific refutation by others, it suggests the conclusion that, while the AMC in general terms denounces terrorism, it does so only by denying that organizations with which it is associated are in fact terrorist bodies, when there is ample evidence to the contrary.

If this is true, then the NCCB and other churches would be backing an organization that lends its support to, among others, the regime in Sudan that is waging genocidal war on Christians, including Catholics. These are very grave charges and demand far more than attacks on Emerson and an unwillingness to engage his specific points. Clearly nobody can spend their time checking up on any and all casual allegations made against colleagues. But a detailed article in the *Wall Street Journal* has to be taken more seriously. Any refusal to tackle the substance of Emerson's contentions would be an abdication of responsibility.

The National Conference of Catholic Bishops seems to be led by a desire to counteract any portrayal of Muslims *tout court* as bomb-throwing, murderous radicals. These are noble motives, and ones I share. Despite devoting two chapters to Muslim persecution of Christians, I have tried consistently to point out that such Muslims are not representative of Muslims at large. I have also noted, all too briefly, the persecution of Muslims in Sudan, Saudi Arabia, Chechneya, Bosnia, Ingushetia, India, China,

Pakistan, Central Asia, and Burma, and that this is only a partial list. In the face of popular American press coverage that leaves the impression that Muslim equals Arab equals terrorist, one can do no less, and acknowledge that this is not enough.

But to place peace with organizations above the responsibility to determine what those organizations are doing would be to pursue peace at any price. If Emerson's charges are true, then peace with the AMC would not be a means of combating "Muslim-bashing." It would simply be another means of "Muslim-bashing," since it would treat the majority of peaceful and moderate Muslims as if they were truly represented by apologists for terrorism.

The NCCB owes Muslims, Christians, and Jews a careful and detailed response to the allegations made about the AMC. Failure to do so would betray the brave stance for religious freedom of other Catholics, and Muslims, throughout the world.[71]

THE END OF FALSE PEACE

There is probably no segment, denomination, or organization of Christians whose response to the persecution of Christians is beyond reproach. None of us has done all that could be done. While this book is intended for an audience with a variety of religious views, it perhaps would not be amiss to close a chapter on the churches with a particularly Christian admonition.

> Then the King will say to those on His right hand.... "For I was hungry and you gave me food, I was thirsty and you gave me drink, I was a stranger and you made me welcome, lacking clothes and you clothed me, sick and you visited me, in prison and you came to see me."
>
> Then the upright will say to him in reply, "Lord, when did we see you hungry and feed you, or thirsty and give you drink? When did we see you a stranger and make you welcome, lacking clothes and clothe you? When did we find you sick or in prison and go to see you?"
>
> And the King will answer "In truth, I tell you, in so far as you did this to one of the least of these brothers of mine, you did it to me."

Then he will say to those on his left hand. . . . "I was hungry and you never gave me food, I was thirsty and you never gave me anything to drink, I was a stranger and you never made me welcome, lacking clothes and you never clothed me, sick and in prison and you never visited me."

Then it will be their turn to ask, "Lord when did we see you hungry or thirsty, a stranger or lacking clothes, sick or in prison, and did not come to your help?"

Then he will answer, "In truth, I tell you, in so far as you neglected to do this to one of the least of these, you neglected to do it to me."

—Matthew 25:33–46 (JB)

CHAPTER EIGHT

Western Secularists: A Deafening Silence

Several thousand Algerians overflowed the tiny Christian cemetery. In silent tribute, they had closed their shops in Tizi-Ouzou and had found their way to the funeral. The villagers were intent on paying their respects to the three elderly Catholic priests who were being laid to rest that last day of December 1994.

The assemblage at the funeral was not a Christian one—it was made up almost entirely of Muslims. They were determined to express their sympathy for the surviving members of the "White Fathers" order, and to honor three men who each had devoted more than forty years of their lives to their beloved Algerian community.

The Muslims' show of solidarity with the slain priests stood in eloquent opposition to the statement of the clerics' murderers, GIA (Armed Islamic Group) terrorists, who stated that their forces were "carrying on with the extermination of Christian crusaders."

An anonymous GIA leader described foreigners such as the priests as "the main coronary artery" of a plan to "colonize" Algeria with non-Muslims.[1]

Six weeks after this scene took place, the *New York Times* wrote a story on Algeria. As usual, it gave a broad and (usually) quite good background survey. However, in its summing up of events, it gave this overview of terrorism:

> The targets of the militants have expanded from police, military, and political figures to include westerners and prominent secular Algerians. Some eighty expatriates and hundreds of secular intellectuals, teachers, writers, unveiled women, and civil servants have been among the victims.[2]

Somehow "secular" deaths are worth mentioning in a story, but not religious ones. Admittedly, priests can also be expatriates, teachers, and writers, so maybe the *Times* also had them in mind. But priests are also priests. And since, along with other Christians, they are one of the GIA's principle targets, don't they bear some mention? Is religion irrelevant, even in discussing a campaign of terrorism by fanatical Islamicists?

There was more than one story. Two weeks later, the *Times* reported:

> Clashes between secularists and Islamic militants have taken at least thirty thousand lives with security officers, Government officials, foreigners, and now secular cultural figures among the main targets.[3]

Apparently Christians don't rate. Nor, for that matter, do moderate Muslim leaders, also slain by the guerrillas.

On June 16, 17, and 18, 1996, the *Baltimore Sun* published an extensive and excellent series on slavery in Sudan. However, while the faith of those enslaved was noted, the fact that it is largely Christians who are being enslaved by agents of a radical Islamic regime drew little attention. The slavery was given only the context of its inherent evil and as countering Louis Farrakhan's denials that it exists. A North American camera crew, in the Sudan at the same time as the *Baltimore Sun* reporters, was asked if the massacre of Christians would itself make their network come to Sudan. They replied no, only the issue of slavery would draw TV companies' interest.

Newsweek has recently given much attention to China, even devoting the better part of an issue to the subject. Subsequent issues have addressed Chinese pop-culture and pornography. But on the world's largest program of religious repression, there is silence.[4]

If we turn to secular news outlets, to academics, to policy analysts, to international relations scholars, to political activists in search of news about the persecution of Christians, we encounter a deafening silence. Of course, as my notes demonstrate, there are many able and committed people in each of these areas who have done careful and excellent work in discovering, publicizing, and inspiring action on these matters, just as there are in the world of the churches. But the overall result is similar. The suffering of Christians is virtually unknown or, when it is known, is passed over in silence.

In this chapter, as in the previous one, I am not trying to provide a survey of what has been done in this area. Rather, I will suggest some reasons for what has been left undone.

> We do no credit to the ideal of religious freedom when we talk as though religious belief is something of which public-spirited adults should be ashamed.
>
> —Stephen Carter[5]

Many secular circles in North America are small, parochial worlds wherein many of the great struggles of human life are unknown, trivialized, or forgotten. Instead, there is an introverted focus on Enlightenment culture, as though this constituted the common opinion of humankind, or the common opinion of *reasonable* humankind, or at least the common opinion of Americans. None of these superstitions bears much relation to the reality of the world in which we live. My complaint is not about Enlightenment views *per se*: People are welcome to hold them. My lament is lack of awareness, openness, and respect for other views.

Boston University sociologist Peter Berger once remarked, referring to people of the Indian subcontinent rather than to Native Americans, that "America is a nation of Indians ruled by Swedes," a nation of fervent, multi-hued faiths overlooked by self-styled, cool rationalists.

It is with such "Swedes," meaning secular opinion-formers, that I am now concerned.

MYOPIC MEDIA

> *It is "crystal clear that advocates of religious human rights must be prepared to encounter in the secular news media less outright hostility or opposition than blank incomprehension."*[6]

There are many reasons why stories about the persecution of Christians are not often found in our major media. What David Stravers wrote so accurately about American Christians can be applied to Americans generally—they "for the most part are not interested in anything that happens outside the boundaries of the United States. . . ." Coupled with this is the fact that many of the atrocities we have described occur in remote areas and, hence, are expensive to report. Editors do not like expensive stories and tend to avoid them, especially if they have no sympathy for the subject. But beyond these particular reasons is a pervasive cultural mindset that is either ignorant of, skeptical of, or occasionally antithetical to religion—especially Christianity. I noted some of these attitudes in Chapter One. One result is that religious persecution is ignored or glossed over.

Numerous surveys show that reporters, columnists, and editors are, by and large, more secular than the majority of the U.S. population. About 60 percent of Americans can be found in a place of worship at least once a month, and the percentage is higher among African-Americans, and probably among Asian-Americans. The corresponding number for people in the media is usually given as about 10 percent. Some of this is related to the attitudes which make a good journalist: skepticism and a willingness to question and challenge authorities, which may be less prevalent among many believers. Many religious believers also self-select out of media careers.

But people with religious faith can also be marginalized. Robert Lichter, codirector of the Center for Media and Public Affairs, testified before the U.S. Commission on Civil Rights that he would advise evangelical

Christians looking for a career in the media to remove hints of their faith from their résumés. "I would say leave it off, just as twenty years ago, if you were a member of a gay rights organization, I would have said leave it off."

Whatever the case, the result is that religion is usually not dealt with seriously in major news coverage.

> We "occasionally field inquiries from junior staff members of newspapers or, more likely, TV shows that reveal a level of illiteracy about Catholicism and about religion that would make the devil weep."[7]

This has major effects even on general news coverage. In the 1994 elections there were complaints that the "religious right" had been running "stealth candidates"—essentially operating hidden campaigns that lulled their opponents into false security until the closing days of the election. The situation was that many of these campaigns were aimed at churchgoers, and leafleting took place outside churches. Since more people go to church than go to work in America, this is obviously a reasonable strategy. Churches are, in this sense, the most public and popular places in the United States.

The media complaint was in reality caused by the fact that, presumably, most political reporters either don't go to church or didn't bother to check with those that do. Thus the media refused to go where most Americans are gathered, then perversely claimed that events were being "hidden" from them. This is akin to someone who doesn't own a television complaining that events broadcast on TV are taking place in secret.

Being assigned to the religion desk, if there is one, of a major newspaper is often considered punishment duty, and maybe a hint that you should get your résumé in order. Of the big three TV networks, only ABC has an explicitly assigned religion reporter, Peggy Wehmeyer. Religion is notably absent in TV entertainment and news. Only about fifty out of sixteen hundred U.S. dailies have even one full-time religion reporter.

More Americans go to church on any given Sunday than attend major league sports events in an entire year.[8] Yet newspapers usually have entire pullout daily sports sections but only provide a few religion columns or occasionally, religion pages once a week. Obviously, the situation is different. Sports are easier to cover than religion, and many people who didn't see a game want to know what happened; whereas, not too many people who missed a sermon want a play-by-play summary. But there is no denying that an entire segment of human life is simply passed over.

As Sir Walter Moberly has pointed out,

> If in your organization, your curriculum, and your customs and way of life, you leave God out, you teach with tremendous force that, for most people and at most times, He does not count. . . . It is a fallacy to suppose that by omitting a subject you teach nothing about it. On the contrary, you teach that it is to be omitted. . . . And you teach this not openly and explicitly, which would invite criticism, you simply take it for granted and thereby insinuate it silently, insidiously, and all but irresistibly. . . .[9]

One of my own complaints is the fact that most political chat shows out of Washington are aired on Sunday morning. They seem to be provided according to time slot for those for whom Sunday worship is the *New York Times* Sunday edition in bed, followed by brunch. Of course, several of the shows can also be seen on Saturday night. Maybe the assumption here is that people who are in church Sunday morning aren't likely to be out on Saturday night. This is an incorrect, and perhaps prejudiced, assumption.

When religion is noticed, the result is frequently myopic. A skilled religion reporter, Peter Steinfels of the *New York Times*, notes that most religion stories have only a few basic themes. One can then fill in the blanks. His list of "Basic Religion Stories" is:

- Religious leader reveals feet of clay (or turns out to be scoundrel).
- Ancient faith struggles to adjust to modern times.
- Scholars challenge long-standing beliefs.
- Interfaith harmony overcomes enmity.

- New translation of sacred Scripture sounds funny.
- Devoted members of a zealous religious group turn out to be warm, ordinary folk.[10]

When the Pope hits town, religion does make it to the front pages but, even then, in a curiously truncated fashion. If the Pope talks about concern for the poor, there is speculation about whether this is a slam at the Republicans. If he talks about family breakdown, there is speculation about whether this is a slam at the Democrats. The fact that the Pope has raised exactly the same concerns in several dozens of countries seems to be ignored, as is most of what he actually says. Judging by most news coverage, the Pope has only one thing on his mind—Americans' sex lives. This is a case of media Freudian projection if there ever was one.

These points concern domestic coverage, but the underlying attitudes cannot help but affect the coverage, or lack of it, of human-rights violations elsewhere. When we turn overseas, several other factors come into play. One is concepts and words that seem designed to hide, or disguise, what is really going on.[11]

Even the *Economist*, which can be penetrating in its coverage, seems to suffer from a type of conceptual schizophrenia. Its special reports can give informed commentary on religious developments, but this rarely penetrates the news pages, which usually portray life as a process of acquiring commodities more or less hindered by government action or inaction.

For example, its recent review of works analyzing Russia, by Russians, notes the pervasive influence of Orthodoxy on the culture. It outlines Communist leader Gennady Zyuganov's claim that there is a political and religious battle between Russia and the West dating from the schism between Rome and Byzantium in 1054, and describes his hopes for the restoration of a "third Rome" on a Byzantine model. But the same issue (June 15, 1996) contains an article on a "Russian Exceptionalism," asking, "Is Russia Different?" This article resolutely ignores religion. Despite ruminations on Russian geography and the Russian soul, the word "Orthodoxy" does not even appear.

Religious activists, such as Islamic or Hindu militants, are always described as "right-wing," whatever that might mean. Maybe they are thought of as budding Ralph Reeds, or vice versa. But most such activists have very detailed plans for state control of the economic order of a kind usually thought of as the staple of "left-wing" views. And what is a "right-wing" or "left-wing" view of whether a Hindu temple should be put on the site of the Babri mosque?

When the vocabulary of left and right has run its tired course, we are left with that old standby term, *fundamentalist*—a word dredged up out of the American past and of dubious provenance and meaning even there. What it might mean for a Buddhist, Hindu, or Muslim is hard to understand. But understanding doesn't seem to be part of the goal.

Basically the term *fundamentalist*, as used in the media, is shorthand (or long-hand) for religious maniac or lunatic, someone to be categorized rather than heard, to be observed rather than comprehended, to be dismissed rather than read. If we want to find out what makes these people tick, we are not going to find it out through our news media. The result is ignorance. One consequence of ignorance is prejudice. One consequence of prejudice is renewed conflict.

ACADEMIC APOLOGISTS

The patterns in the media are paralleled by and, to some degree, stem from the situation in many academic circles. The example of Quentin Skinner was given in Chapter One. Other trends are less extreme but perhaps more influential, and therefore, more destructive. One pattern in contemporary legal and political philosophy is an attempt to exclude religious discourse from public life. Robert Audi suggests: "It is appropriate, however, that citizens apply a kind of separation of church and state in their public use of religious arguments, especially in advocating laws or public policies that restrict liberty."[12]

Audi adds, "Just as we separate church and state institutionally, we should in certain aspects of our thinking and public conduct, separate religion from law and public policy matters."[13] This is not merely a call to avoid legislating standards of belief, a call echoed on every page of this book. It is a call for believers to surrender their faith when they try to find their way through life's major issues.

Similar emphases come to the fore in the distinguished philosopher John Rawls' contention that political discussion should be confined to "public reason."[14] He also demanded that religious people not even *think* about public policy in terms of their beliefs. Rawls suggests: "To check whether we are following public reason, we might ask: How would our argument strike us presented in the form of a Supreme Court opinion?"[15] Here the Court has become the standard not only of law, but of what people may say, and therefore, believe. Similarly, noted liberal philosopher Richard Rorty remarks: "I take religious toleration to mean the willingness of religious groups to take part in discussions without dragging religion into it."[16]

More recently, Rawls and others have been embarrassed by the realization that their argument would exclude not only their apparent intended target, the "religious right," but also Martin Luther King and most of the civil rights movement—not to mention Gandhi, the Dalai Lama, and Desmond Tutu.

One consequence of this secular myopia is a tendency to regard devoted religious believers as weird, even mad. As Stephen Carter notes: "Our culture seems to take the position that believing deeply in the tenets of one's faith represents a kind of mystical irrationality."[17] Rawls earlier argued: "To subordinate all our aims to one end . . . still strikes us as irrational, or more likely as mad."[18]

There is cultural imperialism in Rawls' claims about "our" and "us." To paraphrase Tonto's reply when the Lone Ranger worried that "hostile Indians have surrounded us," "What do you mean 'us', Paleface?" He (Rawls, not Tonto) implies that it is "us Americans," but his view is a minority one. It is probably more the "us" of the Harvard Faculty Club.

Nor is it clear why Rawls tries to speak for America. Polls consistently show that more people in America believe that the Bible sheds light on politics than believe in views of Rawls' type. In fact, polls indicate that more people believe that Elvis is still alive than adhere to views of Rawls' type. He (Rawls, not Elvis) is welcome to persuade people that his views should be adopted, and he is brilliant at doing so. But when he tries to commend them by implicit claims that they *have* been adopted, he merely shows that he doesn't get out much.

In contrast, there are academics who study religion because they appreciate its role in public life. Those non-Muslims who study Islam tend to do so because they have been attracted to it in some way. This is understandable, since anybody who knows Muslims and Islam will find very much to admire and even to envy. However, this attraction can spill over into an apologetic stance toward the object of study, so that negative aspects are ignored or downplayed.

For example, a widely used introductory text, *Islam and the Muslim Community* by Frederick M. Denny, gives a glossary of important Islamic terms, but the terms *dhimma* and *dhimmi* are excluded.[19] Denny also maintains that, of Judaism, Christianity, and Islam, only Islam "has had a major impact on Asia to the point of becoming dominant in some regions."[20] Later, he remarks, "Christianity is not making headway in the Islamic world, but Islam is certainly prospering in countries that have a strong tradition of Christian dominance."[21]

These statements are inaccurate, as anybody who has traveled in Korea, China, or Indonesia can testify. Even one visit to Paul Yonggi Cho's five hundred thousand-member congregation in Seoul, Korea should be enough to disprove them.

They also give a misleading impression of the relation of Islam and other religions. After all, shouldn't any stress on the relative impunity of Islam to defections make at least a teensy mention that imprisonment and the death penalty face many people who might want to leave Islam? The same fate awaits anyone who talks with them about the possibility of doing so. As it is, the theme of religious persecution is absent from Denny's book.

John L. Esposito is one of the most widely respected interpreters of Islam in the West. His works, too, largely pass over the theme of persecution. While he does discuss *dhimmi* status, this is described only as "protected people" who pay "a special poll or head tax. . . ."[22] In his popular *Islam and Politics*, he says that the "revivalist mood and orientation of resurgent Islam has also raised concern about the status and rights of non-Muslims."[23] But these are then described as "tensions and clashes between Muslim and non-Muslim communities" such as "the Copts in Egypt, Ba'hai in Iran, Chinese in Malaysia, Christians in the Sudan and Pakistan." Are these really only "clashes between" such groups? In some cases, this is akin to describing Ku Klux Klan activities as "clashes between" black and white communities. Esposito does go on to describe discrimination against the Copts, Ba'hai, and Chinese, but maintains that most "Muslim states have granted equality of citizenship to all regardless of religious faith," and that the problem is a "traditional attitude toward non-Muslims that, though changed by modern legislation, has remained operative. . . ."[24]

He attributes the rejection by radical Islamic organizations of any role for non-Muslims in government as stemming from their belief that it is "contrary to Islam," but he adds, it is also "in the case of Christians, as recognition of their past ties with Christian, European colonial powers, and their continued association with the Christian West."[25] This would come as something of a surprise to Christians who have lived continuously in the area for two thousand years.[26]

These books are often illuminating treatments of Islam, and I have used them myself in preparing for this work. I would recommend them for much of what they cover. However, if these are used to introduce people to modern Islam, they will leave a distorted picture of contemporary realities.[27]

A better treatment is given in Timothy B. Sisk's *Islam and Democracy: Religion, Politics, and Power in the Middle East*.[28] This provides an invaluable update on many Middle East developments, but while it mentions some Muslim attacks on Christians in Egypt, it lacks any in-depth treatment of the question of religious freedom in Islam. The worsening situation of Christians and other minorities in this area receives no systematic attention.

Even Mark Juergensmeyer's excellent *The New Cold War? Religious Nationalism Confronts the Secular State* succumbs at times to misleading euphemism. He writes of the Copts in Egypt, "They tend to reside in urban areas, and they have prospered as businessmen and professionals. Their prosperity is a cause for some resentment from their Muslim neighbors, and the perception that they were favored during the Nasser regime has been the cause of some hard feelings as well. Nonetheless, the antiquity of their tradition brings them respect. . . ."[29] There is truth in these statements, but only part of the truth. What is not said may be far more vital.

In general, we can say that many academic treatments relevant to the subject matter of the worldwide persecution of Christians tend either to underplay or ignore it.

CULTURAL CONTRADICTIONS

Religious freedom is threatened not only by persecution but by trivialization. One of the most pernicious forms is treating religion merely as an aspect of "culture."

Fareed Zakaria, managing editor of *Foreign Affairs*, correctly notes "from business consultants to military strategists, people talk about culture as the deepest and most determinative aspect of human life." But such talk dangerously misstates the case. It treats religion as background, like ethnicity and language. People just "happen" to have a religion. So, if you have covered Arab "culture," then you have covered Muslims. Covering India covers Hinduism. Covering China covers Confucianism. However, as Princeton theologian Max Stackhouse points out, "All the great religions are already multi-cultural."

While they interact extensively, religion is not merely a product of culture: It is more often the origin and shaper of culture. It touches the deepest commitments about the nature of human life. Treating religion merely as culturally derived makes it seem secondary and subordinate. Certainly, to take two areas of Episcopal preponderance, Inuit (Eskimo) Episcopalians are different from Episcopalians in East Africa. But Iran is not simply the way it is because its culture shaped Islam, but because Islam shaped its culture. This is true for Orthodoxy in Greece, Hinduism in India, Confucianism in China.

This is not a trivial academic quibble: It has real consequences. In contemporary struggles over universal human rights, those countries, such as China, who are repressing religious freedom claim that such repression reflects Chinese "culture." The Mongolian State Intelligence Bureau describes Christianity as a "foreign religion" which new laws imply is "against Mongolian customs." In Armenia, those outside the Armenian Apostolic Church are increasingly being described as "foreign." In Bulgaria, the head of the Baptist Union says the Orthodox Church "believe evangelicals . . . are destroying their culture." In Mexico, mayors in the southern state of Chiapas justify the ongoing persecution of Protestants, claiming they "attack . . . our culture and traditions." Serbs view conversions to Catholicism as "surreptitious movements toward Croatization." Even Lutherans are regarded as "Croats."

Parallel problems exist in the West. Affirmative action is often justified as a means to increase "cultural diversity" on campuses and in workplaces. But religion, one of the key features of human diversity, is resolutely ignored. This resistance is doubly surprising since one of the stated goals of minority hiring is the expression of voices which would otherwise not be heard—the voices of women, African-Americans, Hispanic-Americans, and so forth.

This implies the dubious proposition that there is something which can be called a woman's voice or a black voice. But conservative Catholic women are not well-represented by secular feminists, and vice versa. Nor are African-American Pentecostals well-represented by secular liberals.

United States Civil Rights Commissioner Robert George noted that religion "doesn't seem to be treated as an issue in diversity, even among people who are in roles that give them responsibility for promoting diversity within their organizations."[30] Meanwhile, Christianity, in stunning disregard of history and geography, is treated as dead, white, male, and European. This slighting of religion in efforts to enhance "cultural" diversity is not only ignorant but perverse. It buries many of the real issues of human life. Religion shapes people's view of marriage, culture, and politics. It does most of what "culture" claims to do.

If religion is treated only as an aspect of culture, it will be marginalized. If religious freedom is subordinated to claims of cultural identity, it will be crippled.

ANTHROPOLOGICAL ANIMOSITIES

The negative opinions in the academy and the culture at large might be due simply to the fact that people have read too many misleading potboilers like James Michener's *Hawaii*. However, similar trends appear in some academic anthropologists' cavalier views of religious belief. In recent years, there have been verbal attacks by anthropologists on mission work.

In 1993, University of Michigan anthropologist Ann Stoler said missions promote a "culture of terrorism." In 1994, Donald Pollock claimed missions "extinguish Indian identity." Frank Proschan used accusations of neocolonialism and imperialism to try to expel missions from Asia.

Thankfully, there are signs that the issue is also being addressed more thoughtfully. In June 1994 the Canadian Anthropological Society devoted part of its program to a study of the effect of missions, and this was followed by December sessions at the American Anthropological Association on "Missionaries and Human Rights."

There are certainly examples enough of insensitivity, arrogance, and exploitation by missionaries which need to be exposed and condemned. But to regard these as typical of most mission work is simply to perpetuate worn-out Victorian myths and stereotypes. Mission historian Harold Fuller says they were "the human-rights activists of their day."

The British and other imperialists tried to restrict missionaries in areas such as Nigeria and India precisely because they made life harder for the colonial powers. The Spanish and Portuguese sought to do the same with the Jesuits in Paraguay, a tale well-told in the movie *The Mission*. Missionaries have been in the forefront of struggles against the slave trade and western imperialism. In Korea, they fiercely resisted Japanese imperialism, one reason why the Republic of Korea is on its way to becoming one the world's most professedly Christian countries.

Thomas Headland maintains that if a "missionary family is living in a tribal village, including fundamentalist missionaries with no formal training in anthropology, we generally will not find slave-raiding, wife-beating, gang-raping of girls, and so forth. I dare say that if missionaries had been allowed to live in the Yanomami area of the Amazon Basin when miners raided in the summer of 1993, that massacre would not have occurred."[31]

As Mark Juergensmeyer notes, especially of evangelical missionaries: "The commitment of colonial administrators to a secular-nationalist vision explains why they were often so hostile to the Christian missionaries who tagged along behind them: The missionaries were the liberal colonizers' competitors. The church's old religious ideology was a threat to the new secular ideology that most colonial rulers wished to present as characteristic of the West."[32]

John Barker of the University of British Columbia points out that, while Papua New Guinea is often singled out as a hotbed of missionary problems, the vast majority of the people happily consider themselves Christian. The indigenous churches are large national organizations capable of effective stands against destructive mining and logging, as well as alcoholism and family violence.

Yale anthropologist Lamin Sanneh, a Gambian national, shows that Christian missions protected indigenous cultures by translating the Bible, often creating written languages in order to do so—the same process by which the Russian "Cyrillic" alphabet and German and English were created. Indigenous writing reinforces resistance to governmental and economic forces. The United Nations Educational, Scientific, and Cultural Organization has given grants to mission minority-language literacy programs for precisely this reason.[33]

The charge of western imperialism usually betrays ignorance of history. To repeat: Christianity has been in Africa and Asia for two thousand years. It was in Africa before Europe, India before England, China before the United States. Africa is probably over 50 percent Christian. Three-fourths of active Christians are in the Third World. Much critique doesn't seem to flow from any real study of the issue. Rather, it seems to stem from Victorian stereotypes and a secular bias that, by definition, rejects as inherently imperialist any attempts to convince someone of religious truth.

Critics of those who want to share their faith should ask themselves how they respond when democracy activists, many of whom are Christians, are imprisoned by repressive governments on the grounds that their view of democracy is a "foreign cultural influence"—a notion propagated by the governments of China, Singapore, Burma, and Syria, among others. What if secular academics are repressed as violating cultural traditions, as in Egypt? What if environmentalists are accused of importing western guilt, as in Malaysia? What if feminists are attacked because their views are contrary to the dominant religion, as in Bangladesh? Our response to restrictions on religious believers should be no different.

Any attempt to freeze religion in place is not only nonsense, it is in itself a type of cultural imperialism. Behind at least some of this antipathy, there seems to be a functional view of religion wherein belief is treated either as an unquestionable inheritance, a secondary expression of culture, or a sublimation of power relations. What rarely enters this mindset is that believers are talking about things important in themselves, that may or may not be worth knowing. This paternalist attitude, while pretending to protect traditional religions, in fact trivializes all religion. Some western secular anthropologists may not care what religious beliefs people adopt. Usually, missionaries and the people they live and work among do. And they want to exercise their human rights to do so.

Those anthropologists who want to are welcome responsibly to propagate their European view that religion is merely a reflection of culture, or a means of social adaptation, or a projection of power relations. But if they demand that political authorities enforce policies based on these views in order to repress others, then they attack freedom of speech as well as freedom of religion. They will also undercut some of the major defenders of the rights of indigenous peoples.

PAROCHIAL POLITICS

> *Only a great fool would call the new political science diabolic: It has no attributes peculiar to fallen angels. It is not even Machiavellian, for Machiavelli's teaching was graceful, subtle, and colorful. Nor is it Neronian. Nevertheless, one may say of it that it fiddles while Rome burns. It is excused by two facts: It does not know that it fiddles, and it does not know that Rome burns.*[34]

Downplaying religion has major effects on our understanding of international politics and foreign policy. Strategic theorist Edward Luttwak remarks that recent intellectual currents "prohibited any sustained intellectual interest in religion itself. . . . As for religious motivations in secular affairs, they were disregarded or dismissed as mere pretense, and because this could not be done in the case of the entire history of Byzantium, the quandary was resolved by simply abandoning its study."[35]

Some decades ago during my own doctoral studies in political science, in reviewing comparative politics and trying to make some systematic sense of foreign countries, I learned that these countries were all busily "modernizing," "rationalizing," and above all, "secularizing." In foreign affairs, they seemed to spend their lives either lining up with the West or with its opponents. This seemed a far cry from some of what I was reading in many newspapers. But professional political analysts replied with some pride that one should look beyond, or perhaps beneath, the ephemera contained in the media.

It is true that we need to move beyond day-to-day events to grasp underlying factors, trends, currents, and structures. However, this only made the problem doubly puzzling. These trends and currents didn't come to very much fruition, even in the long run. At times, I entertained the suspicion that we were not looking beneath the surface, but beyond the world itself. Religion was a topic that almost never arose, except in relation to past and passing superstitions.

Political history, and indeed political theory, suffer, *mutatis mutandis*, from the same problems. Histories of western political thought often take flying leaps from the history of Greece and Rome to the Renaissance, coming down only for Augustine and Thomas Aquinas, who are treated as honorary Greek political theorists. The influence of specifically Christian, Jewish, and Islamic elements in western thought and in western politics is usually passed over. Meanwhile, in contemporary liberal political thought, religion is either ignored, or else introduced merely to make the point that it *should be* ignored.

This divorce of religion from intelligent and polite company remains, even among foreign policy and intelligence professionals, who one might have thought by now would have been mugged by religious realities.

> *"Policymakers, diplomats, journalists, and scholars who are ready to over-interpret economic causality, who are apt to dissect social differentiations more finely, and who will minutely categorize political affiliations, are still in the habit of disregarding the role of religion, religious institutions, and religious motivations in explaining politics and conflict, and even in reporting their concrete modalities. Equally, the role of religious leaders, religious institutions, and religiously motivated lay figures in conflict resolution has also been disregarded—or treated as a marginal phenomenon hardly worth noting.*
>
> *This does not necessarily have anything "to do with personal attitudes toward religion" but with "a learned repugnance to contend intellectually with all that is religion or belongs to it—a complex inhibition compounded out of the peculiar embarrassment that many feel when faced by explicit manifestations of serious religious sentiment."*[36]

This secular embarrassment can have painful consequences. When the CIA was trying to get a handle on events in Iran shortly before the Ayatollah Khomeini took power, there was one recorded proposal to analyze "the attitude and activities of the more prominent religious leaders." "This attempt was vetoed on the ground that it would amount to mere 'sociology,' a term used in intelligence circles to mean the time-wasting study of factors deemed politically irrelevant."[37]

This was not a novel blindness. In Vietnam, "every demographic, economic, ethnic, social, and, of course, military aspect of the conflict was subject to detailed scrutiny, but the deep religious cleavages that afflicted South Vietnam were hardly noticed." The "tensions between the dominant Catholic minority, a resentful Buddhist majority, and several restless syncretic sects were largely ignored until Buddhist monks finally had to resort to flaming self-immolations in public squares, precisely to attract the attention of Americans so greatly attentive to everything else in Vietnam that was impeccably secular."[38]

This pattern continues. In recent U.S. negotiations with Vietnam about diplomatic recognition, the issue of religious persecution was never raised. When recognition was achieved, Vietnam embarked on an intensified campaign of persecution against its religious minorities. Similar, though less striking, tales can be told of Bosnia, Lebanon, the Philippines, Nicaragua, India, Israel and the Palestinians, Sudan, and Indonesia.[39]

Much world conflict is tied to religious history. Chronic armed confrontation in the world is currently concentrated on the margins of the traditional religions, especially the boundaries of the Islamic world. The Middle East, the southern Sahara, the Balkans, the Caucasus, Central Asia, and the Indian subcontinent are zones of perennial conflict. They are also where the boundaries of Islam, Christianity, Judaism, and Hinduism intersect.

These are not necessarily wars about religion in the sense that one side represses and kills the other simply because they have different religious views. The immediate causes are as myriad as the forms of human evil. Many are wars over dynasties, colonialism, or territorial boundaries. Others coincide with geographical, tribal, and language divides. Others are precipitated when mineral wealth is discovered.

My point here is not about religious war and persecution per se. The question at this juncture is not so much *why* people fight, but *where* they fight. Since religion shapes culture and civilization, people on either side of these boundaries have different histories and different views of the nature and purpose of human life. Hence, they are more likely to differ from and to oppose one another. Regardless of the particular reason for conflict, these are the areas where conflict occurs. They are the religious fault zones, the places where political earthquakes erupt.[40]

Religion also shapes forms of government. In Eastern Europe, authoritarian governments find it easier to hold on in areas where the Orthodox churches, with their long history of association with the state, have held sway.[41] The new boundaries of Eastern and Western Europe are tending to fall along the old divide between Orthodox and Catholic/Protestant.[42]

In East Asia, the current economic dynamo of the world, economic growth is strongest in areas rooted in a Confucian ethic. They combine this with authoritarian government, and the jury is still out on whether they can continue to do so. But it is becoming increasingly difficult to understand the roots of development without taking religious factors into account.[43]

The role of religion affects conflict, persecution, political order, and economic development. It is germane to almost every human-rights question. Despite western secular predictions and hopes germinated in the sixties and seventies, there is no sign that this influence is diminishing. The trends point in the other direction.

HIDEBOUND HUMAN RIGHTS

> Freedom of religion is indeed the oldest of the international recognized human freedoms. . . .
>
> —John P. Humphrey, the principal writer of the Universal Declaration of Human Rights[44]

The first effective national Bill of Rights in the world—the American—starts its First Amendment with guarantees of religious freedom. Even before freedom of speech, freedom of the press, the right to assemble, or the right to trial, the Bill of Rights establishes the free exercise of religion. It is tragic and even dangerous that in practice, if not intent, some of its putative heirs ignore this. Any failure to take religion with the utmost seriousness not only endangers explicit religious freedom but endangers human rights of any kind.

The Contents of the 1994 *Harvard Law School Guide to Human Rights Research* lists rights to housing and food, the rights of refugees, children's rights, women's rights, rights pertaining to sexual orientation, labor rights, development rights, human rights, and the environment. . . . but nothing at all on religion. Its lists of categories, bibliographies, newsletters, information services, and activist organizations ignore the myriad religious bodies involved in this work.[45]

Consequently, anyone who looks to the *Guide* for guidance will get a highly informed and professional outline of a truncated view of the world. Whole areas of human life are excluded. Harvard usually prides itself on setting trends. In this case a western, secular myopia leads it askew.[46] This trivializes the plight of hundreds of millions of believers around the world who suffer for their faith. The single largest factor in persecution in the world today is religious belief. Most of this falls on Christians, but Muslims experience some of the most violent repression, often at the hands of

Muslims with a different view. Smaller groups such as Ba'hai and Jews have lived in fear for much of this century.

A closed, secular mindset also distorts our grasp of other rights. For most human beings, religion is the core of existence. For good and ill, it sustains their lives, shapes their ethics, animates their dreams, provides their hopes, and comforts their sufferings. Throughout the world, religion is interwoven with human life and human rights.

SIDESTEPPING SLAVERY

Jesse Jackson "is busy with affirmative action. . . . Right now slavery is not on his agenda."

Some of the major civil-rights organizations are also weak in their treatment of this issue. This has come to the fore in a striking way in the matter of slavery. Slavery is not, of course, the same as the persecution of Christians. In Mauritania, for example, those who are enslaved are nearly all Muslims. However, in the case of Sudan, slavery is intimately tied to the treatment of Christians, and so the two concerns overlap.

One might expect that, given the history of slavery in the United States, the present enslavement of black Africans would be a matter of some concern and attention, especially among civil-rights groups. One might expect so. But in most cases, one would be wrong.

In early 1995, Samuel Cotton raised this issue in a series of articles in the *City Sun*, a New York City newspaper with a largely African-American readership. This was followed up by the *Daily Challenge*. However, they have had little effect. Charles Jacobs, the director of the Boston-based American Anti-Slavery Group, says, "Every schoolchild in America knows that women have been raped in Bosnia. . . . Everyone knows the whales have to be saved. But no one seems to realize you can buy a black woman as a slave for as little as fifteen dollars in Khartoum."[47]

Jacobs reports that almost everywhere he has turned in the last three-and-a-half years—"The eminent human-rights agencies, the women's groups, the church councils, the civil rights coalitions—they have encountered the same response: Yes, we know about the slaves. No, we're not prepared to fight for their freedom."[48] Augustine A. Lado, president of the human-rights group Pax Sudani Network says the "Congressional Black Caucus, Trans-Africa, the Rainbow Coalition, the Nation of Islam, and the NAACP [have] forsaken us. . . ."[49]

The Nation of Islam has denounced anti-slavery efforts and, in turn, has spoken in defense of Sudan, one of Louis Farrakhan's stops on his grand tour of terrorist governments. Farrakhan's international representative, Akbar Muhammad, fresh from the Islamic Conference in Khartoum, thought it worthwhile to add to his justification for dismissing this issue the fact that the American Anti-Slavery Group's research director, Charles Jacobs, is "a Jew. . . ."[50]

Maybe one might expect little else from Farrakhan who, according to reports, has received money from some of the governments he has extolled. However, while certainly not criticizing anti-slavery efforts, the NAACP has done little on the issue itself. In 1993, Representative Frank Wolf sent Benjamin Chavis, now a Farrakhan associate, then executive director of the NAACP, two letters about slavery in the Sudan and asked whether the "NAACP is willing to step forward." There was no response. The NAACP passed a resolution in May 1995, condemning Sudan and Mauritania, but anti-slavery has not become a major issue for the organization.[51]

Jacobs himself says, "For two years we tried to get Reverend [Jesse] Jackson on the record against slavery. . . ." He "returned our document packages unopened. A staff person told us that Jackson wouldn't touch the issue because it seemed anti-Arab." In explaining why Jackson wouldn't even give Samuel Cotton an anti-slavery statement, an aide explained that the Reverend "is busy with affirmative action. . . . Right now slavery is not on his agenda."[52]

HUMAN-RIGHTS ORGANIZATIONS

The movement for "freedom of belief" precedes every other in the history of the struggle for human rights and fundamental freedoms.[53]

Similar criticisms cannot be made of the mainstream international human-rights organizations. Most of these are already overstretched, and there are more than enough other human-rights violations in the world to fill their time. Furthermore, as will be apparent from my notes, these organizations do vastly more than most in this world to call attention to religious persecution. However, there are problems in several of their treatments.

First, by and large, these international organizations do not deal much with questions related to freedom of worship and to religious speech. But this is an area as important as freedom of the press or freedom of political opposition. Freedom of worship is something for which people are willing to give their lives. The fact that this seems strange to many in the West should not cause us to underestimate its importance as a human-rights issue.

Another tendency is to restrict questions of freedom of religion only to freedom of worship. But religion is a matter of the pattern of one's life, of the freedom to live out one's beliefs each day. Freedom House, for example, has in its past surveys remarked on relative freedom of worship around the world but has usually not gone much beyond that.

A third problem is passing over the religious identity of the people who are suffering. In surveys of abuse, there is often a particular focus on what happens to human-rights activists, to political-opposition figures, to academics, to trade unionists, to journalists, to women, and to intellectuals. But there is usually no specific attention to matters of faith.

For example, while Amnesty International has produced some excellent reports on Sudan, it gives little attention to the overtly religious dimensions of the repression. At one point its *Sudan: The Tears of Orphans* says, "Bigots on all sides, Muslims and Christians alike, have exploited religion, making it a significant factor in the continued fighting." This statement is literally true, but it gives a distorted picture of a conflict involving Christian resistance to a fervently Islamicizing government. As in the *Baltimore Sun* articles, the specifically religious dimensions are treated as an overlay on what is "really" an ethnic or territorial conflict.[54] However, in a conflict which has, by one side, been pronounced a *jihad*, which involves widespread forced conversion to Islam, sometimes on penalty of death, and in which government troops machine-gun altars and tear the figure of Jesus off crucifixes, religion is no mere veneer.[55]

This pattern continues even in surveys of religion itself. When Morton A. Winston, chair of the board of directors of Amnesty International U.S.A., testified before House hearings on "Religious Intolerance," his introduction to Sudan mentioned "widespread human-rights violations based on religious affiliation," but thereafter, the religious dimensions recede. The word *Christian* appears only once, in noting that the South includes Christians and followers of "traditional African religions."

The issue of forced conversion and the execution of those who leave Islam is ignored. The imposition of Shari'a law is described as an attempt to "arabize" the country, something which would come as a shock to the 75 percent of Muslims throughout the world who are not Arabs. It is hard to escape the impression that Winston has taken a basic Amnesty overview of Sudan, added on some religious reference, and introduced it as "religious intolerance."

Similar patterns occur elsewhere in the testimony. Attacks on Christians in Nigeria are ascribed to "religious tensions between the Northern Muslim-dominated part of the country and members of the Christian minority in the North. . . ." This seems to have things backward. The attacks have usually led to the tensions, not vice versa.

The testimony also says that "Christians are not singled out from other minority religions for persecution" in the "Asia-Pacific" region. If this means only that some governments persecute all religions and that, in the region as a whole, one can find persecuted people of many religions, it is true. But as a description of particular countries or regions, it is ambiguous or wrong. Some countries like Vietnam "single out" Christians and Buddhists—or like Burma, Christians and Moslems—or, like Bhutan, Christians and Hindus. In Nepal and the Southern Philippines, Christians have particularly been "singled out," and in India they are the only religious group that cannot even have untouchable status. Laos seems to single out Christians and not Buddhists. Mongolia is similar. The key point is that, throughout the region, Christians are particular, though not the only, objects of persecution. The Amnesty testimony obscures this point.

There are other problems, such as passing over the situation of Christians in Egypt and Turkey, and Protestants in Mexico. But we need not belabor the matter, except to say that Amnesty is comparatively weak in its treatment of religious persecution in general and Christian persecution in particular.[56]

In many cases, the difference is not about the specific *people* who are suffering. After all, many Christians are also human-rights activists, journalists, trade-union figures, opposition leaders, academics, intellectuals, and members of ethnic groups, not to mention being women and children. Human Rights Watch, Amnesty International, and Freedom House call attention to many of these same people but often without identifying the religious element.

For example, in the case of Amnesty, such people are usually treated under the category of "prisoners of conscience." This is the category around which Amnesty has built its work, and it is a good one: It embraces people who suffer for the peaceful expression of their beliefs. However, Amnesty is often willing to identify people as "ethnic," "political leaders," "intellectuals," or "secular intellectuals." Religious categories, such as "Christian," are much less frequent in their reports. One result is that, though instances of the persecution of Christians and other religious figures may be covered, we lose a recognition of the extent of religious persecution that exists in the world.

In other cases, there seems simply to be less interest in religious matters. Human Rights Watch has "Special Initiatives" to deal with prisons, business and human rights, drugs and human rights, lesbian and gay rights, and standard setting. Religion does not appear as a focus of special attention.

Perhaps if I had been working instead on trade-union rights or children's rights, I might feel equally that these were under-represented in general human-rights books. Nevertheless, I do think that there are avoidable gaps in their coverage of religion.

These gaps are sometimes reflected not so much in the more specialized reports, several of which I have used throughout this book, but in the yearly overviews produced by human-rights organizations. Clearly, any attempt by any organization to summarize a world's and a year's worth of persecution and death within the covers of one volume is always going to miss some things. I have learned a little about these constraints. Some prisoners, some deaths, and even some countries such as Laos and Peru, find their way only into a note—and some not even that. It may be because good confirmation cannot be gained, or the event seems less important than other things which are included. How can one say that someone's death is not important? And yet, by implication, I have already done that.

Even after sensing a little of what it must be like to summarize a far larger amount of information on human-rights violations of all kinds, some things about these reports need comment. *Amnesty International Report 1995* devotes attention to the persecution of Christians in some of the more prominent instances we have covered, such as Vietnam, China, and Egypt. However, for Burma, there is a focus only on "ethnic" conflict. For Algeria, only human-rights activists, lawyers, journalists, academics, political activists, and so forth, are mentioned as targets of radical Islamic groups. The targeting of Christians is passed over. This is also true of places such as Cuba or Morocco.[57]

At times Amnesty uses its limited space in strange ways. For example, its 1995 report devotes about as much space to the Netherlands as it does to Oman, Mauritania, or Malaysia, and more than it does to Kazakhstan, Mongolia, or Qatar. This is doubly surprising in that the coverage of the Netherlands largely concerns an incident in the Netherlands Antilles where a police officer punched a bus driver in a dispute over a parking offense.

Clearly, the amount of attention which can be given to places like Mauritania and Kazakhstan reflects the limits imposed by their governments on what can be investigated there. Amnesty also needs to avoid charges of political bias, and so spreads its reports and its criticisms widely. The result is that small events can be highlighted, thus squeezing out the space and attention devoted to more brutal offenders.

Human Rights Watch's general surveys can have similar problems. Its 1996 report does not deal with religion in discussions of Ethiopia, Liberia, Nigeria, Mexico, or Turkey. In its introductory overview of human-rights violations in the Middle East, the word *Christian* does not appear.[58]

The U.S. State Department's Annual Survey of Human Rights, except for its (decreasing) tendency to adjust some of its findings to the priorities of U.S. foreign policy, often gives a better summary of events. However, here too are problems. Nina Shea summarizes them well:

> Two general problems arise in the State Department's coverage of religion: First, the Country Reports in some cases do not adequately distinguish among the various Christian denominations in a particular country, but instead generalize the experience of the dominant religious group that usually has the most freedom.
>
> Second, the Country Reports in some important instances also fail to address the role of society in persecuting religious minorities, concentrating instead on active government involvement in religious intolerance while ignoring the government's own passive role in the face of societal terror, which can be quite extreme. It is worth noting that in the section on "women" in the Country Reports, societal violence is often the main focus of the reporting.
>
> Both of these shortcomings in the reporting lead to serious distortions in the profiling of countries in the area of religious freedom. . . .
>
> Ethiopia is a prime example of a Country Report that ignores the plight of a minority religion—in this case, evangelical Protestants. The Country Report makes no mention at all of the evangelicals or any other Christian group, limiting its religious discussion to a riot within a mosque that was the result of an inter-Muslim dispute.
>
> The discussion on religion in the Sudan Country Report misses the big picture by failing to address the reasons for the devastating war that has already left 1.5 million dead. The war is being fought over Khartoum's policy of Islamicization. What is taking place in Sudan today is essentially a war against non-Muslims and Muslim minorities. By neglecting to take this into account, the Country Report's Religion Section under Sudan only gives sketchy details of the bloody onslaught faced by Christians and other non-Muslims, focusing primarily on the more trivial incidents of harassment, discrimination, and arrest. It neglects to acknowledge the element of religious persecution in the discussion of slavery, mayhem, and other atrocities.

> . . . By late 1995, Chinese Christian leaders from the banned house-church movement were stating that they were experiencing the worst persecution since the pre-Deng period in the late 1970s and four Roman Catholic bishops had been detained. An arrest warrant with the names of three thousand evangelicals was circulating and more Christians were in jail or under house arrest than any other country in the world. By failing to note this trend, the Country Report allows for only a dim understanding of the extent of religious persecution in China today.

Meanwhile, James Sasser, the U.S. ambassador to China, reports that his "soft approach" in the area of human rights "has worked."[59]

With State Department reports, as Nina Shea's testimony verifies, there are also important, direct, practical effects:

> Immigration judges around the country have relied on these Country Reports to deny political asylum to a Sudanese Christian activist whose employer was executed for religious reasons; a Pakistani Christian who was acquitted of blasphemy but feared mob retribution; over twenty Iranian Christian clergy who fled last year after four of their colleagues were gunned down by Islamic extremists; numerous Chinese Christian women fleeing coercive abortions and sterilizations; and one of the most prominent evangelical preachers from Ethiopia, who came to the U.S. after managing to escape imprisonment and torture by fanatical Muslims in his homeland. It is extremely important that these Country Reports give accurate accounts of religious persecution.[60]

Freedom House has usually been consistent in reporting the status of religious groups and religious freedom, but, in its specific focus on the structures of government, its references in the past have been all too brief, usually commenting only on constitutional guarantees of freedom of worship. However, its 1995 incorporation of the Puebla Program on Religious Freedom shows signs that its coverage is quickly improving. Even here, the program urgently needs additional staffing and funding.

Religious human rights deserve more than to remain a neglected chapter in the universal endeavors to ensure observance of and respect for human rights.[61]

EARS THAT CANNOT HEAR

Several of my remarks have dealt with understandings of religion in North America. My concern is not with intra-American disputes *per se*, but with how a secular myopia ignores the role of religion in the world at large. It produces astonishment at events which are entirely predictable, insofar as anything in human life is predictable, and surrenders the intellectual equipment necessary to deal with the actual patterns of the world.

But, beyond this, it ignores the suffering and death of countless women and men of all races and cultures because its eyes do not see, and its ears do not hear. Consequently, the largest pattern of persecution in the world is allowed to pass in a "deafening silence."

There is a widely shared intuition that says ". . . religion is like building model airplanes, just another hobby: something quiet, something private, something trivial. . . ."[62]

CHAPTER NINE

Forging a Way Ahead

During last week's Passover Seder, our family read the Haggadah portion charging us to think of ourselves as the slaves our forebears had been during Pharoah's time. Given our blessed lives as Americans, it would not have been easy to fulfill the Seder admonition had I not known of the courage and faith practiced daily by tens if not hundred of millions of believers in countries such as China, Saudi Arabia, Cuba, Iran, Sudan, indeed and still, even the land of Egypt. Thinking of my friend Getaneh M. Getaneh—now subject to a recent Immigration Service deportation order despite having been suspended by his feet for hours while guards punished his ministry activities by pouring hot oil on the soles of his feet and lashing them with steel cables—it was not hard for me at the Seder to renew my pledge not to suffer any such further martyrdom silently.[1]

WHY THIS ISSUE?

After having described human suffering, it seems superfluous, even cynical, to suggest some reasons why we should try to do something about it. If we don't already understand that human suffering is *in and of itself* a call to human action, there is usually no means of persuasion, for such matters do not live at the level of arguments. Nevertheless, perhaps there are some additional things that should be addressed.

One is, why focus on *Christian* persecution? This is a good question. There are many people of all religions, races, and cultures who suffer throughout the world in the myriad wars, oppressions, and tyrannies that human evil can devise. There are millions of women and men of all religions, races, and cultures who also suffer persecution. If we are concerned about human rights, we need to be concerned about the rights of *all*, wherever and whoever they are. Christian teaching itself emphasizes that all human beings are made in the image of God.

Concern for some human-rights issues does not mean becoming less concerned with others. When we learn something about what goes on in the world, we also quickly learn—and want to learn—about what happens to others. Human-rights issues are not usually closed tunnels but opening paths.

One of the few reports on the persecution of the three million Muslim Beja people in Eastern Sudan has come from Christian Solidarity International, who learned of them through their other work in Sudan. A call to take up the issue of the persecution of Christians is not a call to ignore Amnesty International or Human Rights Watch, or to give up on a wide range of other human rights. But it is a call to take up something much neglected.

The suffering of Christians demands a particular and concrete focus. First, while it is right that we should act on behalf of Muslims in Bosnia, it is not right that school children know about this alone and not about massacres in the Sudan, in Nigeria, in India, in China, in Mexico. At the least, we need to begin to bring our attention to the persecution of Christians up to the level of our attention to the persecution of others.

Second, the regimes which persecute Christians are also the regimes which are the world's most regressive and repressive. This association is not accidental. For, while most Christians throughout the world have no desire to be thought of as westerners, they are, by and large, agents for positive change in their own countries. Newer Christians, especially, find in their faith a discipline and a commitment that enables them to contribute to economic renewal—in their families, in their villages, and in their countries at large.[2]

As we noted in Chapter One, Christians embody the confession that there is another Authority beside and beyond Caesar. This, in and of itself, challenges the claims of authoritarian political power. As Peter Berger has noted, totalitarians lust for "a world without windows" in which no other light can shine in their closed and false universe. This is why religious freedom is a priority target for tyrants. It is also why religious freedom is the seedbed of democracy, as it was in the United States.

In the twentieth century, Christians have been among the major forces for the spread of democracy.[3] As we noted earlier, Samuel Huntington argues that changed attitudes toward freedom within the Roman Catholic Church since the Second Vatican Council have produced a "third wave of democracy" which has helped depose dictators in much of the world, including the Philippines, Eastern Europe, and Latin America.[4]

For Americans above all people, this must be a priority. Many of those coming to these shores did so in search of religious freedom, and the Bill of Rights enshrined this in its opening words. Turning away from religious persecution would be a betrayal of America's own founding.

Third, an attempt to deal with *everything* has the consequence of dealing with nothing. We need to work on *particular* matters, not because they are the only important issues in the world but because they have become, to use a theological term, our vocation. Many people are deeply immersed in other issues and deserve our support. But many more of us are not involved in much at all.

Fourth, if we don't do it, *who will?* Americans have contacts throughout the world and a greater ability than any other country to influence events around the globe. Especially the Christian churches have the possibility of contact with believers throughout the world. Many suffering Christians will not talk about their situation to anybody except other believers simply because they have learned, to their cost, that many others are not very interested, so that the best they can expect is that they will continue to be ignored. Sometimes the news that they have spoken to someone may reach the authorities or the terrorists, and their suffering will increase. For this reason, many of those who are enduring persecution will not even talk to other believers. But Christians have at least the greater possibility of fruitful contact. With ability comes responsibility. Here, Christians have some ability.

There is a fifth reason, particularly important for those who are not Christians. The United Sates has over the last decades experienced growing political activity by, especially, evangelical, charismatic, and fundamentalist Christians. Despite the fevered claims by some of their opponents, these movements are marked not by desire for any incipient theocracy, but by a defensive, and often bewildered, reaction to seeing their lives and their children's lives spiritually undercut by a thoughtless secularism. They are not ayatollahs from Iran, but housewives from Houston and businessmen from Boston.

One thing that often does mark them is ignorance or indifference to the world outside the U.S. and, consequently, little knowledge of and concern for international human rights. Since concern for some human rights usually leads to concern for others, mobilizing this constituency in defense of other Christians can lead to a major increase in support for other rights. If even a small proportion of the 15–30 percent of voters who claim to be some sort of evangelical take this matter seriously, the results could be profound. United States debates on Most Favored Nation Status for China or Vietnam will no longer be human-rights organizations and some committed members of Congress against the trading lobbies, but a vast lobby of (usually) conservatives committed to struggling against international human-rights violations. This is a difficult goal, but it is an achievable, realistic one.

Before turning our attention to what we need to do, it is worth cautioning about what we should *not* do.

SUPPORT, NOT "CRUSADES"

The dangers of doing the wrong thing can be greater than the dangers of doing nothing. This is no reason for passivity or paralysis, but it is a reason for clear thinking. Consider the following call to action on human rights:

> *Most overseas Christianity is being destroyed by non-Christians in crushing defeat and, like cattle, they are every day being murdered, and Christians are being exterminated.*

This has a certain contemporary ring. It is, in fact, quite an old sentiment. It is taken from a letter written in the 1070s by Pope Gregory VII to the German King Henry IV.[5] It was part of the Pope's campaign to summon a crusade. The facts behind the claim were quite true, since the Christian population under Islam in the Eastern Mediterranean—probably then a majority of the total population—was undergoing a wave of intense persecution. But, while the facts are true, the response was as destructive as the problem. Apart from immediate bloodshed, the resulting crusades helped to poison relations between Christians and Muslims and between Orthodox and Catholic Christians in ways that persist to this day. Many Christians in the Middle East who had no part in the Crusades, and also suffered under them, nevertheless bear the legacy of centuries of hatred and frequently have the epithet "crusader" spat in their faces.

While a crusade of this type is as unlikely as it is unwanted, we should beware of falling into the same mindset. It is no help to Christians overseas to think of them as western clones. It does them no favors in their own country, and can make their situation worse, since they may be falsely branded as agents of "imperialism."

Egyptian Christians are Egyptians. They fought against European attempts to take over their country. Malaysian Christians are Malaysians and, while they have problems with their government, most are usually as proud as other Malaysians about the country's economic progress. Christians in Eastern Europe are fearful of the cultural onslaught of things western. Our calling is to genuine solidarity with others, not to a cultural projection which assumes that they are just like us.

This also means that our actions have to be tied to the needs, desires, and wishes of those who are actually suffering persecution. Normally, we should not act except with the agreement of those for whom we are trying to act. This is not an iron rule since, as we saw with the history of the World

Council of Churches, the question of who speaks for suffering Christians can be a difficult one.

Even if we are dealing with people who genuinely represent their communities, there is still a need for discernment. To put the matter crudely, if a haggard man in prison, with an official by his side and two guards standing behind him, tells you that everything is fine and that you needn't do anything, it is wise to be skeptical. Nevertheless, unless we have good reasons to think otherwise, our presumption must be in favor of deferring to the expressed wishes of those who themselves are suffering.

THE DANGERS OF STEREOTYPES

Crusades may not only give "aid" to people who might not want such aid, they may also stereotype whole swathes of people. As we have seen, some churches and academics have shied away from the issue of the persecution of Christians because, they claim, it might lead to anti-Arab or anti-Islamic prejudice. The danger is real, though the proposed lack of action is irresponsible. One might equally well ignore any persecution in the world, since action against it could lead to stereotyping those who share some characteristics with the persecutors. Anti-Nazi activities probably do lead to some stereotyping of Germans. But it would be a poor excuse for stopping anti-Nazi activities.

The solution is quite simple in principle, though difficult in practice. It is to be precise and definite about *who* is doing the persecuting, and to make clear that this does not include whole races, cultures, or religions. The idea that all Arabs or all Muslims hate and attack Christians is obviously a cruel and false parody.

Earlier, we described the thousands of Algerian Muslims who closed their shops and workplaces and, at risk to themselves, went to the funeral of the murdered White Fathers. It is possible that more Muslims in that one town went to the funeral than comprise the entire GIA, the terrorist faction that carried out the murders.

Many Muslims are themselves persecuted. Bosnia, we hear about. Chechneya, we hear a little about. Yet the suffering of the Rohingya

Muslims in Western Burma and the Beja Muslims in Eastern Sudan rival the worst of the stories we have told here.

Throughout the world, there are people of different religions who live alongside each other happily, peacefully, and harmoniously and who defend one another from persecution, sometimes at their own cost. Mubarak El Mahdi, the grandson of the legendary Mahdi of Khartoum, has been struggling to end the persecution of Christians in Sudan. This is true not only for Muslims but for Hindus, Buddhists, and others. When they sought to call attention to their plight, Buddhists in Vietnam set fire to *themselves*, not to others.

I have not the slightest wish that the facts described here should be taken as a blanket condemnation of any religious group. The people who have contributed to this work come from many religious backgrounds. My inclusion of a chapter about Christian-on-Christian persecution should emphasize this point.

The complexities of the relations between Christians and Muslims can be shown in the testimony of Sultan Hassein Karabus, a representative of the Muslim community in the Nuba Mountains of central Sudan. It is worth quoting at length:

> *I am a chief of the Koalib tribe from Dellame District. The government has destroyed many villages and completely depopulated large swathes of land. The government of Sudan troops took livestock, burned crops, and looted all household property. Many churches and mosques have been burned down. The male captives were killed, while most of the women and children were sent to "peace camps."*
>
> *When they arrive, the captives are given a little sugar, rice, and clothing, but . . . suffering soon begins again. The people are separated in the camps by sex and by age so that the family structure is destroyed. Non-Muslims are forced to become Muslims. They have to take Muslim names, learn about ablutions, and how to recite Muslim prayers.*
>
> *Every morning the people have to assemble in the camps. The men are then taken in trucks to three big plantations near Dellame (Shaq El Kitir, Falastine, and Malabak) and one near Heiban (Kortala). The army sells*

these captives to the plantation owners. The plantations produce grain, sesame seed, and ground nuts.

The plantation slaves receive no money for their labor, only a minimum of food for their survival. Most of the women are sent to work on small plots near Dellame. Women are divided among the soldiers and forced to have sexual relations. One example was given of a woman, Nura Hamat, who said she was a Christian and refused to commit adultery and was shot (in 1993). Boys usually do small jobs in the town or are conscripted into the army.

The most recent offensive began when the government recaptured Dere on March 18, 1995. On the following day, they put the torch to Dere. The Church of Christ churches in Dere and in nearby Kuman were set alight. At the same time they also burned down the mosque in Kilbaba, a one-hour walk from Dere. All the people fled to the mountaintops when the army started to burn the crops. Those that the army caught were loaded onto trucks and taken away to the "peace camps."

My own village is Sabbath. It was destroyed in January 1992. At that time a convoy arrived. The soldiers killed nineteen men, took four thousand cows, and looted all the property before the village was set ablaze. Among those killed were Reverend Thomas Kodi of the Church of Christ, and two catechists, Tigani Koumi and Magadem Said. The captured women were taken to the town.

There are very good relationships between Christians and Muslims—to the extent of intermarriage of Muslim men with Christian women and vice versa.[6]

It is not only Muslims, Hindus, or Buddhists that can be invidiously stereotyped. The practice of stereotyping Christians is also rampant, not only in lands abroad, but in North America.

Ed Knippers, an accomplished visual artist, describes how, when he appeared to testify in favor of continued funding for the National Endowment for the Arts and it was noted that he was a "Christian" artist, many in the audience responded with boos and hisses.

More recently, he had some of his paintings torn up by a fundamentalist Christian who thought them blasphemous and pornographic. Reflecting on these, he said, "Of the two, personally I prefer the fundamentalist. He at least desires to defend what he believes is true. The NEA crowd trumpet their openness, and then act with the worst of prejudices."[7]

There are other types of prejudice, some of them close to home.

In 1992, I met Romulo Saune, a Quechua native from the central mountains of Peru. Shining Path guerrillas had killed many members of his family, including his eighty-three-year-old grandfather, who had his hair torn out, his tongue cut out, and had then been scalped. While Romulo did not idealize Inca civilization, he was proud of his heritage and appeared dressed in the traditional robes and headdress of his people. I still have some tapes of him playing the haunting quena flute music of the high Andes. He was a preacher and a Bible translator.

From somewhere deep within my own prejudices, I assumed that, though he was a man of very great faith, he was probably of simple beliefs.

The next day I heard him discussing Hebrew word meanings in a conversation with a visiting Lutheran.

I said to him, "I didn't know you knew Hebrew."

He replied, "I studied linguistics in the United States and lived in Israel for a time."

A moment's thought might have told me that Bible translators need to know languages, but sometimes we have barriers to a moment's thought. Weeks later he was killed, whether by the Peruvian Army or the Shining Path is still not known.[8]

We need to avoid generalized descriptions of any people, of any religion. But we need to call *persecution* by its name. Murder and repression by Communists, Hindus, Buddhists, Muslims, and other Christians needs to be called by name, denied any excuse, and fought with all our power.

GUIDELINES FOR DIALOGUE

Given the fact of pervasive stereotyping, we need dialogue with others. Still, the fruits of dialogue should not be overestimated, since, while it is certainly possible to dialogue with, for example, Muslims, the Muslims who actually participate in dialogue are not usually the ones engaged in murder, kidnapping, or the rape of Christian women.

Nor should we think that education or dialogue is the solution to all such violence. The people engaged in persecution are neither stupid nor uneducated. Turabi, the principle power in Sudan, has law degrees from London and Paris as well as from Khartoum, and he chats with westerners all the time. He is probably happy to dialogue until the cows come home, or at least until the Dinka cows come into Khartoum. As diplomats well know, dialogue can also be an effective strategy of delay, and of avoiding action. We will not understand persecution if we think it is a mere misunderstanding to be resolved through more education and chatty conferences.

Nonetheless, what some dialogue *can* do is clear away misunderstandings between those who are open to realize that they may have misunderstandings. They also allow us to distinguish the different elements of religions which make for persecution and for toleration. Dialogue does not end persecution, but it can help clarify areas of dissension.

At the same time, for all the dangers of stereotyping, it needs to be emphasized that the facts described in this book are true. Certainly not all Muslims are persecutors. But millions of Christians *are* suffering persecution from Muslims. The same is true at the hands of Hindus, Buddhists, and other movements throughout the world. It helps no one to repeat the World Council of Churches' whitewashing of persecution lest it hinder dialogue.

Some guidelines for Christian-Muslim dialogue prepared by a working party in London are useful here. While these are specific to Christian-Muslim relations, they can offer some perspective for dialogue between several religions:.

> We support the pursuit of Muslim-Christian dialogue on issues of human rights and religious liberties as an essential aspect of our understanding, relationships, and responsibilities. . . .
>
> We urge that in the continuance of this dialogue internationally,

the participants represent the broad range of perspectives within the states and religious communities, including representatives of Christian communities within predominantly Muslim countries, and representatives of Muslim communities within predominantly non-Muslim countries. . . .

Meaningful dialogue requires that parties freely state their serious concerns, fears, and grievances. We, therefore, believe it essential to enumerate our grave concerns over . . . the following:

a. *The formal, legal, and institutionalized denial of equal civil and political rights to persons or groups based solely on their religious views.*

b. *Denials of persons' religious liberty to adopt a religion of their choice and their freedom to change their religion.*

c. *Laws restricting or penalizing conversion.*

d. *The linkage of spiritual goals with military or terrorist agendas.*

e. *Denials of equal opportunities in employment, education, and family life to persons on the basis of their religious identity.*

f. *Discrimination affecting legal rights, including access to law, and the denial of equal rights in civil and criminal courts and legal process.*

g. *The intrusion into the internal life of religious communities by governments, including the subordination of religious leadership to serve political ends.*

No dialogue ought to affirm or reinforce any rigid classifications of the world into religious territories based on religion or some neo-colonialist recognition of spheres of influence. Political and religious patterns are appropriately fluid.[9]

The patterns of legal and institutional discrimination against Christian *minorities in some* Muslim *states should not be glossed over. . . .* While *certainly there are elements of discrimination against* Muslims *which arise in western states, the scope of legal handicaps in most western states is not*

> *only relatively limited, but many mechanisms for publicly and legally challenging such discrimination exist; whereas, the discrimination against Christian minorities in some Muslim states is legal, formal, and systematic, with little procedural or substantive basis for challenges. Indeed, minority religious communities may feel intimidated in any challenge to the prevailing practices. . . .*
>
> *[We] must address the Muslim formal, legal, and apparently theologically grounded commitment to dhimmi status for non-Muslims. Any temptation to treat this formal discrimination as justified on the basis of cultural differences or political autonomy must be as firmly opposed. The interest in "agreement" and collaboration must not mask serious confrontation on issues of fundamental freedom.*
>
> *It is incumbent to press for the recognition of full legal status for converts, and oppose any state-enforced sanctions or disabilities imposed on converts. . . .*

As David Forte has said, "In the deepest sense, to defend Christians who are being persecuted by extreme Muslims is to defend Islam, a religion that was unusually tolerant for its era and one that has always permitted a wide variety of practices and customs within its fold. To speak up now against religious persecution on behalf of Christians, is to give mainstream Muslims heart. . . . If done with courage, determination, openhandedness, and consistency, Muslims from around the world will join with Christians against those tyrants that seek to destroy both faiths."[10]

Dialogue is important, especially for the churches, but there are also other church responsibilities.

CHURCHES

> *Years ago, I used to drive up Bathurst Street on my way to work in Toronto. I would pass synagogues of varying strictness, but each had a sign for the passing cars, "Remember Soviet Jews." I did remember, since I was reminded every working day. Christians too need to be remembered. Where are the signs on the churches?*

Relations with persecuted Christians should be part of western churches' *daily* life. It cannot be a "crusade," in the sense of a frenetic short-term focus. There is clearly a need for urgent and speedy action. But this cannot be all. Persecution will not disappear easily or quickly. If "crusades" don't succeed fairly quickly, people tend to get disillusioned and give up. They often stay disillusioned and don't bother joining the next crusade. What is also needed is a plan of action for the long haul. It must be an issue addressed in each Sunday's prayers, each newsletter, each campaign, and each election.

Church members are often more enthusiastically mobilized by the plight of a persecuted person, family, or congregation than by the abstract issue of religious persecution itself. When a church group is introduced to the circumstances of specific cases of imprisonment or other suffering, they will most likely be motivated to launch petition drives, media blitzes, postcard mailings to strategic agencies or offices (such as the White House), the printing of signs and bumper stickers, and other means of demanding official action on behalf of the victims. By "putting a human face" on the subject of religious persecution, the subject continues to be addressed, but with a more focused approach. Ultimately, however, it is essential to remember that the system itself must be changed.

Congregations need to make considered plans regularly and systematically to acquire information about persecuted Christians. They need to maintain contact by phone, letters, fax, e-mail, and personal visits directly with Christians overseas in a relationship of partnership. They need interaction with organizations addressing this issue. (See Appendix A.) They need contacts with international businesses to find out how they relate to persecution, asking them to make this an issue. This should be done by encouragement—buttressed, when necessary, by product boycotts.

Church action also needs to include direct contact with governments and groups engaged in persecution, challenging them to change and publicizing their actions. It needs coordination with human-rights groups such as Amnesty International, Freedom House, or Human Rights Watch. It needs to pressure the secular media, foundations, and universities to further publicize this issue. And it requires explicit political pressure on the government to make this a real part of a real human-rights agenda.

SECULAR ORGANIZATIONS

The first priority for media, academics, rights organizations, and others is the same as for the churches—learn what is happening. For the media, the imperative is even stronger, since these are organizations directly in the information dissemination business.

This requires committing funds and personnel to the task of dealing with religion seriously. Hiring skilled and informed religion reporters is one aspect. Also, an additional "diversity" check should be made through the newsroom, not asking "who represents an ethnic minority?" or "how many women are here?" but discovering and using the skills of those who take religion seriously and know what they are talking about. Anything less makes a mockery of any claims to expand religion perspectives in the news. Any news organization that doesn't do this deserves to be mocked and, more to the point, deserves to be dismissed as incompetent and out of touch with the world.

At this point, I'm not concerned with the coverage of events within the U.S. But unless media organizations take religion seriously, they cannot deal with very real death and suffering overseas. Foreign correspondents need to do less hanging around hotels in the capital and chatting with a coterie of diplomats and domestic journalists who operate with the same mindset. Instead, they should visit churches (and temples and mosques). Cultivate a range of contacts within religious bodies, since religion is often the single most pervasive reality. A correspondent who can discourse on Asian economies but knows little about Christian-Buddhist relations should be regarded as uninformed and unprofessional.

The same responsibilities apply to human-rights organizations. I noted earlier that I want to be careful in my criticisms here, since many of these organizations *are* doing something. But there are still problems which need to be addressed—in some cases, severe ones. Academic bodies like the Harvard Law School Program in Human Rights should be asked why religion does not rate in their materials. If this is not dealt with, then it should no longer be regarded as an institution on which to rely for clear thought and good information, but as a parochial ax-grinder who deserves downgrading in institutional academic rankings.

This problem does not occur with, say, Human Rights Watch. But since it has specific programs devoted to arms, children, free expression, women, prisons, business and human rights, drugs and human rights, lesbian and gay rights, standard setting, and mechanisms of international law, it may want to consider dealing with the persecution of Christians or, at least, with religious persecution in general. Amnesty International could provide a clearer breakdown of its category of "prisoners of conscience" so that not only peaceful political dissidents, but also religious believers, come into clearer focus. In its Puebla Program, Freedom House has an excellent beginning focus on religious persecution, but this initiative desperately needs strengthening, and its focus needs to permeate the whole organization.

The State Department is better discussed in the context of overall government policy.

GOVERNMENT

In May 1993, President Clinton threatened tough trade measures against China unless it improved its human-rights record within the year. The following week a ship, the Golden Venture, ran aground off New York carrying three hundred desperate Chinese, a large proportion of them Christians, escaping from their government's repression—especially its forced abortion and birth-control policy.

Two days after coming ashore, the refugees were shipped to prisons throughout the U.S. The largest group was sent to York County Prison in Pennsylvania, where they stayed for over a year. The women, for reasons unexplained, were transported to New Orleans Parish Prison. Later, some were transferred to California, where they still remained three years later in Lerdo Prison, awaiting return to China. Several of the claimants eventually found refugee status in Ecuador. Ecuador admitted them partly on humanitarian grounds, since the refugees had already been in U.S. prisons for a year, which implies that asylum was granted less because of their treatment by China than by America.

"One of the men is Catholic," said Claudia Tsao, who was volunteering her time. "When it was time for his immigration hearing, his interpreter didn't know anything about Catholicism and didn't know how to translate the religious terms."

A Chinese-American man from a local church was there in the hearing, and he realized that translating mistakes were "so terrible, serious," that the man's claim of religious persecution would be rejected summarily. The man from the local church called from the back that the interpreter wasn't doing a good job—and the judge had a guard throw him out of the courtroom.

"I know his religious claim was valid," Ms. Tsao said, "but it wasn't communicated."

In 1989, a U.S. immigration court in the case of "The matter of Chang," said China's forced birth-control and abortion policy need not itself be grounds for asylum. (Canadian Courts have required that it be accepted as grounds in Canada.) During the Reagan and Bush administrations it continued to be almost automatic grounds, but after Clinton became president, this was stopped.

On May 26, 1994, President Clinton announced that he would keep China's trade privileges with the U.S. but would "stay engaged with those in China who suffer from human-rights abuses." As he said this, several such sufferers had fled to asylum in Latin America after a year in U.S. prisons.

Others had been deported back to China. In August 1996, Representative Bill Gooding received a phone call describing the fate of one of these deportees. "When they [Chinese authorities] summoned his family, they told them, 'We broke his legs well enough so he'll never run away again.'"[11]

Granted, the U.S. government has a legitimate interest in deterring the smuggling of people into the U.S. But it is still hard to escape the conclusion that, as an institution, the U.S. government, especially in its immigration and foreign-policy branches, doesn't know much about religion and that either it doesn't *know* or doesn't *care* that it doesn't know much. United States government's ignorance of religion contributed to debacles in Iran and Vietnam, and nearly so in the Philippines and Indonesia. As noted, when James Sasser was appointed ambassador to China and met with human rights NGOs about the situation in the country to which he was going, he asked the famous question, "What's a *house church*?"

The fault might be less his since, with the politicization of ambassadorial appointments, many ambassadors neither know, nor are expected to know, very much at the beginning about the countries to which they are posted. For many (not Sasser, a former senator) their chief talent has been an ability to make deposits in the accounts of presidential campaigns. But if Sasser didn't know about house churches, then the people at the State Department and the intelligence services who briefed him didn't know about them either, or else they didn't think house churches were worth mentioning. In any case, many people in the U.S. government ignored the largest situation of religious persecution in the world.

United States immigration policy and officers require urgent attention. Richard Cizik, of the National Association of Evangelicals, estimates that evangelicals are the largest group that seeks asylum and sponsorship in the U.S. Their appeals are routinely denied by a bureaucracy that seems oblivious to religion around the world.

Immigration officers have denied asylum to Sudanese Christians, whose associates have been executed, Pakistani Christians arrested for blasphemy, Iranian Christian clergy fleeing after their church leaders were assassinated, Chinese Christian women escaping forced abortions, and an Ethiopian Christian preacher tortured under the Communist Dergue and suffering a similar fate to Islamic radicals.

"In the case of Christian refugees from Iran, the U.S. has simply turned over the question of the determination of asylum to the Muslim police in Turkey (where the refugees usually arrive) who summarily deport them back to Iran. Not one of some twenty clerics and religious leaders who fled Iran in the last two years received asylum in the United States."[12]

In the latter case, James Halmo, director of the Office of Asylum Affairs, claimed, "There is no evidence to confirm suggestions or allegation of a government-sponsored campaign of persecution of evangelical Christians in Ethiopia." One Ethiopian claimant, who had been tortured twenty-five times, was advised by his lawyer that he had little chance of gaining asylum in the U.S. because Christian claims of persecution were not taken seriously.[13]

The State Department often doesn't seem to take it seriously either. In the case of Robert Hussein, convicted of apostasy in Kuwait in late May 1996, the Department said the following:

> We are following this case very closely. Mr. Hussein, who is a natural-born Kuwaiti citizen, was sued by a private group in Kuwait, following his conversion to Christianity and divorce from his wife, in order to strip him of certain rights that Muslim men are automatically entitled to under Kuwaiti Muslim law.
>
> After several hearings, the Kuwaiti court found that Mr. Hussein was an apostate, meaning that he was no longer a Muslim and thus he loses his custody rights to his children and inheritance rights to his father's estate that would be given to a Muslim. These are the only ramifications of the Court's decisions.

If the State Department means that these are the "only ramifications" of the Court's decision as far as the Kuwaiti government and *direct* court action is concerned, it may well be right. But this evades the main issue. What the Court itself may now initiate is not the point. Under Shari'a law, as applied in many countries, Mr. Hussein may be killed by any Muslim with immunity. The judge in his case said he should be killed and he has received death threats.

The situation has parallels with that of Salman Rushdie. The *fatwah* pronounced on Rushdie by the Ayatollah Khomeini did not call on the Iranian authorities to kill him but declared him an apostate, saying that he may and should be killed. Rushdie is not an American citizen either. Has the State Department "not been involved" in his case either, "except to monitor the human-rights aspects?" Even the British government, not often noted for its strong human-rights stance, took an interest in the Hussein affair, as have British newspapers and British parliamentarians of all parties. Why the difference?[14]

United States' concern for rights in foreign policy (insofar as it now is concerned with anything other than copyrights) needs to devote specific attention to the persecution of Christians in the world. There should be no shame or embarrassment about taking up this issue as if it were some parochial matter. A pattern of repression that affects some two hundred million women, men, and children worldwide deserves attention, if anything in the field of human rights deserves attention.

A good summary of some basic steps is provided in the Statement of Conscience issued by the National Association of Evangelicals, endorsed by the Episcopal Church and the Southern Baptists, and commended by the Presbyterian Church (USA). It has also drawn support from groups and individuals as diverse as Amnesty International, Bob Dole, and Barney Frank, as well as from long-standing opponents of religious persecution such as Congressmen Chris Smith (R-NJ), Frank Wolf (R-VA), Tony Hall (D-OH), Tom Lantos (D-CA), John Porter (R-IL), and Senators Sam Nunn (D-GA), Jesse Helms (R-NC), and Richard Lugar (R-IN). (More detailed sections of the Statement are given in Appendix B.)

- There must be public acknowledgment of widespread and mounting anti-Christian persecution in the world and a public commitment by the president to public diplomacy openly condemning such persecution.
- The president should appoint a knowledgeable, experienced, and compassionate special adviser to the president for religious liberty to prepare a report outlining the changes in policy needed.
- Ambassadors and other diplomatic officials need to meet regularly with willing church leaders and dissidents.[15]
- The United States delegate to the United Nations Commission on Human Rights needs regularly and forcefully to raise this issue.
- Trade and other international negotiators should link their negotiations with the need for constructive changes.
- The State Department's Human Rights Reports need to add a specific

focus on such persecution, and reporting officers should be equipped to be able to distinguish the different types of groups affected.

- Immigration officials need to be informed of and to consider anti-Christian persecution in dealing with the claims of refugees.
- Foreign assistance to countries which do not take action to end this persecution should be terminated.

President Clinton agreed in late 1995 to appoint an adviser, and the White House assured Nina Shea that, subject to "paperwork processing only," she would be designated as the president's special adviser on religious persecution. However, the appointment was held up, reportedly by conflicts between the president's political staff and the State Department.

The president then promised in a meeting at the Oval Office that he would attend the March 1996 convention of the National Association of Evangelicals and speak on the subject of its Statement of Conscience. This was then canceled, with White House staff telling NAE officials that there was not enough money in the president's budget to allow him to fly to their convention in Minneapolis.

Meanwhile, the Saudi government, the China business lobby, and the National Council of Churches, among others, have begun lobbying to make sure that little happens on this score.[16]

By the fall of 1996, political pressure along the lines suggested by NAE was building. On September 17, the Senate passed a resolution highlighting religious persecution, especially of Christians. In the meantime, the World Evangelical Fellowship called a World Day of Prayer on September 19, 1996. It was observed in one hundred and ten countries. On September 24 the House of Representatives passed a similar resolution. In November the State Department announced the formation of an Advisory Committee to the Secretary of State on Religious Persecution. There are many able people among the commissioners, but its composition and terms were so broad that it carried the danger of diffusing the issue rather than focusing it. The facts that it will be staffed by the State Department, will meet only two or three times a year, and, according to John Shattuck, assistant secretary of state for Democracy, Human Rights, and Labor, will not be "action-oriented," make it a far cry from a special adviser to the president.[17]

The outcome of these struggles will depend on each of us, and what we do about them. While countries resist criticisms of their human-rights records and claim to ignore such criticism, most *will* change in order to avoid international censure and trade restrictions if other governments and peoples have the courage to raise them. And democratic governments *will raise them* when their people *pressure them to do so*.

This pressure needs to be intense, continuous, persistent, focused, and intelligent. There are people now, as I write . . . as you read . . . who are being imprisoned, raped, sold into slavery, and tortured to death. Christians should note that in orthodox Christian theology, this must be treated the same as Jesus being tortured to death. I know of no greater challenge facing the churches today.

It is no mercy to spare the feelings of others by allowing the suffering of millions to pass by in silence. It is no humility to accept the death of others. It is no love to be quiet in the face of oppression. We may indeed be called to turn the other cheek in attacks on ourselves. We have no such call in attacks on others. The call to escape self-centeredness and self-justification is meant to free us to be servants of others. A just politics is a means of such service.

Ignoring the plight of Christians abroad while voting and lobbying in defense of local Christian interests cannot be excused. In orthodox Christian theology, it is crucifying Christ once more. The evangelical and Catholic communities include over half of the American public. It is not unreasonable nor unachievable for Christians to make it clear that nobody seeking federal office in the United States can get substantial support or votes from Christians unless he or she makes an explicit and believable commitment to contribute to the ending of the persecution of Christians. Compared to the courage and commitment of others around the world, it is a small thing.

I [Akuac Amet] was caught in my home on March 25 [1995], in Sudan. They beat me unconscious with a big club. Now my legs are paralyzed and I can only crawl. They then shot my four sons who were tending cattle and abducted my fourteen-year-old daughter, Ajak. The raiders left with all of my property. My husband died in the great famine. I am now completely destitute. The owner of this tukul is helping me to survive.

When we revisited Akuac Amet . . . we found her dying in the tukul . . . of . . . Adut Wol Ngar. [Adut] is currently caring for sixty-two victims of the March raid. She recalled that day. . . .

The enemy came early on March 25; this woman was too old to run; so they caught her and beat her so badly it was impossible to know if she was alive or dead. The enemy returned and killed her four sons and kidnapped her daughter. She can be returned, if the money can be found—but there is no one to pay the money. . . . I came and took care of this old lady and have looked after her. . . .

About three hundred people were killed. . . . The enemy divided into two groups—some on horseback, some on foot. . . . We ran with the children to try to hide them in the long grass but they found us and drove the older children away. Any who refused to go, they killed them. . . . Those who went were tied with rope and pulled like cows behind horses. Some children were as little as seven years old. Some died of thirst. . . . They were not given any water. . . .

The families of those who were captured are still trying to find the money to pay for their children. . . . If they have no money, they can be told that their children are still alive, but are unable to buy them back. . . .

We are happy you have come to meet us, to see how we are suffering; how our children have been taken by the enemy and how we are having to live without our children. . . . and how we have to eat fruits and grass. . . . We are grateful to you for coming to see our situation. . . . Thank you for coming to us. . . . We pray that God will bring our children back to us. . . .[18]

APPENDIX A

U.S. Offices of Groups Fighting Religious Persecution

Advocates International
7002-C Little River Turnpike
Annandale, VA 22003
ph: 703-658-0070 fax: 703-658-0077
e-mail: sam.ericsson@gen.org

Advocates takes a long-term approach to religious liberty, focusing on the education of lawyers, judges, and legislators around the world.

Amnesty International
U.S. office: 322 Eighth Avenue
New York, NY 10001
ph: 212-807-8400 fax: 212-989-5473
homepage: www:http://www.amnesty.org
e-mail: aimember@aiusa.usa.com

Prominent international organization, which monitors and advocates on behalf of human rights. Amnesty has worked for the release of people imprisoned for the peaceful exercise of their religious beliefs. It also reports on the persecution of religious minorities.

CARDINAL KUNG FOUNDATION
P. O. Box 8086
Ridgeway Center
Stamford, CT 06905
ph: 203-329-9712 fax: 203-329-8415

Monitors religious liberty abuses against Catholics in China.

CHRISTIAN LIFE COMMISSION OF THE SOUTHERN BAPTIST CONVENTION
901 Commerce, Suite 550
Nashville, TN 37203-3696

An arm of the Southern Baptist Convention, America's largest Protestant denomination. Seeks to draw the attention of Baptists and others to religious persecution, and lobbies for changes in U.S. government policy.

CHRISTIAN SOLIDARITY INTERNATIONAL
U.S. office: 1101 17th Street, NW
Suite 607
Washington, D.C. 20036
ph: 540-636-8907
e-mail: csiusa@rma.edu

An interdenominational human-rights organization headquartered in Switzerland that works for persecuted Christians and other victims of oppression. Conducts relief-work, fact-finding trips, and organizes campaigns on behalf of persecuted believers.

COALITION FOR THE DEFENSE OF HUMAN RIGHTS UNDER ISLAMIZATION
231 East Carroll
Macomb, IL 61455
ph: 309-833-4249

Focuses on the situation of religious minorities in the Islamic world.

COMMISSION ON SECURITY AND COOPERATION IN EUROPE
("Helsinki Commission")
234 Ford House Office Building
Washington, D.C. 20515-6460

ph: 202-225-1901
e-mail: csce@HR.house.gov

A Congressional commission established in 1976 to monitor and encourage progress in implementing the provisions, including human-rights provisions, of the Helsinki Accords on East-West cooperation. Several staff members monitor religious liberty developments in the Helsinki countries.

COMPASS DIRECT NEWS SERVICE
P. O. Box 27250
Santa Ana, CA 92799

A highly informative newsletter on the persecution of Christians, published by Open Doors.

FREEDOM HOUSE'S PUEBLA PROGRAM ON RELIGIOUS FREEDOM
1319 18th Street, NW
2nd Floor
Washington, D.C. 20036
ph: 202-296-5101 fax: 202-296-5078

Freedom House is a national organization dedicated to strengthening democratic institutions. With the addition of the Puebla Program, directed by human-rights veteran Nina Shea, the group now also gives special attention to religious freedom. In 1996 they published an excellent booklet on the persecution of Christians around the world, In the Lion's Den. *An expanded version will be published in early 1997 by Broadman and Holman.*

HUMAN RIGHTS WATCH
485 Fifth Avenue
New York, NY 10017-6104
ph: 212-972-8400 fax: 212-972-0905
homepage: www:gopher://gopher.humanrights.org:5000/11/int/hrw
e-mail: hrwnyc@hrw.org

An independent international human-rights organization that conducts regular investigations of human-rights abuses in about seventy countries around the world. It has produced several reports about religious rights abuses, especially in China.

INSTITUTE ON RELIGION AND DEMOCRACY
1521 16th Street, NW, Suite 300
Washington, D.C. 20036
ph: 202-986-1440 fax: 202-986-3159

Publicizes instances of religious persecution and monitors the response (or non-response) of U.S. churches.

INTERNATIONAL CHRISTIAN CONCERN
2020 Pennsylvania Avenue, NW
#941
Washington, D.C. 20006
ph: 301-989-1708 fax: 301-989-1709
homepage: www:http://esoptron.umd.edu/icc/ics.html
e-mail: icc@ids2.unline.com

An independent Christian organization that mobilizes grassroots prayer and activism on behalf of persecuted Christians around the world.

IRANIAN CHRISTIANS INTERNATIONAL
P. O. Box 25607
Colorado Springs, CO 80936
ph: 719-596-0010 fax: 719-574-1141

An evangelical organization that monitors the persecution of Christians inside Iran, works to help Iranian Christian refugees, and does advocacy work with the U.S. government.

JUBILEE CAMPAIGN
U.S. office: 9689-C Main Street
Fairfax, VA 22031
ph: 703-503-0791 fax: 703-503-0792
e-mail: ann.buwalda@gen.org

The U.S. arm of this British-based Christian group conducts campaigns on behalf of human rights and religious liberty around the world.

MIDDLE EAST CONCERN
P. O. Box 295
Macomb, IL 61455

Publicizes oppression and discrimination against religious minorities, especially Christians, in the Middle East.

NATIONAL ASSOCIATION OF EVANGELICALS
P. O. Box 28
Wheaton, IL 60189
ph: 630-665-0500
email: NAE@nae.net website http://www.nae.net

A cooperative of approximately 42,500 evangelical congregations nationwide from 47 member denominations and individual congregations from an additional 30 denominations whose executive serves on the White House Advisory Committee on Religious Freedom Abroad. NAE's landmark "Statement of Conscience Concerning Worldwide Religious Persecution" is available on the web.

OPEN DOORS WITH BROTHER ANDREW
U.S. office: P. O. Box 27000
Santa Ana, CA 92799
ph: 714-531-6000

A large international, evangelical organization formed to help suffering Christians throughout the world. Members deliver materials to persecuted Christians, conduct training sessions for indigenous leaders, and work to mobilize and educate churches to become more involved in helping persecuted Christians. It now publishes an informative newsletter called Compass Direct.

PARLIAMENTARY HUMAN RIGHTS FOUNDATION
1056 Thomas Jefferson Street, NW
Washington, D.C. 20007

This Foundation is increasingly employing technology, specifically the Internet, to promote human rights internationally. Having parliamentarians from various countries on its board of directors, it seeks to pressure governments, which have the main responsibility to enhance human rights."

THE RUTHERFORD INSTITUTE
P. O. Box 7482
Charlottesville, VA 22906-7482
ph: 804-978-3888 fax: 804-978-1789
homepage: http://www.rutherford.org
e-mail: rutherford@fni.com

An international legal and educational organization "dedicated to the preservation of religious liberty, the sanctity of human life, and family autonomy." The bulk of their work is on U.S. cases, but they have a growing international division focusing on religious persecution around the world, especially Latin America.

VOICE OF THE MARTYRS
P. O. Box 443
Bartlesville, OK 74005
ph: 918-337-8015 fax: 918-337-9287
homepage: www:http://www.iclnet.org/pub/resources/text/vom/vom.html
e-mail: vomusa@ix.netcom.com

Nonprofit missionary organization working with persecuted churches in more than fifty countries around the world. Provides practical assistance to oppressed Christians and informs Christians in the West about ongoing religious persecution.

WORLD EVANGELICAL FELLOWSHIP RELIGIOUS LIBERTY COMMISSION
U.S. Office
2309 139th Street, SE
Mill Creek, WA 98012
ph: 206-742-7923
homepage: http://www.xc.crg/wef/wefintro
e-mail: WEF NA@XC.Org

The Singapore-based World Evangelical Fellowship is an umbrella group of evangelical associations worldwide and draws together some 180 million people from over one hundred countries. From its main office in Finland, the Religious Liberty Commission coordinates the work of its members on issues of religious freedom.

These are groups that do significant work on the persecution of Christians. There are many other human-rights organizations with diverse foci whose work also touches on this issue.

APPENDIX B

Selections from the "Statement of Conscience of the National Association of Evangelicals"

Washington, D.C., January 23, 1996

"If, though it is true, the United States government cannot end all evil throughout the world, it can nonetheless adopt policies that would limit religious persecution and ensure greater fulfillment of inalienable and internationally recognized rights to freedom of religious belief and practice. . . . We respectfully call for the following actions to be taken by the government of the United States:

I. Public acknowledgement of today's widespread and mounting anti-Christian persecution and the adoption of policies condemning religious persecution whether it results from official policy or from unchecked terrorist activity.

- A major policy address by the president initiating a new public diplomacy commitment to openly condemn anti-Christian persecution wherever it occurs and further announcing a lesser reliance on today's private diplomacy and case-by-case appeals to curb such persecution.
- Issuance of instructions to all ambassadors or surrogates to meet regularly with willing church leaders and dissidents in countries where religious persecution occurs.

- Appointment of a knowledgeable, experienced, and compassionate "special adviser to the president for religious liberty," charged with preparing a report indicating needed changes in policies dealing with religious persecution, and with recommending remedial action.

- Issuance of instructions to the United States delegate to the United Nations Commission on Human Rights, to regularly and forcefully raise the issue of anti-Christian and other religious persecution at all appropriate Commission sessions.

- Issuance of instructions to consular officials acknowledging the mounting evidence of religious persecution and instructing them to provide diligent assistance when the victims of religious persecution seek refugee status.

- Issuance of instructions to senior officials engaged in trade or other international negotiations, when dealing with officials of countries that engage in religious persecution, to vigorously object to such religious persecution and to link negotiations with the need for constructive change.

II. Issuance by the State Department's Human Rights Bureau and related government agencies of more carefully researched, more fully documented, and less politically edited reports of the fact and circumstances of anti-Christian and other religious persecution.

To that end, we respectfully recommend that the following steps be taken:

- Issuance of instructions to human-rights officers to distinguish between the treatment of different Christian groups within countries and to no longer assume that all such groups are similarly dealt with.

- Issuance of instructions that Human Rights Bureau annual reports are to make explicit findings of whether anti-Christian or other religious persecutions occur, thereby eliminating from these reports an "option of silence" regarding such persecutions.

- Clarifying and upgrading the role of embassy human-rights officers in countries where anti-Christian or other religious persecution is ongoing and pervasive, and ensuring that such officers carefully monitor religious liberty violations on an ongoing and prioritized basis.

III. Cessation of the indifferent and occasionally hostile manner in which the Immigration and Naturalization Service often treats the petitions of escapees from anti-Christian persecution.

To that end, we respectfully recommend that the following steps be taken:

- Issuance of an Attorney General's Bulletin to INS hearing officers acknowledging mounting anti-Christian persecutions in many parts of the world, and directing such officers to process the claims of escapees from such persecution with priority and diligence.
- Issuance of instructions by the attorney general directing preparation of annual INS reports describing its processing of religious refugee and asylum claims.
- Issuance of regulations requiring written opinions from INS hearing officers clearly stating the grounds for any denial of religious refugee and asylum claims.
- Establishment of INS listening posts in countries to which refugees from anti-Christian persecution frequently flee.
- Cessation of INS delegation of refugee processing functions to foreign and United Nations agencies.

IV. Termination of foreign assistance to countries that fail to take vigorous action to end anti-Christian or other religious persecution, with resumption of assistance to be permitted only after a written finding is made by the president that the countries have taken all reasonable steps to end such persecution, and arrangements are made to ensure that religious persecution is not resumed.

APPENDIX C

The Meaning of Religious Freedom

By *religious freedom*, I mean what is contained in the United Nations Declaration on the Elimination of All Forms of Intolerance and of Discrimination Based on Religion or Belief, 1981:

Article 1

1. Everyone shall have the right to freedom of thought, conscience, and religion. This right shall include freedom to have a religion or whatever belief of his choice, and freedom, either individually or in community with others and in public or private, to manifest his religion or belief in worship, observance, practice, and teaching.

2. No one shall be subject to coercion which would impair his freedom to have a religion or belief of his choice.

3. Freedom to manifest one's religion or beliefs may be subject only to such limitations as are prescribed by law and are necessary to protect public safety, order, health or morals, or the fundamental rights and freedoms of others.

Article 2

1. No one shall be subject to discrimination by any state, institution, group of persons, or person on ground of religion or other beliefs. . . .

Article 5

1. The parents or, as the case may be, the legal guardians of the child have the right to organize the life within the family in accordance with their religion or belief and bearing in mind the moral education in which they believe the child should be brought up.

2. Every child shall enjoy the right to have access to education in the matter of religion or belief in accordance with the wishes of his parents or, as the case may be, legal guardians, and shall not be compelled to receive teaching on religion or belief against the wishes of his parents or legal guardians, the best interests of the child being the guiding principle. . . .

Article 6

. . . the right to freedom of thought, conscience, religion or belief shall include, inter alia, the following freedoms:

(a) To worship or assemble in connection with a religion or belief, and to establish and maintain places for these purposes;

(b) To establish and maintain appropriate charitable or humanitarian institutions;

(c) To make, acquire, and use to an adequate extent the necessary articles and materials related to the rites or customs of a religion or belief;

(d) To write, issue, and disseminate relevant publications in these areas.

(e) To teach a religion or belief in places suitable for these purposes;

(f) To solicit and receive voluntary financial and other contributions from individuals and institutions;

(g) To train, appoint, elect, or designate by succession appropriate leaders called for by the requirements and standards of any religion or belief;

(h) To observe days of rest and to celebrate holidays and ceremonies in accordance with the precepts of one's religion or belief;

(i) To establish and maintain communications with individuals and communities in matters of religion and belief at the national and international levels.

These articles do not contain a clear internal definition of the right to *change* one's religion. But, as an authoritative commentator, Natan Lerner, observes, "There is no doubt, however, that the final text recognizes the right to change one's religion or beliefs, to abandon a religion, and to adopt a different one. This liberal interpretation is supported by the discussion during the preparation for the Covenant."[1] A new Article 8 was added to reinforce this point. This states that:

> Nothing in the present Declaration shall be construed as restricting or derogating from any right defined in the Universal Declaration of Human Rights. . . .

The 1948 Universal Declaration, in turn, states in Article 18 that "Everyone has the right to . . . change his religion or belief. . . ."[2]

The United Nations Human Rights Commission further emphasized this point in its authoritative 1989 clarification that article 18 (1) of the International Covenant on Civil and Political Rights emphasizes "the right to replace one's current religion," and says "the freedom to . . . adopt a religion (is) . . . protected unconditionally. . . ." and "cannot be derogated from, even in time of public emergency. . . ."

Even apart from specific rights of religion, we also need to refer to rights of free speech, since freedom of religion does not exist in a corner but manifests itself through, among other things, the rights of free speech, free expression, and freedom of association. The right to propagate one's religion is a right of free expression. The Universal Declaration of Human Rights states in Article 19 that:

> Everyone has the right to freedom of opinion and expression; this right includes freedom to hold opinions without interference and to seek, receive, and impart information and ideas through any media and regardless of frontiers.

This was given more formal legal expression in Article 19 of the 1966 International Covenant on Civil and Political Rights, which states:

1. Everyone shall have the right to hold opinions without interference.
2. Everyone shall have the right to freedom of expression; this right shall include freedom to seek, receive, and impart information and ideas of all kinds, regardless of frontiers, either orally, in writing, or in print, in the form of art, or through any other media of his choice. . . .

The above rights are what I mean by *religious freedom*.

APPENDIX D

The Meaning of Terms and Numbers

Many terms, such as "Christian," "persecution," and "genocide" are both ill-defined and controversial. The accuracy, precision, and meaning of the numbers of those persecuted are equally ill-defined and controversial. There is no way here, and probably no way anywhere else, to resolve all of these questions. But what I would like to do is explain and give some justification for how I use them.

Religious Persecution

By *religious persecution* I mean, in general, the denial of any of the rights of religious freedom. I also use a series of other terms such as *genocide*, *harassment*, *and discrimination*. Except for *genocide*, none of these terms has any widely agreed meaning. While I have avoided terms like "holocaust," I have used the term *genocide* to refer to what is contained in the 1948 United Nations Convention on the Prevention and Punishment of the Crime of Genocide. There, it means:

> . . . any of the following acts committed with intent to destroy, in whole or in part, a national, ethnical, racial, or religious group, as such:
>
> a) Killing members of the group;

b) Causing serious bodily or mental harm to members of the group;
c) Deliberately inflicting on the group conditions of life calculated to bring about its physical destruction in whole or in part;
d) Imposing measures intended to prevent births within the group;
e) Forcibly transferring children of the group to another group.[1]

On occasion, I have used the term *persecution* as a general expression to cover the whole range of denial of rights. At other times, I use it to refer to instances which are severe but are somewhat less than genocide. The context usually makes the meaning clear.

By *harassment*, I mean a situation where people are not systematically imprisoned, nor are denied the basic possibility of following their faith, but where they suffer from legal impediments and are interfered with by the authorities or others, and face arbitrary arrest and possible physical assault.

By *discrimination*, I mean a situation where people may have basic freedom of worship and other forms of religious freedom, but where the law places them at a consistent civil and economic disadvantage for exercising such freedoms.

"Christian"

The word *Christian* can also be used in a variety of ways. Most of the meanings grade into one another, but we can usefully distinguish four or five common meanings.

One is what can be called "census Christians." These are people who, in answer to a question of what their religion is, would say "Christian." It says nothing at all about what they actually believe or whether they participate in any real way in the life of a Christian community. It is almost a cultural term.

The second can be called "member Christians." These are people who claim membership in a particular Christian church. It does not necessarily imply that they have ever actually shown up in such a church. It includes those who simply want to get baptized, married, and buried by one.

The third category can be called "practicing Christians." These are people who participate in the life of the church, attend worship services, and maintain the basic forms and rituals of the Christian faith.

The fourth I have tended to call "believers," or "committed believers." These are people for whom their Christian faith is a central aspect of their lives and who are committed as much as possible to living out their faith and communicating it to others.

I have not always taken pains to distinguish these groupings, since they can shade imperceptibly into one another and people may be one or the other at different times in their lives. Nevertheless, we should be aware of the different meanings, especially as persecution is often different for different groups. It is usually the fourth category who suffer the most intense persecution and who comprise the members of the "underground" or "house" churches. The members of the third group are often given more lenient treatment as long as they keep quiet, but they still suffer significant disabilities. It is usually only the most fanatical Islamicists that make specific efforts to target the first and second groups.

It may be useful to note a fifth category, which can be called "hidden Christians." These are people who believe as Christians but, for fear of persecution, keep that belief entirely to themselves, hidden even from family and friends. We know of such people in the history of Japan and China and Saudi Arabia. Such people do not suffer direct external attack, but this is simply because external threat has driven their religious life totally inward, itself an intense form of persecution and denial of human rights.

Persecution of Christians

The fact that Christians suffer is not in and of itself a sign of persecution since, after all, many people suffer—in war, famine, and the other myriad forms of human misery. Nor is the fact that Christians are persecuted *itself* a sign of what I have called "Christian persecution," since Christians may be persecuted alongside, and in the same way, as others who do not share their faith. What I mean by the persecution of Christians is persecution that stems, at least in part, from the fact that they *are Christians*.

A possible demarcation point of Christian persecution is to ask whether, if they had other religious beliefs, would it still be happening to them? If the answer is yes, we probably should not call it specifically Christian persecution, though not for a second should we forget that it is real persecution and that real people, Christians and others, suffer it. Examples of this might be the sufferings of Quechua Christians under both the Shining Path guerrillas and the brutal Peruvian military responses, or the death of hundreds of thousands of Tutsi Christians in the genocide in Rwanda, or the murder of nuns and priests engaged in human-rights work in Central America.[2]

When we turn our attention to those who are actually doing the persecuting, similar complexities may arise. When I speak of the persecution of Christians, it does not necessarily imply, for example, that Muslims who are persecuting Christians are doing so for specifically Muslim reasons, but only that it is Christians that they are persecuting in a situation where they would not be persecuting others.

Nor does the use of the term *Christian persecution* necessarily imply that Christians' *identity* is the *only* reason for their persecution. Since religious freedom involves the freedom to live out one's religion, it is also a question of what Christians' faith leads them to be and to do, so that their actions rather than their identity can become the object of others' rage.

Nor does the fact of Christian persecution imply that this is the *only* factor involved in the persecution. There may also be ethnic tensions, territorial claims, economic advantages, and many other forms of human greed involved. But it does mean that Christian identity and Christian commitment are among the real factors.

Categories of Countries

In trying to provide a brief survey of developments in over sixty countries, it is important to categorize the countries in a way that reveals the overall patterns. The alternative would be simply to give an alphabetical listing of countries. This would have the virtue of being relatively complete and, on this point, uncontroversial. But it has the defect of being boring and unilluminating.

Clearly, any classification of countries has an artificial quality since countries form a continuum of patterns and trends rather than a set of discrete categories. There is no wholly satisfactory classification, but we must try to provide some crude division.

I have divided the sites of persecution into the Islamic world, the Communist world, Christian-on-Christian persecution, and then a set of countries in Asia largely comprising traditionally Hindu and Buddhist societies. I wrestled for a long time whether to include persecution in the name of nationalism as a discrete category. I decided not to do so, since such a category would take up nearly all of the countries that I discuss. With the exception of fervently Islamic countries like Saudi Arabia, every instance of persecution also involves a government or a community claiming it is defending a nation or a traditional culture from "foreign religious influence." This is true for countries as varied as Mexico, Egypt, India, and Vietnam.

Since almost every instance involves nationalism, we then would face the problem of dividing up types of nationalism. In one sense, this is what I have done. The categories of countries comprising the chapter outlines can, in most cases, be understood as referring to a symbiosis of particular religious forms with nationalism.[3] For example, the government of Egypt has treated Islam as part of its national character. Radical Hindus treat Hinduism as the essence of Indian culture. Mongolians treat Christianity as a threat to national traditions. Nearly all of the religious categories I use are interwoven with nationalism.

One particular problem arises with the countries of Eastern Europe and the former Soviet Union. In many of these countries, there is a chauvinism which tries to screen out foreign influences. The governments are often simply holdovers, at least in personnel, from the old Communist days. These functionaries, such as the present leaders of the Serbs, now use nationalism and religion as rallying cries to shore up their faltering legitimacy and to instill national loyalty. The Serb example is a particularly striking case since (ex)-Communist thugs such as Milosovic in Serbia and Radovan Karadzic and General Ratko Mladic, who were thorough-going Communist cadres, now wrap themselves in the cloak of the Orthodox Church, though without any obvious manifestation of piety.

Obviously, there is an artificial quality to categorizing these as "Orthodox" instances of persecution. The problem is further exacerbated when we consider Albania, which combines an authoritarian "post-Communist" government with attempts to use nationalism and Islam in an effort to reject western, Greek, and Orthodox influences.

In any case, it should be understood that religious categories are intertwined with forms of reactionary nationalism. Usually, my categories refer to the general religious identity of specific forms of nationalism.

The Agents of Repression

Religious repression can have a variety of sources. One is direct repression by officers of the state, such as in Vietnam or Cuba. A second is extra-legal, community-led violence against religious minorities, such as is common in Nigeria and Pakistan. A third is when radical opposition groups directly target Christians for assault, as in Algeria and India.

These forms are often intertwined. For example, a government may oppose the agenda of radical groups in their assault on Christians, but do comparatively little to stop these assaults, either because the government is weak, or because it wants to placate the radicals. The same is true with more widespread communal violence. In many countries, the government is not initiating attacks on Christians but, in all too many cases, its attempts to stop such violence are extremely weak. Even where there is no direct government action, there can be government complicity.

The Meaning of Numbers

I have usually tried to provide current figures for the number of Christians present in and persecuted in the countries described. Obviously, these figures are approximate. Especially in the case of Christians who are "underground," numbers are extremely difficult to estimate. In the case of "hidden" Christians, the numbers are *by definition* impossible to know. While noting these severe limitations, we still need to give the best figures we can. David B. Barrett gives the figures for mid-1996 of:[4]

- 1,960,000,000 "Christians . . . of all kinds"
- 1,790,000,000 "affiliated church members"
- 1,300,000,000 "practicing Christians"
- 740,000,000 "active Christians"

While the definitions are different, these groups could roughly parallel the first four categories of the meaning of *Christian* that I described above. Breakdown by continents of "affiliated church members" is as follows:

- Africa—300,000,000
- Asia—290,000,000
- Europe—530,000,000
- Latin America—440,000,000
- North America—200,000,000
- Oceania—22,000,000

Some 60 percent of Christians live in the Third World. Since "Europe" here includes much of Russia, the figure for non-western Christians is somewhat higher. The number of Christians in the "West"—Western Europe, North America, and parts of Oceania—would be about 25–30 percent of total "membership" Christians.

The category of "member Christians" inflates the proportion of Christians in the West compared to the figures for "practicing Christians" and "active Christians." "Member Christians" include those for whom membership is a formal matter, perhaps simply denoting baptism as a child. While there are people like this in many countries, including the Middle East, Latin America, Africa, and Asia, they form a conspicuously large proportion of the European population, where the number of "active Christians" is sometimes less than 5 percent of the "member Christians."

In the rest of the world, where being Christian can create problems, there is less likelihood that anyone who claims a Christian commitment would do so in a purely formal way. If it meant little to them, they are more likely to abandon it rather than face discrimination. This also implies that church attendance and active Christian commitment involve a higher proportion of Third World "member Christians." Consequently, it is likely that the West contains a fifth or less of the world's "active Christians."

Some consequences of this may appear surprising, at least to secular westerners. For example, as noted in the text, it is likely that more Christians attend Sunday worship in China than do in the entirety of Western Europe. It may even be the case that more Christians attend Sunday worship in Indonesia, the world's largest Muslim country, than do in Western Europe. *There is absolutely no excuse for thinking of Christianity as either western, white, or male*. It may be the largest Third World religion, having slightly more adherents in that part of the world than Islam and far beyond Hinduism and Buddhism, the next largest categories.

For the year 1980, Barrett gave the figure of 605,000,000 for Christians "living under political restrictions on religious liberty," and the figure of 225,000,000 for Christians "experiencing severe state interference in religion, obstruction, or harassment." These would correspond roughly to what I have called "harassment" and "persecution" respectively. The current numbers would be similar, reflecting both the decrease of persecution with the collapse of many Communist countries and the corresponding expansion of the church and rise of increased persecution in the rest of the world. For 1996, Barrett suggests that the average rate of martyrdom is about 159,000 Christians per year. (He defines a *martyr* as "a believer in Christ who loses his or her life prematurely in a situation of witness as a result of human hostility.") This figure strikes me as too high, but I have no alternative one to suggest.

In general we can say that, currently, two hundred to two hundred fifty million Christians are persecuted for their faith, and a further four hundred million live under non-trivial restrictions on religious liberty.

APPENDIX E

Spreading the Faith

Many persecutors try to justify their actions by claiming to defend a tradition against "foreign" or novel ideas. But even apart from the fact that this is no justification for denying human rights, it ignores the nature, geography, and history of most religions. Religious beliefs spread and change. A thousand years ago probably the largest Christian church was the Nestorian Church, spread throughout Asia. Many Nestorians were massacred by Tamerlane. There were bishops in Afghanistan and monasteries in China over a millennium ago. Over half of Europe was under Islam for centuries. We may have forgotten this but, to the cost of many, the Serbs haven't; nor have the Russians. However, should we claim that the retreat of Islam from Europe in the last five hundred years is a historical mistake? Should we go back to the *status quo* of, say, the year 1400? If not, what year? Or is 1996 the privileged year, when all human change in religion must come to a halt?

Changes in religion can be illustrated by Mongolia. According to tradition, Mahayana Buddhism was introduced into Mongolia over two thousand years ago by Buddhists traveling along the Silk Road. Other religions including Manicheanism, Nestorian Christianity, and Islam traveled the same route and left their mark on the country. The present form of "Yellow Hat" Tibetan Buddhism did not arrive until the thirteenth century, when Kublai Khan, then emperor of China, named a Buddhist lama from Beijing as the head of the faith for Tibet,

Mongolia, and China. The monasteries function in the Tibetan language, look to the Dalai Lama as a spiritual authority and, in the 1990s, have had the ambassador from India as a leading spiritual source.[1]

In short, the current leading religious forces have their seat of authority outside the country and are only the most recent of the successive religions which have had influence. This is not intended as any slight on their legitimacy; it is simply a fact about their history. Despite this, Mongolian governments in the 1990s have sought to prevent further changes and have given legal preeminence to Buddhism. A 1993 law asserted the "predominant position of the Buddhist religion," forbade the "propagation of religion from outside," and "banned religious activities alien to the religions and customs of the Mongolian people."[2]

We can sympathize with Buddhist attempts to defend their beliefs, and they have every freedom to argue against newer beliefs and seek to refute them. However, attempts to repress other beliefs are illegitimate.

Firstly, it treats a people's religious beliefs as if they had simply been dominant from time immemorial. But, in fact, many countries and regions of the world now have different beliefs from those of previous centuries, or even previous decades.

Secondly, it ignores the fact that the currently predominant religion displaced much of a previous religion.

Thirdly, most religions in most of the world have their point of origin "outside."

Religions are fluid, and they spread. Any attempt by repressive means to freeze present demographics flies not only in the face of justice, but in the face of history and of faith itself. Religions, like political and other ideas, interact, evolve, and change. We cannot seize a point in time as the just religious distribution so that attempts to change it are "intrusions."

We should treat repression of the spread of religion as we should repression of any other belief. Liberal North Americans should consider how they react when conservatives complain, for example, that the traditional Judeo-Christian basis of the country is being undercut. They would accept conservative attempts to *argue* that traditions should be maintained. But they would surely say that any conservative attempt to ban anything "untraditional," or to imprison anybody who argues otherwise, is a violation of human rights. We should react the same way when Hindus in India, Buddhists in Nepal, Muslims in Egypt, or Catholics in Mexico attempt to do the same.

> *Our respect for the culture of others is therefore rooted in our respect for each community's attempt to answer the question of human life. And here we can see*

> *how important it is to safeguard the fundamental right to freedom of religion and freedom of conscience, as the cornerstones of the structure of human rights and the foundation of every truly free society. No one is permitted to suppress those rights by using coercive power to impose an answer to the mystery of man.*[3]

Even claims about "outsiders," illegitimate as they are, do not usually apply. Christianity has native adherents in almost every country and territory on the globe. There is an almost comic quality in listening to people who claim that Christianity is being spread only by foreigners. This claim is made even in India, where the indigenous Christian population outnumbers any foreign workers by a factor of some twelve thousand to one.

The idea that Christian ideas are being "imposed" on people is also faintly ludicrous, since in the situations we are discussing, Christians are usually minorities, are often poor and, invariably, the *victims* of coercion, not its practitioners.

It is also noteworthy that most of the regimes which repress "foreign religions" are those governments which repress *anything* that might weaken their grasp on power.

But beyond all these considerations is the fact that the people being persecuted are simply exercising their human rights as outlined in any genuine democratic constitution and as defined in international human rights law. These are fundamental human freedoms.

There is no law or valid norm that forbids people from believing that their beliefs are true and from trying to share those beliefs with others. This is precisely what human-rights activists, journalists, intellectuals, environmentalists, democrats, and feminists of all stripes do—committedly, persistently, and continually. This is the core of what free speech, free expression, and free association are all about. The freedom to express views and to attempt to persuade in the religious field is the same. As Michael Roan puts it, "The right to hold and assert truth claims is precisely what the freedom of religion or belief is about."[4]

Nor should minority groups, even minority groups that many people find annoying, be stigmatized as "sects." The United Nations special rapporteur on religious intolerance notes that there is no meaningful legal distinction between religions and sects. Religions are merely sects that have become successful. The repression of "sects" is simply one more form of religious persecution and should be opposed. The fact that most of us encounter Jehovah's Witnesses only when they knock on our door at the most inconvenient time is no excuse for failing to realize that they are simply exercising religious freedom and, worldwide, are among the most persecuted people.

It is true that many religious efforts can be insensitive and/or intensely annoying to the objects of their attention. Many observers, including Russian and western evangelicals, found the rapid influx of some American organizations into the former Soviet Bloc after its political collapse to be ill-advised, insensitive, and appalling.

But this is no grounds for the legal repression of organizations that upset others. There are no laws against being annoying. Journalists are frequently annoying: Often it's part of their job. Human-rights activists are annoying. Political opponents, especially radical ones, are annoying. In fact, anyone who challenges a given situation usually annoys people who are happy to remain in that situation.

In any situation where we are tempted to advocate repression of an unpopular religious group, we should ask ourselves whether we would accept similar controls if the group were journalists, or feminists, or were advocating the defense of other human rights. We should be as reluctant to control groups in the religious sphere as we are in any other sphere.

The right to free speech includes a right to be annoying, since if the speech in question never upset or challenged anybody, then the issue of restricting it would never even arise. In the religious sphere as in other spheres, the proper response to annoying people is to criticize them, argue against them, or ignore them. But not to imprison or kill them.

The British used to have a joke about the late, unlamented East German car—the mother of all lemons—the Trabant. Question: "What's the difference between a Trabant and a Jehovah's Witness?" Answer: "You can close the door on a Jehovah's Witness."

There are, of course, instances where attempts to spread beliefs involve coercion or manipulation. But such events involve a minuscule proportion of what is described in this book. These instances should not lead to any blanket condemnation of, or restriction on, freedom of expression in the religious field. As the UN special rapporteur notes, "These instances properly fall under the strictures of good criminal law." This covers "respectful public order, trickery, fraud, non-assistance, prostitution, illegal practice of medicine, etc. Genuine hazards posed by religious sects are adequately covered by such laws; laws which specifically target smaller religious groups are not needed, and raise dangers of their own." He adds, "In the last analysis, it is not up to the state or any community to assume the guardianship of the conscience of people or to censure religious beliefs."[5]

APPENDIX F

A Brief History of Orthodoxy

The Orthodox churches trace themselves back through the Roman Empire. After the western half of the Empire collapsed in the fifth century, the East continued for another thousand years based in Constantinople (now Istanbul), the city of Constantine, who first made Christianity its official religion. Byzantium, the eastern branch of the empire, maintained close links between the emperor and the church. Though they had distinct tasks, they were united in a "symphony," a joint mission. This pattern, symptomatic of the "second Rome," was dominant in the eastern Mediterranean, the Middle East, and North Africa. On its home ground, it lasted until the Ottoman Turks conquered Constantinople in 1453.

Fearful of having the center of the Holy Roman Empire under the control of Islam, Orthodox authority was transferred north to Moscow, which had accepted Orthodoxy nearly five hundred years earlier. Russian rulers married into the family of the last Byzantine emperor, and Ivan III appropriated the title of Caesar, rendered in Russian as *Czar*. Philotheus of Pskov, in a famous and well-remembered prophecy, proclaimed to Czar Basil III that: "Two Romes have fallen. A third stands fast. A fourth there cannot be."

These roots have made the Orthodox more likely to become intertwined with state power.[1] Other branches of Christendom have also shown such tendencies, but Orthodoxy's subsequent, and often tragic, history has reinforced them.

Since the Orthodox churches existed in the original heartland of Christianity, they were those most affected by the early spread of Islam. The churches in the Arabian Peninsula and North Africa were consumed almost entirely. Those in Egypt, Palestine, Syria, and Armenia came under Muslim control that often exists to this day.[2]

The same pattern was repeated further north. Christianity spread into the Ukraine from 988 onwards. The word "Cyrillic," describing the Russian alphabet, is derived from Cyril, who along with Methodius, was the original Orthodox missionary to the Slavs. Cyril composed the alphabet to help the spread of Christian teaching.

Two hundred years later, this area also fell under Muslim control with the sack of Kiev by the Mongolian Tartars. Islamic control lasted from the thirteenth to the fifteenth centuries (longer than the Crusader incursions into the Middle East). The name "Slav" comes from the fact that many were sold as slaves to Muslim countries. The trade was so pervasive that the name "slave" came to be applied to an entire people.

The Ottoman Turks, after taking Constantinople, subsequently conquered Southeastern Europe and advanced as far as Vienna. In the case of Greece, this control ended only in this century. One consequence of the Ottoman control is the Muslims of Bosnia. Though much of this history is forgotten in the West, it is remembered ferociously in the East. Many Serbs now castigate the Bosnian Muslims as "Turks," and try to identify them with their own ancient oppressors.

Islamic control of the Orthodox has affected them in three ways relevant to our concerns. Firstly, they were shaped by a history in which religious bodies set the rules for the entire society—by force, if necessary. The other patterns are related to the *millet*, the Turkish variety of the *dhimmi* system.[3]

Within this system, Christian (and Jewish) communities were allowed to manage their internal affairs, not just as congregations but as entire communities, providing that their external relations were controlled by the Islamic authorities, and that they accepted a subordinate status. This had two consequences. One was that the expression of nationality, the sign of who they were, became the church. The second was that church leaders became the central authorities within the subordinate Christian community. They administered the community's affairs and represented it to the higher authorities.

The history of the Orthodox churches under this occupation was, and is, often a brave one. Many of them have survived under a situation of oppression for up to thirteen hundred years and have been largely forgotten by the outside world. This past has often led them to identify themselves with the nation and the nation with themselves. It is doubtful whether they could have survived otherwise. Nevertheless, it has reinforced Orthodox claims to have exclusive religious jurisdiction over the people in its territory. Other religious bodies are often cast as "interlopers."

In Russia, the experience of the church under the Czars reinforced this. The Czars understood themselves, or pretended to understand themselves, as Christian emperors, inheritors of the Holy Roman Empire, and defenders of the faith. They sought to control the church while the church, in turn, saw itself as an associate of the state in governing the Russian people.

It was in this setting that the Bolshevik Revolution took place in 1917. Even this revolution drew on much that had gone before. But the Communists introduced a level of discrimination, repression, and massacre beyond that of previous tragic Orthodox sufferings. The Orthodox churches in the Old Soviet Union have only, in the last five years, begun to emerge from a nightmare which few of us can imagine. They are emerging into a plural world in which ideas and movements are spreading rapidly in areas they had previously regarded as their own. And they are emerging shaped by a history which has given them little experience for dealing with it.

APPENDIX G

Christianity in Soviet Russia

The Russian Communists experimented with, developed, and perfected many of the techniques of repression and control described in Chapter Four on current Communism. Already, in January 1918, Lenin instituted regulations to control the church. It was forbidden to have legal status, its land was removed, and it was forbidden to be involved in education. From 1921, the content of sermons was controlled. In 1922, the regime began a policy of demanding that churches register, and then refusing to register them, thus making them illegal. In 1923, many churches were expropriated: Two-thirds of the monasteries were closed.

In March 1922, Lenin told the Politburo that as many as possible "representatives of the reactionary clergy" should be shot, to teach "such a lesson that they will not dare think about any resistance whatsoever for several decades."[1] In the first six years of Soviet rule under Lenin, twenty-eight Russian Orthodox bishops and more than twelve hundred priests were killed.[2]

The Communists also instituted a program of daily discrimination against believers, restricting them from employment and educational opportunities. The Party made particular efforts to ensure that capable and qualified clergy were excluded from the church. Through Party control, the government sought to ensure that candidates for the priesthood were, as much as possible, drawn from the less qualified. It also took particular delight in elevating corrupt clergy. As Lenin wrote to Gorky in 1913, Communists ought to tolerate "a priest who violates young girls," but not one upright and well-educated.[3]

In this period, the church leaders struggled, often with great suffering and great courage, to resist Communist control. The first patriarch under Bolshevism, Tikhon, was imprisoned for his resistance. Despite the fact that after his release in 1923, he expressed loyalty to the Soviet state, he died in 1925, probably at the hands of the secret police.

His acting successor, Metropolitan Peter, refused to register the church under the prevailing conditions, and he too was imprisoned. His replacement, Sergei, felt that he had to seek registration, but he still resisted so that in December 1926, he too was arrested, along with 117 other bishops. The authorities tried to persuade Metropolitan Kirill to succeed him, but he resisted. The day of his interview, he was sent back into Arctic exile, where he died seventeen years later.[4]

After Kirill, the regime tried to use Sergei again and, after his prison term, he was a little more compliant. During this period, large numbers of bishops and clergy were exiled to camps in the Arctic. In the prison camp on the Solovetiky Islands, formerly a monastery, three hundred were executed on a single night in October 1929.

Other examples could be given. The history of the Orthodox Church under Communism has never been one of simple subservience. Many of those who cooperated with the regime did so because they believed that some measure of cooperation and compromise was preferable to the outright eradication of the church which they thought would ensue if they did not go along. Even those who seemed to cooperate too much did so often only after a spell in prison.

People who have never faced such a situation should not easily judge those who have. In the same circumstances, most of our performances would likely be far worse.[5]

And here I have only written of the *official*, the "above-ground" church. Very many Orthodox developed underground, or catacomb, churches.[6]

Under Stalin, from the late 1920s onward, the repression became worse. By 1933, five hundred out of Moscow's six hundred churches had been closed. By 1941, ninety-eight out of every one hundred churches were closed.[7] In the 1920s and 1930s approximately two hundred thousand Russian Orthodox priests, monks, and nuns were slaughtered. A further half-million were imprisoned or deported to Siberia.[8] Of those sent to the Gulag Archipelago, 80 to 90 percent died in the camps. Many others of Stalin's tens of millions of victims also died simply because they were believers. According to the Russian State Commission investigating the NKVD and KGB archives, "Most priests were shot or hanged, although other methods used by Communist death squads included crucifying pastors on their church doors [or] leaving them to freeze to death after being stripped and soaked in water during winter."[9]

This frozen hell lasted until World War II when Stalin, seeking for any legitimacy and source of morale that he could find, wrapped himself closely in the flag of Russian nationalism and called on the Orthodox Church to rekindle the nationalist memories of "Holy Rus." For this to happen, they needed to have a public presence and so, gradually, restrictions were lifted. When the church tried to reconvene its Synod, it found that fewer than twenty of its bishops were still alive in the camps.

The next phase of repression began in the late 1950s and early 1960s under Nikita Khrushchev. Despite his reputation as something of a liberal in the West, Khrushchev's control of the churches, especially in the period 1959 to 1964, was worse than that of Stalin's later years. In a form of repression that even Americans might understand, priests had an income tax rate of 81 percent.[10] Additional legal methods were developed in order to further incriminate believers, and they were subject to violent assault.[11]

These patterns continued under Leonid Brehznev. By the time Mikhail Gorbachev came to power, there were fewer churches open in the Soviet Union than there had been when Stalin died.

ENDNOTES

Chapter One

1. William J. Kole, "France Mourns Monks Beheaded in Algeria by Muslim Militants," Associated Press, May 25, 1996. On August 1, 1996, Pierre Claverie, the Roman Catholic Bishop of Oran, was killed by a car bomb when returning from a ceremony honoring the slain monks, Associated Press, August 2, 1996.

2. Richard Land, president of the Christian Life Commission of the Southern Baptist Convention, testimony to hearing of the House Committee on International Relations, Subcommittee on International Operations and Human Rights, February 15, 1996.

3. Quentin Skinner, "Who Are We? Ambiguities of the Modern Self," *Inquiry 34* (1991), p. 148, an extended review of Charles Taylor, *Sources of the Self: The Making of the Modern Identity* (Cambridge, MA: Harvard University Press, 1989). See also Paul Marshall, "Quentin Skinner and the Secularization of Political Thought," *Studies in Political Thought 2* (1993), pp. 87–104.

4. Charles Taylor, "Comments and Replies," *Inquiry 34* (1991), p. 242.

5. James Finn, "The Cultivation and Protection of Religious Human Rights: The Role of the Media," pp. 161–189 of J. D. van der Vyver and J. Witte Jr., eds., *Religious Human Rights in Global Perspective: Legal Aspects* (The Hague: Martinus Nijhoff, 1996), p. 188.

6. World figures are given in Appendix D. Fifty-one percent of African Americans claim to be "born again" compared to national figures of 31 percent. Comparable figures for "religion very important in own life" are 82 percent vs. 58 percent. See "More Than Worship," *Orange County Register*, August 1, 1996. On the spread of Christianity throughout the world, see Samuel H. Moffett, *A History of Christianity in Aisa, Vol. I: Beginnings to 1500* (San

Francisco: Harper, 1992); Aziz S. Atiya, *A History of Eastern Christianity* (Kraus Reprint: Millwood, NY, 1991). In an otherwise distinguished essay, Samuel Huntington says, "Western Christians now make up perhaps 30 percent of the world's population, but the proportion is steadily declining, and at some point in the next decade or so the number of Muslims will exceed the number of Christians." Here there is some confusion between "Western Christians" and "Christians." The proportion of Western Christians is indeed declining but the proportion of Christians is increasing. Depending on definitions, the number of Muslims worldwide is one-half to two-thirds the number of Christians. See Huntington's, "The West: Unique, Not Universal," *Foreign Affairs*, November/December 1996, pp. 28–46, esp. p. 40.

7. Samuel P. Huntington, *The Third Wave: Democratization in the Late Twentieth Century* (Norman: University of Oklahoma Press, 1991).

8. George Weigel, "Catholicism and Democracy: The Other Twentieth Century Revolution," in Brad Roberts, ed., *The New Democracies: Global Change and U.S. Policy* (Cambridge, MA: MIT Press, 1990), pp. 20–25.

9. Vaclav Havel, *Letters to Olga: June 1979–September 1987* (London: Faber and Faber, 1988), p. 150.

10. *China: Religious Freedom Denied* (Washington: Puebla Institute, 1994), p. 13.

11. Matthew 2:7–9, 12, 16–18 (NJB).

12. Armando Valladares, *Against All Hope* (New York: Alfred A. Knopf, 1986), pp. 199–200, 380.

13. February 9, 1996. A preliminary survey of this persecution is given in Kim Lawton, "The Persecuted Church Stands Faithful," *Christianity Today*, July 15, 1996, pp. 54–61, 64.

14. *Detained in China and Tibet* (New York: Human Rights Watch, 1994), p. 2.

15. The Baroness (Caroline) Cox and John Eibner, "Report to United Nations Human Rights Commission: Evidence On Violations of Human Rights in Sudan," *Christian Solidarity International*, April 1996, p. 4.

CHAPTER TWO

1. *The Observer*, London, June 5, 1994.

2. David Little, John Kelsay, and Abdulaziz Sachedina, *Human Rights and the Conflicts of Culture: Western and Islamic perspectives on Religious Liberty* (Columbia: University of South Carolina Press, 1988).

3. I am deliberately avoiding the word *fundamentalist*, a word of American origin to describe an American phenomenon and of doubtful and unclear meaning even there. It psychologizes religion and suggests invidious parallels as though American Christian fundamentalists were budding "ayatollahs." One does not need to sympathize with such so-called fundamentalists to realize that this is a vicious parody. The word *fundamentalist* should be abandoned as the piece of pop sociology it is. The University of Chicago Press has published a multivolume series as a world survey of fundamentalism in a project called "The Fundamentalism Project." The material provided by the project is insightful and worthwhile, and its leader Martin Marty is a careful and considerate scholar. But unless it assumes it from the outset, the project is not having much success in showing that there *is* a discrete phenomenon which can properly be called fundamentalism. See Martin Marty and R. Scott Appleby, eds., *Fundamentalisms Observed, Fundamentalisms and Society, Fundamentalisms and the State, Accounting for Fundamentalisms* (Chicago: University of Chicago Press, 1991–1994).

4. There is a tendency in the West to describe the Shi'a as extremist and the larger Sunni schools as moderate. This is misleading. The difference is not in depth or fervency of commitment to Islam, but in a different "denominational" understanding of the way Islam is to be followed. If we were looking for some sort of western parallel, the Shi'ites might be akin to charismatic Pentecostals, and the Sunni to strict Presbyterians. The Shi'ites actually can be more open to Islamic innovation than Sunnis, but unfortunately, this usually means stricter innovation.

5. "Widespread enslavement of Black African Southern Sudanese by Arabic PDF Militia," report on visit to Sudan, October 23–28, 1995, *Christian Solidarity International*, Zurich, October 30, 1995.

6. *Economist*, June 24, 1995.

7. See Joseph R. Gregory, "African Slavery 1996," *First Things*, May 1996, p. 37–39.
8. For example, there is an almost universally ignored conflict in northeastern Sudan in the Eritrea-Sudanese borderlands. Here, the war is wreaking devastation upon approximately three million Beja people who are non-Arab Muslims. See CSI Draft Preliminary Report on visit to this area January 7–15, 1996, Zurich, January 15, 1996.
9. See, for example, *Sudan: Monitoring Human Rights* (London: Amnesty International, October 1995); *Sudan: The Tears of Orphans—No Future Without Human Rights* (New York: Amnesty International, January 1995).
10. Testimony by Kevin Vigilante, representing the Puebla Program on Religious Freedom of Freedom House before the House Subcommittee on International Operations and Human Rights, March 13, 1996. See also *Sudan: Progress or Public Relations?* (New York: Amnesty International, May 29, 1996). See also "The Flourishing Business of Slavery," *Economist*, September 21, 1996.
11. CSI report on visit to Sudan, October 23–28, 1995, Zurich, dated October 30.
12. Puebla testimony, March 13, 1996.
13. Reports of crucifixions were presented by several organizations to the forty-ninth meeting of the UN Human Rights Commission in Geneva, February 1993. Sections 167 and 168 of the 1991 Sudanese Penal Code include possible punishment for highway robbery of execution followed by crucifixion, if the offense involved murder or rape. Also see *Tears of Orphans*, Amnesty International.
14. March 12, 1996. Author was present during Biro's verbal testimony.
15. Bernard Levin, "Martyred for his Faith," *The Times*, February 15, 1994. Haik's church does not have bishops, but he was often called "bishop" as an honorific.
16. Kim A. Lawton, "Iran: Mehdi Dibaj," *Charisma*, October 1995, p. 59.
17. Yossef Badansky and Vaughn S. Forest, "Islam Against the Church," Task Force on Terrorism & Unconventional Warfare, House Republican Research Committee, U.S. House of Representatives, January 19, 1994, pp. 6–7.

18. "Killings of Church Leaders Signal New Crackdown," *The First Freedom*, Fall 1994, p. 10. On or about September 25, 1996, another church leader was found dead in suspicious circumstances. Mohammed Bagher Yusefi was allegedly found hanging from a tree and the authorities have refused to release his body. He had helped raise the two sons of Mehdi Dibaj after he had been murdered in 1996, *Compass Direct* news bulletin, October 3, 1996.

19. Robin Wright, *In the Name of God: The Khomeini Decade* (New York: Simon & Schuster, 1989), p. 181.

20. *Iran 1994: The Year of Assassinations*, Report by Middle East Concern, (Loughborough, UK, 1995) p. 10.

21. *International Herald Tribune*, August 2, 1994.

22. *The Continued Escalation of Persecution of Christian Minorities in the Islamic Republic of Iran*, Colorado Springs, Iranian Christians International, Inc., October 1, 1996. See also *The Status of Human Rights of Ethnic Armenian/Assyrian Christians in the Islamic Republic of Iran*, Iranian Christians International, Inc., October 1, 1996.

23. "Saudis Cracking Down," *On Being*, November 1993.

24. *News Network International*, "Two Baptist Filipinos Reported Released from Prison," November 22, 1995.

25. *News Network International*, op. cit.

26. Statement of Nina Shea, director of Puebla Program on Religious Freedom, to U.S. Congressional Human Rights Caucus, March 7, 1996.

27. *National and International Religion Report*, vol. 10, no. 1, December 25, 1995.

28. David F. Forte, "Apostasy and Blasphemy in Pakistan," *Connecticut Journal of International Law*, vol. 10:27, Fall 1994.

29. Statement before the Subcommittee on Near East and South Asia Affairs, U.S. Senate Committee on Foreign Relations, David F. Forte, professor of law, Cleveland State University, March 6, 1996. Forte quotes from the U.S. State Department, *Country Reports on Human Rights Practices for 1992*, p. 1171 (Washington D.C.: 1993).

30. *Frontier Post*, April 21, 1994.

31. *Patriot* (India), April 22, 1994; August 16, 1994.

32. Here and elsewhere, there is great difficulty in determining the exact Christian population of these countries. The governments in question have every interest in minimizing the number. For Pakistan, the *Economist* gives the figure of 1,200,000. Lahore Bishop Alexander John Malik puts the figure at over 4,000,000, *Asian Age*, February 13, 1995. Other Christian sources often put the number as double that. While Christians may exaggerate, most fairly secular sources consistently understate religious commitment because they have less contact with it.

33. *Patriot*, August 16, 1994.

34. *Asian Age*, March 8, 1996.

35. The bishop prefers to remain anonymous; interview with the author, December 8, 1994.

36. "Blasphemy Law," *Toronto Star*, February 19, 1995.

37. *The Observer*, London, June 5, 1994. There are also examples of intolerance and kidnapping by Coptic Christians. See "Coptic Girl Resists Abduction by Her Own Family," *Compass Direct*, August 22, 1996.

38. Again, exact numbers are impossible to come by. The government gives estimates of 4–5 million, some Christian groups estimate 12–13 million.

39. On this see Makram Samaan and Soheir Sukkary, "The Copts and Muslims of Egypt," *Muslim-Christian Conflicts: Economic, Political, and Social Origins*, ed. Suad Joseph and Barbara L. K. Pillsbury, (Boulder, CO: Westview Press, 1978). Barbara Watterson, *Coptic Egypt* (Edinburgh: Scottish Academic Press, 1988).

40. *Christian Science Monitor*, February 24, 1995.

41. "Two More Christians Murdered by Muslim Militants," *Compass Direct*, August 22, 1996. While in previous years the Egyptian Organization of Human Rights has done excellent work in defending Christians, as well as others, who suffer in Egypt, there are concerns that since 1993, they have been infiltrated by the Muslim Brotherhood and are, consequently,

downplaying the mistreatment of Christians. For example, in the case of Bothina Nienaa Faragallah, allegedly kidnapped by Islamists, EOHR did not investigate the case and merely published the answer of the police in November 1994. It did not publicize attacks on villages around Qena in September 1993, though this was carried even in Islamic newspapers such as *el-Shaab*, on September 17, 1993 and was reported directly to EOHR. When EOHR deals with the cases of converts, it tends to deal with them only as cases of torture, and usually only the well-known cases. They use the previous Muslim names of the converts and have not helped to get new ID documents. They are reluctant to have Christian lawyers in their team. While it still defends intellectuals, it seems to be less active than before 1994. Taken from a report on the EOHR, Cairo, January 6, 1996. Author wishes to have his name withheld.

42. *Christian Science Monitor*, loc. cit.

43. See Youssef M. Ibrahim, "The Fury of Egypt's Muslim Militants Is Falling on the Country's Christians," *The New York Times*, March 15, 1993.

44. Warren Cofsky, "The Implications of Egypt's Islamization for Coptic Christians: A Conversation with Muslim Author and Columnist Rifaat Said," *News Network International*, March 26, 1993, p. 38.

45. *Open Doors News Brief*, June 1992.

46. See stories in *The Times* (London), April 19, 1996; *Daily Telegraph*, April 19, 1996

47. Montgomery Watt, *Muhammad at Medina* (Oxford: Clarendon Press, 1956) Excursus F, v. 16, p. 359. My thanks to Dudley Woodberry for calling my attention to this.

Chapter Three

1. See Caroline Cox and John Eibner, *Ethnic Cleansing in Progress: War in Nagorno-Karabakh* (Zurich: Institute for Religious Minorities in the Islamic World, 1993), p. 54.

2. Let me emphasize again that there are very tolerant Muslim movements. One striking example is Crown Prince Hassan of Jordan and the Royal

Institute for Interfaith Studies, which he founded to promote dialogue and understanding between different religious groups. His 1995 book, *Christianity in the Arab World*, is hailed by many as an excellent work explaining to Muslims what Christianity is about. "New Royal Book and Institute Battle Religious Ignorance in Arab World," *News Network International*, November 17, 1995.

3. *Religious Liberty and Human Rights in Nations and in Religions*, ed. Leonard Swidler (Philadelphia: Ecumenical Press, 1986); M. Khadduri, *War and Peace in the Law of Islam* (Baltimore: The Johns Hopkins Press, 1955).

4. See David Little, John Kelsay, Abdulaziz Sachedina, *Human Rights and the Conflicts of Culture: Western and Islamic Perspectives on Religious Liberty* (Columbia: University of South Carolina Press, 1988), pp. 7f. See also Ann Elizabeth Mayer, *Islam and Human Rights: Traditions and Politics* (Boulder, CO: Westview Press, 1991). Mayer credits classical Islam as being less opposed to human-rights values than some of its more modern variants.

5. Bernard Lewis, *The Jews of Islam* (Princeton: Princeton University Press, 1984), p. 8. Sachedina, in Little et al, op. cit. p. 89, complains that Lewis' view contradicts various Qu'ranic stipulations. Lewis might even agree with this, but his point is not the ways in which the Qu'ran might be read but what has been the dominant practice in the Islamic world. For an excellent survey, see also Lewis' *The Middle East: A Brief History of the Last Two Thousand Years* (New York: Scribner's, 1996).

6. See Little et al., op. cit. pp. 8f; Muhammad Iqbal Siddiqi, *The Penal Law of Islam* (Lahore: Kazi Publications, 1979); Abdulrahman Abdulkadir Kurdi, *The Islamic State: A Study based on the Islamic Holy Constitution* (London: Mansell Publishing Limited, 1984).

7. *Human Rights Watch World Report, 1996* (New York: Human Rights Watch, 1995), p. 273.

8. Daniel Pipes, "The Western Mind of Radical Islam," *First Things*, December 1995, pp. 18–23; also see Abdullahi Ahmed An-Na'im, "Human Rights in the Muslim World: Socio-Political Conditions and Scriptural Imperatives, A Preliminary Inquiry," *Harvard Human Rights Journal*, vol. 13, 1990, pp. 13–52.

9. Mark Juergensmeyer, *The New Cold War? Religious Nationalism Confronts the Secular State* (Berkeley: University of California Press, 1993), p. 177.

10. The situation in Indonesia combines relative openness for Christians in most of the country with oppression in areas such as East Timor.

11. On April 6, 1995, U.S. Representative Ileana Ross-Lehtinen, chairperson of the House Subcommittee on Africa, said, "It is clear that Islamic extremists and militant groups pose a direct threat to regional stability, to the fragile democracies of the African continent, and to U.S. Security interests," Brittney A. Lindsey, "Experts Warn of Security Threat from African Islamist Expansion," *News Network International*, April 21, 1995.

12. Willy Fautre, "Two More Catholic Nuns Assassinated," *News Network International*, September 22, 1995; Richard Nyberg, "French Nuns Assassinated in Continuing Violence," *News Network International*, November 17, 1995.

13. *Los Angeles Times*, May 25, 1995.

14. See stories from *The New York Times* in Chapter Eight.

15. Abdelfattah Amor, *Report to UN Commission on Human Rights by Special Rapporteur on Religious Intolerance*, Geneva, December 1994, p. 10. Translation of last testament of Christian de Chargé provided by the monks of Mt. St. Bernard Abbey, Leicester, England, and printed in *First Things*, August/September 1996, p. 21.

16. Barbara Baker, "Salvadoran Christian Banned from Morocco for Five Years," *News Network International*, February 10, 1995.

17. *Human Rights Watch World Report, 1996*, p. 301.

18. *Freedom in the World: The Annual Survey of Political Rights and Civil Liberties* (New York: Freedom House, 1995), p. 91. Abdelfattah Amor, op. cit., p. 415; *Impact*, No. 6, January 1996, p. 2. In response to inquiries from the United Nations special rapporteur on religious intolerance, the Moroccan government said that while the Moroccan penal code forbids proselytism, it does not forbid conversion to Christianity as such. Abdelfattah Amor, op. cit., p. 61.

19. *Impact*, loc. cit.

20. Barbara Baker, "Extremists Attempt to Bomb Greek Orthodox Patriarchate," *News Network International*, June 14, 1994; "Fanatic Islamist Group Bombs Istanbul's Greek Patriarchate," *Compass Direct*, October 17, 1996.

21. Hans Chabra, "Assyrian Christians Report Increased Pressure from Muslim Kurds," *News Network International*, June 14, 1994.

22. Abdelfattah Amor, op. cit., pp. 102–103.

23. An excellent survey of the situation in Turkey is given in "La Turquie face à ses minorites," *Droit de l'Homme san frontierès* (Brussels), vol. 7, nos. 1–2, 1995.

24. *Freedom House News*, May 29, 1996.

25. Barbara Baker, "No Arab Has Walked This Road Before," *Compass Direct*, April 23, 1996; "Kuwait Religious Court Finds Christian Convert Guilty of Apostacy," Press Release, *Freedom House News*, May 29, 1996; "Support Grows for Christian Sentenced to Die," *The Times* (London), July 8, 1996. Hussein left Kuwait for an undisclosed location in the United States in late August 1996. Sources close to the situation also report that Hussein is facing difficulties adjusting to his new circumstances.

26. *Freedom in the World*, p. 347.

27. "Punishing the Victim: Rape and Mistreatment of Asian Maids." *Middle East Watch, Women's Rights Project*, vol. 4, issue 8, August 1992.

28. See *Human Rights Watch World Report, 1996*, pp. 293–296.

29. Andrew Wark, "Christians Say Religious Liberty Endangered by Government's Islamic Policies," *News Network International*, September 19, 1994.

30. *Freedom in the World*, p. 582.

31. Barbara Baker, "Dubai Court Jails Briton for Distributing New Testaments," *News Network International*, December 21, 1993. British Vice Consul David Gessing said, "As far as we're concerned, the law has taken its course. It's not for myself or anyone else to question the laws of the UAE."

32. *Freedom in the World*, p. 473. Two Indian Christians, M. V. Babu and Samuel Philip, were arrested in January 1993 for holding an unauthorized prayer meeting, *Amnesty International Report 1995* (London: Amnesty International, 1995,) p. 240.

33. *Freedom in the World*, p. 444.

34. In July 1994 radical Islamic elements ransacked a Catholic church used by expatriates, *Freedom in the World*, p. 610. Members of the Sisters of Charity and the Salesian Fathers, who focus on work with the poor and the sick, have been harassed since July 1994. Abdelfattah Amor, op. cit., p. 109.

35. *Freedom in the World*, p. 565.

36. op. cit., p. 397.

37. op. cit., p. 519.

38. op. cit., p. 91; Abdelfattah Amor, loc. cit.

39. Richard Nyberg, "Isolated Island-Nation Remains Closed to Christians," *News Network International*, May 5, 1995.

40. *Freedom in the World*, p. 388.

41. *Amnesty International Report*, op. cit., pp. 205–206.

42. op. cit., p. 69.

43. Ajay Ghosh, "Muslims Push for Adoption of Blasphemy Law," *News Network International*, July 6, 1994.

44. Andrew Wark, "Muslim Extremists Demand Expulsion of Korean Missionaries," *News Network International*, March 24, 1995.

45. Abdelfattah Amor, op. cit., p. 19.

46. Ajay Ghosh, "Christians Fear Political Crisis Could Yield Blasphemy Law," *News Network International*, February 10, 1995.

47. See Kirk Albrecht, "Christians Continue to Face Pervasive Discrimination," *News Network International*, February 23, 1994.

48. Federal Constitution, Article 124, Section 3b, ii., One "who professes the religion Islam, habitually speaks the Malay language, (and) conforms to Malay custom," *Asia Week*, August 3, 1994.

49. Personal interview by author with Archbishop Soter Fernandez, head of the Catholic Church in Malaysia, August 18, 1994.

50. Personal interview by author with Daniel Ho and Oo Chin Aik, Kuala Lumpur, August 17, 1994.

51. See Andrew Wark, "Malaysia Consolidates its Islamization Campaign," *Special Report: News Network International*, August 17, 1994; "Christians in East Malaysia Fear Encroachment of Islamic Society," *Special Report: New Network International*, September 7, 1994. The situation varies in the different Malay states. In Sabah and Sarawak, on the Island of Borneo, and with a larger Christian presence, there is far more openness than in the parts of Malaysia attached to the Asian mainland. In the 1980s, the government gave grants toward the construction of churches in these two states.

52. Some estimates put the number of immigrants as high as 800,000 out of a total population of about 1.5 million, *Economist*, February 26, 1994.

53. Abdelfattah Amor, op. cit., p. 59.

54. *Economist*, January 22, 1994.

55. There are also reports that officials have banned religious worship among Vietnamese refugees, *Orange County Register*, May 17, 1996.

56. *Economist*, March 30, 1996.

57. For background, see *Indonesia and the Rule of Law* (Geneva: International Commission of Jurists, 1987), especially pp. 141–145, "Freedom of Religion and Belief."

58. Paul Marshall, "Irian Jayans Say Policies Undercut Traditional Christians," *News Network International*, September 7, 1994; interviews in Ambon and Timor.

59. "Ten Churches in Indonesia destroyed by Muslim Mobs," *Compass Direct*, June 20, 1996; "Muslim Rioters Kill Five Christians and Torch Churches in Indonesia," *Compass Direct* news bulletin, October 16, 1996. Abdurrahman Wahid, the chairman of Nahdlatul Ulama, apologized to the churches for the incident and called on people of all faiths to help the Christians rebuild the churches, "Muslims Offer Olive Branch to Christians," *Compass Direct*, November 22, 1996. Indonesia's other major Muslim leaders also denounced the attacks.

60. Andrew Wark, "Church Worker Murdered in Northern Sumatra," *News Network International*, June 14, 1994.

61. *The Straits Times* (Singapore), August 6, 1994.

62. Some situations are hard to classify. These include Lebanon and the areas under the new Palestinian Authority. Palestinian Christians have suffered along with other Palestinians in the conflict with Israel and the region's various wars. Now they suffer an additional burden due to the increase of radical Islamist movements among Palestinians, particularly Hamas. Many fear for the future, and large numbers of Palestinian Christians have fled abroad. Meanwhile, in Lebanon in late 1993, Hezbollah, the Iran-backed, radical Shi'ite group, warned Lebanese Christians not to celebrate Christmas. Lebanon's own Shi'ite Leader, Sheikh Muhammad Mahdi Shamseddine, has condemned such action. Both he and Sheikh Muhammad Fadlallah publicly welcomed the Pope's proposed visit. cf. Kirk Albrecht, "Christians Fear New Wave of Violence," *News Network International*, March 15, 1994. The situation in Albania is hard to place in terms of the classification we have been using. At present, it has an authoritarian "post-Communist" government which, with some Muslim backing, has sought to exclude a role for the country's significant Greek and Orthodox minority. The Constitution of 1994 required that the heads of "large religious communities" be Albanian citizens, born in Albania, and have residence in Albania for twenty years. See "Albanian Church Seeks Support to Protect 'Religious Freedom,'" *ENI Bulletin*, October 24, 1994, p. 3. Consequently, bishops appointed by the Ecumenical Patriarchate in Istanbul to help Archbishop Anastasios have been refused entry. When the archbishop protested, there were rumors that he, too, might be expelled. Edmond Doogue, "Albanian Archbishop Astonished at Government Threat," *ENI Bulletin*, October 24, 1994, p. 4. This problem is compounded by the fact that, under Communist leader Enver Hoxha, the activities of the Orthodox and other religious groups were repressed so that the church within the country lacks resources and trained clergy. See Abdulfattah Amor, op. cit., p. 9.

63. Personal interviews with Timorese students, July 27, 1994. See also *The Weekend Australian*, July 9–10, 1994. Information on further demonstrations and killings is given in "Indonesia/East Timor: Deteriorating Human Rights in East Timor," *Human Rights Watch/Asia*, February 1995.

64. The sometimes quoted number of two hundred thousand seems to include all the deaths in the period, but many of these would, of course, have occurred anyway. I have taken the one hundred thousand figure from a letter from the Congressional Human Rights Caucus of the U.S. House of Representatives to President Clinton on November 16, 1993.

65. Foreign minister Ali Alatas calls it "gravel in our shoes." See *The New York Times*, November 13, 1994.

66. *The Times* (London), July 8, 1994.

67. The situation of the church in East Timor is described by EDA—Agence d'information des missions étrangerès de Paris, see, for example, *Dossier et documents—églises d'Asie*, no. 143, November 16, 1992; no. 164, November 1, 1993; no. 169, January 16, 1994.

68. *Economist*, February 18, 1995.

69. Personal interview, July 18, 1994.

70. For background see John G. Taylor, *Indonesia's Forgotten War: The Hidden History of East Timor*, (London: Zed Books, 1991).

71. "Gunmen Massacre Fifteen Non-Muslims in Southern Philippines," *News Network International*, June 14, 1994; Andrew Wark, "Gunmen Massacre Nine Non-Muslims in Bus Attack," *News Network International*, December 21, 1993.

72. *South China Morning Post*, April 6, 1996.

73. Andrew Wark, "Church Officials Fear Muslim Violence During Papal Visit," *News Network International*, January 16, 1995.

74. Andrew Wark, "Muslim Guerrillas Attack Christian Town, Killing Dozens," *News Network International*, April 21, 1995.

75. A good survey is given in "Intolerance et discriminations religieuses dans 40 pays d'Afrique," *Droits de l'Homme sans frontières* (Brussels), 6e année, no 3, 1994.

76. Richard Nyberg, "Christians on Alert Following Muslim attacks," *News Network International*, February 24, 1995.

77. Ayodele S. Gbode, "New Round of Violence Targets Christian Community in Kano," *News Network International*, July 15, 1995.

78. Nyberg, op. cit.

79. Richard Nyberg, "Muslim-Christian Tensions Grow After Attack on Churches," *News Network International*, February 24, 1995; "Religious and Ethnic Tensions High Following Clashes," *News Network International*, April 7, 1995; See also Ben Ephson, "Muslims Attack Christian Evangelistic Rally," *News Network International*, July 28, 1995.

80. Ben Ephson, "Christian Leaders Condemn New Round of Religious Clashes," *News Network International*, December 22, 1995.

81. Abdulfattah Amor, op. cit., p. 58.

82. *New York Times*, quoted in *The New Republic*, May 20, 1996, p. 9.

83. Brittney A. Lindsey, "Muslim-Christian Tensions Rise in Northern Liberia," *News Network International*, March 24, 1995.

84. Personal Interviews, Cyprus, December 1995.

85. Abdelfattah Amor, op. cit., pp. 56–57.

86. See articles by Richard Nyberg, *News Network International*, December 21, 1993. On December 27, 1993, the Reverend Greg Denysschen, a Reformed minister in Natal Province, South Africa, was threatened with assassination by Dawah College leader Rashi Suliman unless he apologized for comments made about Islam ten years earlier. This seems to be an isolated incident, but the likelihood is that such incidents will increase in South Africa's future. There are also reports from Chad of increasing harassment of Christians by Islamic militants. See "Christians Harassed and Threatened in Central Chad," *Compass Direct*, September 19, 1996.

87. *Globe and Mail* (Toronto), March 13, 1995.

88. Barbara Baker, "New 'Secret Law' Restricts Religious Literature," *News Network International*, May 19, 1995.

89. Felix Corley, "Religious Liberty Still a Casualty in East-West Crossroads," *News Network International*, November 3, 1995.

90. Barbara Baker, "Government Threatens Non-Muslim Religious Groups," *News Network International*, June 14, 1994.

91. Cox and Eibner, op. cit., p. 59.

92. John Le Carré has called some attention to the treatment of the Ingush in his latest novel, *Our Game* (London: Coronet, 1995). See also *The Ingush-Ossetian Conflict in the Prigordnyi Region* (New York: Human Rights Watch, 1996).

93. Rafik Osman-Ogly Kurbanov and Erjan Rafik-Ogly Kurbanov, "Religion and Politics in the Caucasus," pp. 229–266 of Michael Bourdeaux, ed., *The Politics of Religion in Russia and the New States of Eurasia* (London: M. E. Sharpe, 1995), p. 232.

94. "Report: Mission to Armenia and Nagorno Karabakh," *Christian Solidarity International*, October 7–12, 1995.

95. Cox and Eibner, op. cit., p. 45.

Chapter Four

1. Brother David with Lela Gilbert, *Walking the Hard Road, Wang Ming Tao*, (London: Marshall-Pickering, 1990); *Top Ten Priority List: Chinese Christians Persecuted for Religious Reasons*, (Puebla Program on Religious Freedom, Washington, D.C., December 1995).

2. Kent R. Hill, *The Soviet Union on the Brink: An Inside Look at Christianity and Glasnost* (Portland: Multnomah, 1991), p. 94. See also Appendix G on the Orthodox Church in the Soviet Union. On the complexities of registration, see Alex Buchan, "To Register or Not To Register," *Compass Direct*, September 19, 1996.

3. Personal conversations with several people present at the meeting.

4. *Detained in China and Tibet: A Directory of Political Prisoners*, produced by Asia Watch (Now called Human Rights Watch/Asia), (New York: Human Rights Watch, February 1994). See also the lists in Abdulfattah Amor, special rapporteur on religious intolerance, 1995 Report to United Nations Commission on Human Rights (Geneva: December 1994), pp. 135–143; "China: Religious Persecution Persists," *Human Rights Watch/Asia Report*,

vol. 7, no. 16, December 1995. This last report is a copiously detailed survey of the situation of religious believers. See also "Chinese Christians Persecuted for Religious Reasons," Puebla Program on Religious Freedom, May 1995 Update, pp. 7–8. See also the cover story, "China: God is Back" in the *Far Eastern Economic Review*, June 6, 1996.

5. On instances of repression of Christians, see *Amnesty International Report, 1995*, (Washington D.C.: Amnesty International, 1995).

6. *Freedom in the World* (New York: Freedom House, 1995), p. 191.

7. Nina Shea, "Free Harry Wu," *The First Freedom*, Summer 1995, p. 2.

8. "Out of the Chinese Gulag: In Conversation with Harry Wu," *Freedom Review*, November/December 1995, p. 47. Harry Wu, in a famous 1995 incident, was imprisoned by the Chinese government, something which has happened to him many times before, and has taken the lead in the West of exposing the *laogai* system.

9. Sometimes the CPA and the Roman Catholic Church are not entirely distinct since some CPA clergy privately recognize the Vatican, and Pope John Paul II has recognized several CPA appointed officials. See *China: Religious Freedom Denied* (Washington: Puebla Institute, 1994), p. 11.

10. These stories are taken from an advance review, "China's Savage Secret," by Ross Terrill of Zheng Yi's *Scarlet Memorial*, to be published in June 1996 by Westview Press, published in *The Washington Post National Weekly Edition*, April 1–7, 1996, p. 25.

11. *China: Religious Freedom Denied*, pp. 33–34.

12. *Detained in China and Tibet*, pp. 228–230.

13. Lists are given in *China: Religious Freedom Denied*, pp. 37–66. A beautiful, brief photographic essay on China's Catholics is given in "Chine: Les Catholiques du Silence," *L'Express*, April 4, 1996.

14. "China: Religious Persecution Persists," p. 8.

15. Nina Shea, testimony before the "Members Briefing on Religious Persecution" of the Congressional Human Rights Caucus of the U.S. House of

Representatives, dated March 7, 1996; "China: God is Back," *South China Morning Post*, June 10, 1966; "China Has More Catholics, More Repression," *Washington Post*, October 6, 1996.

16. "Letters from Christians in China," *China Insight*, May/June 1994.

17. P. H. Mullen, "New Eugenics Law and Population Control Program Spell Disaster for Chinese Catholics," *The First Freedom*, Spring 1995, p. 3. See also "Coercive Population Control in China," hearing before the U.S. House of Representatives Committee on International Relations, Subcommittee on International Operations and Human Rights, May 17–July 19, 1995.

18. Anthony P. B. Lambert, "Estimates of Fifty Million or More Christians In China Are Unrealistic," *News Network International—Special Report*, September 19, 1994, p. 8; "China Update," on Internet, September 23, 1996. See also Chan Kim-Kwong, "China's Protestant Reformation," *Far Eastern Economic Review*, November 3, 1994.

19. *Chang Ming* (Hong Kong, May 1995) quoted in *China News and Church Report* (Hong Kong), June 2, 1995.

20. *China News and Church Report*, loc. cit. A translation of the document is given in Human Rights Watch/Asia, "China: Religious Persecution Persists," pp. 41–42.

21. *South China Morning Post*, December 24, 1994, quoted in *China News and Church Report*, January 13, 1995.

22. Editorial, *Toronto Globe and Mail*, August 23, 1994.

23. *The Observer* (London), September 17, 1995.

24. As is the case with most repressive regimes, the Laotian Constitution contains provisions for religious freedom. However, in day-to-day practice, these provisions are simply ignored. Links with believers in other countries require government approval, and the importation of religious publications is restricted. Laos' government continues to regard most religious expression, especially Christian expression, as violating the doctrine of, and control by, the Communist Party. At the same time, it "openly encourages Buddhism and supports Buddhist organizations. High-ranking government officials routinely attend religious functions and Buddhist clergy are prominently

featured at important state and party functions." (U.S. State Department Human Rights Report, 1995, Section on Laos.) Catholics and Protestants can operate in some parts of the country, particularly the central and southern areas. There seems to be a strategy whereby the government allows churches to remain open in areas more readily accessible to foreigners. However, in remote areas, the treatment is more draconian and information harder to acquire. Most of Laos' Protestant churches are severely controlled and have been forcibly closed. In Xiengkhuang, the government has driven Hmong Christian families into Vietnam. One woman in Phonsavan was forced to sell her home after Christians met there. In Sayabuly and Luang Prabang, Christian villagers have been forced to sign statements saying they would leave the Christian church. Government troops blockaded villages until the people signed. Buavan, the previous leader of the church in Luang Prabang, was arrested in Tha Kaek in June of 1994 and later that year police informed Christian leaders that he had died in custody. (Information drawn from December 30, 1994 letter from Laos quoting eyewitness reports. Author wishes to remain anonymous.) Late 1994 seemed to mark a new repressive phase. As of September 1995, all known Protestant and Catholic churches in the northern Laotian provinces of Sayabuly, Luang Prabang, and Xieng Khuang have been forced to cease operations due to a government campaign to coerce Christians into renouncing their faith. Similar tactics have been reported in Bolihmasy, Cham Muon, and Attopeu provinces and, since July 1995, several churches in the province of Vientiane have been forced to meet in homes. A senior church leader from Luang Prabang, Reverend Tong La, remains imprisoned despite the fact that his six-month sentence (for cutting down trees on his own property) has expired. Government cadres have gone through villages demanding that Christians sign affidavits in which they agree "not to propagate religious faith, not to attend church, and not to pray for divine healing when sick." Andrew Wark, "Tribal Christians Still forced to Recant Faith," *News Network International*, May 5, 1995. This seems to stem from a May 1995 directive to Communist Party cadres that they must combat two enemies in the coming year—corruption and Christianity. Andrew Wark, "Officials Continue to Harass Protestant and Catholic Churches," *News Network International*, September 11, 1995.

25. *Vietnam: Free Market, Captive Conscience* (Washington, D.C.: Puebla Institute, 1994), pp. 50–52.

26. A good survey is given in *Freedom in the World* (New York: Freedom House, 1995).

27. *The First Freedom: A Newsletter of the Puebla Institute*, Spring 1995, p. 2.

28. An excellent survey is given in *Vietnam: Free Market, Captive Conscience*.

29. *Vietnam: Free Market, Captive Conscience*, pp. 40f.

30. Abdulfattah Amor, special rapporteur, 1995 Report on Religious Intolerance, *United Nations Commission on Human Rights*, pp. 106–109.

31. Amor, op. cit., p. 108.

32. *Human Rights Watch World Report, 1996*, p. 183.

33. Nina Shea, testimony before joint hearings by the U.S. House of Representatives Subcommittees on International Operations and Human Rights and on Asia and the Pacific, November 7, 1995 (Testimony dated November 8, 1995). An August 1996 letter from Vietnam, "Some Protestant Prisoners of Conscience in Vietnam as of August 1996," (author's name withheld) lists thirteen recently imprisoned Protestants; "Christian Symbol Lands American in Vietnam Jail," *Washington Times*, November 19, 1996.

34. Andrew Wark, "Vietnam at the Crossroads," *News Network International*, February 23, 1994.

35. "Castro Bears Down on Evangelicals," *The First Freedom*, Fall/Winter 1995, p. 7; *Human Rights Watch*, op. cit., p. 86; *Compass Direct*, April 23, 1996, p. 5.

36. A good political overview is given in *Freedom in the World 1994–95*, pp. 208–210.

37. The best survey of the treatment of religion is in *Cuba: Castro's War on Religion* (Washington, D.C.: The Puebla Institute, May 1995.) See especially pp. 7–11.

38. *Human Rights Watch World Report, 1996*, p. 86.

39. *Cuba: Castro's War on Religion*, p. 21.

40. "The relatively few remaining Cuban nuns have continued to be allowed to tend homes for the aged, lepers, and the mentally retarded. Castro himself

has roundly praised their efforts, saying, 'Eighteen sisters can do the job of two hundred nurses.' In 1987, Mother Teresa's order, the Sisters of Charity, finally obtained permission to operate in Cuba after being refused for many years. In 1988, Castro told a visiting American inter-faith delegation that nuns 'work hard and do with little; they are model Communists, and we could use one thousand more.'" *Cuba: Castro's War on Religion*, p. 13.

41. "Cuba Survey," *The Economist*, April 6, 1996.

42. *Cuba: Castro's War on Religion*, pp. 34–35.

43. "Evangelical Christians Face Troubling Times," *News Network International*, February 6, 1996.

44. *Washington Post*, October 23, 1995.

45. Letter from a North Korean Christian to Reverend Isaac Lee, director of Cornerstone Ministries, quoted by Andrew Wark, "North Korea's Hidden Church," *News Network International*, January 16, 1995.

46. In one of history's more tragic developments, it is likely that the first Christian to set foot in Korea was a Catholic chaplain attached to the marauding army of the Japanese Shogun, Hideyoshi, in the late sixteenth century.

47. Conversation with Korean church historian Dr. Horace Underwood, Seoul, April 16, 1996.

48. See surveys in *Freedom in the World; Amnesty International Report, 1995*.

49. Ann Himmelfarb, "Christianity in North Korea: Politics by Other Means," *America*, May 9, 1992, p. 411.

50. See Chapter Seven on the WCC and Erich Weingartner, "North Korean Christians: First Official WCC Visit," *One World* (An official WCC publication), April 1986.

51. In January 1995, on a visit to the United States, hosted by evangelist Billy Graham, Chang Jae Chol, chairman of the Korean Catholic Association, said that "if and when" South Korea's Cardinal Stephen Kim visited the north, he would be asked to ordain a North Korean priest. See Andrew Wark, "North Korea Invites South Korean Catholic Priest to Pyongyang," *News Network International*, February 24, 1995.

52. Himmelfarb, op. cit., pp. 412–413. Himmelfarb also notes that the congregation might appear lifeless not necessarily because they were insincere but because any display of enthusiasm could mark them out to security officials. See also testimony by Nina Shea to the "Members Briefing on Religious Persecution" of the Congressional Human Rights Caucus of the U.S. House of Representatives, March 7, 1996.

53. See Andrew Wark, "North Korea's Hidden Church," *News Network International*, January 16, 1995.

54. Wark, op. cit.

55. Amnesty International, op. cit., p. 184.

56. Wark, op. cit.

Chapter Five

1. "Two Christian Women Stripped, Molested," *Pioneer* (India), July 13, 1994.

2. See, for example, the official response by India of November 17, 1994, to the UN special rapporteur on religious intolerance, given in Abdulfattah Amor, *1995 Report on Implementation of the Declaration on the Elimination of All Forms of Intolerance and of Discrimination Based on Religion or Belief* (Geneva: United Nations, December 22, 1994).

3. Mark Juergensmeyer, *The New Cold War? Religious Nationalism Confronts the Secular State* (Berkeley: University of California Press, 1993), p. 80.

4. "Ultimate Sacrifice," *The Week* (India), March 26, 1995.

5. John Stratton Hawley, "Naming Hinduism," *Wilson Quarterly* (Summer 1991), pp. 20–34.

6. "Religion in Elections," *Hindustan Times*, January 1, 1996.

7. For a summary of these developments and their background, see John F. Burns, "Hindu Die-Hards Seizing Their Day in the India Sun," *New York Times*, May 20, 1996.

8. Quoted by Bindeshwar Pathak, "Fate of Dalit Converts," *Patriot* (India), September 19, 1994.

9. See B. A. V. Sharma, "Secular State and Civil Service" in V. K. Sinha, ed., *Secularism in India* (Bombay: Lalvani, 1968), pp. 44–70.

10. "Extend Benefits of Reservations to Dalit Christians," *National Herald* (India), March 2, 1994; "Christian Rally Demands Scheduled Caste Privileges," *Times of India*, March 3, 1994; "Uplift of Dalit Christians Urged," *Hindustan Times*, March 2, 1994.

11. In early 1995 the Kerala High Court quashed another form of discrimination concerning Christian marriage. Whereas other women could seek divorce on the grounds of adultery, cruelty, or desertion, for the previous fifty years, under Section 10 of the Indian Divorce Act, a Christian woman had to prove that her husband had been living in "incestuous" adultery, or adultery coupled with cruelty, or coupled with desertion. See "Christian Women," *Indian Express*, February 25, 1995.

12. Arun Schourie, *Maharastra Herald*, January 30, 1994, quoted in Ajay Ghosh, "Hindu Journalist Criticizes Christian Missionaries," *News Network International*, February 23, 1994; Figures are calculated from the U.S. Department of State Human Rights Report, India, 1996.

13. "Priest, Nun Held for Forced Conversion," *The Pioneer* (India), January 26, 1996.

14. Sometimes Hindus try to resolve this question by allowing people to be Christian as long as they are "Hindu Christians." A group of women in Sivakasi in the state of Tamil Nadu are types of "secret Christians." They say they are attracted to Jesus and accept him as their teacher. Their husbands accept this as long as they do not remove themselves from membership in the Hindu community. They cannot accept baptism or become members of local Christian communities, but will meet with other Christian women for prayer.

15. "Tension Over Priests' Murder," *Sunday Statesman* (India), September 4, 1994. See also Andrew Wark, "Five Catholic Nuns Beaten by Intruders at Convent," *News Network International*, April 21, 1995.

16. Sunil Dasgupta, "Assault on the Innocent," *India Today*, April 30, 1995.

17. "Bishop's Guidelines Scare Congress in Kerala," *Sunday Observer* (India), February 25, 1996.

18. "Crusade Against Christians," *India Today*, December 31, 1995.

19. Anil Stephen, "Security Concerns Rise for Nuns and Other Christian Workers," *News Network International*, September 8, 1995.

20. Herb Schlossberg, *A Fragrance of Oppression: The Church and Its Persecutors* (Wheaton: Crossway, 1991), p. 52.

21. The patron of the Nepal Buddhist Society, Prem Bahadur Shakya, in a paper entitled "The Wonder of Nepal," delivered in London in July 1989, claimed, "perhaps in no other country is there such a degree of religious tolerance as one finds in Nepal. . . . There is complete freedom in our country to practice any kind of religion." When he was asked why he did not mention Christians imprisoned in Nepal for practicing their religion, or the recent letter from members of the U.S. Congress to the king, complaining about the lack of religious freedom, Herb Schlossberg reports that "his answer was unintelligible." See *Church-State Relations and the Freedom of Conscience*, proceedings of the Third World Congress on Religious Liberty, July 23–26, 1989, p. 83, quoted in Schlossberg, op. cit., p. 55.

22. Ajay Ghosh, "Two Protestant Nationals Briefly Detained: Christians Fear Regression on Newly-Gained Religious Liberties," *News Network International*, March 15, 1994.

23. "Nepal Stumbles on Road to Religious Freedom," *The First Freedom*, Winter 1994.

24. Elisabeth Farrell, "Nepali Church Leader Identifies Eleven Detained Christians," *News Network International*, November 22, 1994.

25. Andrew Wark, "Church Leaders Optimistic Communist Victory Will Not Erode Religious Liberty," *News Network International*, December 8, 1994. The Communists were subsequently defeated in September 1995.

26. "Puebla Appeals to U.S. Embassy on Christians in Nepal," *The First Freedom*, Fall/Winter 1995.

27. In June of 1995, a Christian was arrested in the district of Surkhet and held for two weeks for an incident involving conversion in 1993. Andrew Wark, "Eleven Detained Christians Still Awaiting Trial," *News Network International*, July 14, 1995.

28. Ajay Ghosh, "New Alliance Seeks More Protection for Independent Churches," *News Network International*, February 24, 1995.

29. Edmund Doogue, "Sri Lanka's Conflict is Not Religious, Says President," *ENI Bulletin*, No. 12, June 20, 1995. A good overview is given in *Alliance* (Dehiwali, Sri Lanka), January/March, 1996, pp. 1–3.

30. Andrew Wark, "Christians Attacked in War with Tamil Rebels," *News Network International*, July 28, 1995. For background, see David Little, *Sri Lanka: The Invention of Enmity* (Washington D.C.: U.S. Institute of Peace, 1994).

31. Mark Juergensmeyer, op. cit., pp. 99f.

32. Ajay Ghosh, "Bishops Express Regret for Papal Remarks on Buddhism," *News Network International*, January 16, 1995.

33. Ajay Ghosh, "Uproar Over Papal Visit May Signal New Interreligious Tensions," *News Network International*, January 27, 1995.

34. Ajay Ghosh, "Christians Fear NGO Registration May Lead to Restrictions," "Christians Debate Issue of Induced Conversions," *News Network International*, May 10, 1994.

35. Andrew Wark, "Parliament Sidelines Controversial Religion Law," *News Network International*, May 19, 1995.

36. "Religious Liberty and Christianity in Sri Lanka," *Direction*, August 1994, p. 11.

37. Abdelfattah Amor, op. cit., p. 82. See also Ajay Ghosh, "Evangelicals Report Continuing Buddhist Aggravation," *News Network International*, May 10, 1994.

38. *Human Rights Watch World Report, 1996* (New York: Human Rights Watch, 1995), p. 173.

39. Juergensmeyer, op. cit., pp. 118, 121.

40. Abdulfattah Amor, op. cit., p. 62.

41. Official Statistics claim some 2,500 Christians, both Catholic and Protestant. Unofficial estimates put the figure as high as 10,000, *Reuters*, May 26, 1996.

42. Andrew Wark, "Mongolia to Strictly Regulate Christian Activities," *News Network International*, December 21, 1993.

43. Kim Lawton, "Constitutional Court Strikes Down Passages of Controversial Religion Law," *News Network International*, January 21, 1994.

44. Juergensmeyer, op. cit., p. 117.

45. Kim Lawton, "Christians Allege Deteriorating Social Climate for Non-Buddhists," *News Network International*, May 19, 1995; see also Abdulfattah Amor, op. cit., p. 63.

46. *Reuters*, May 26, 1996.

47. Shirley MacLaine, *Don't Fall Off the Mountain* (New York: Norton, 1980).

48. "Freedom Around the World," *Freedom Review*, January/February 1996, p. 66.

49. Department of State, *Human Rights Report*, Bhutan, 1995.

50. Abdulfattah Amor, op. cit., p. 21.

51. Dr. Martin Panter, "The Karen" report for Christian Solidarity International, 1994.

52. Department of State, *Human Rights Report*, 1995, Burma.

53. "Burma: Rape, Forced Labor, and Religious Persecution in Northern Arakan," *Human Rights Watch/Asia*, May 7, 1992.

54. Reports on this area tend to emphasize the ethnic character of these people, but their Christian character is also very important.

55. Dr. Martin Panter, "Report on a Visit to the Thai/Burmese Border February 6–10, 1995 for Christian Solidarity International," February 12, 1995.

56. Panter, "The Karen", loc. cit.

57. Panter, "The Karen", p. 4.

58. Melinda Reist, "Australian Committee Reports Allegations of Christian Rights Abuses," *News Network International*, November 17, 1995.

59. Reist, op. cit. See also the "Report On the Situation of Human Rights in Myanmar," prepared by the United Nations Special Rapporteur, Yozo Yakata, in early 1995.

60. *New York Times*, February 23,1996.

61. *Economist*, February 4, 1995.

62. Singapore has put restrictions on Jehovah's Witnesses and on Christian evangelism if it leads to any disruption of "public order." This could, in itself, be a legitimate type of restriction, one mentioned in international human-rights law. However, the Singapore government has a very expansive view of what might count as a threat to public order, reminiscent of some homeowners' associations in California or Florida. Anything that might disturb governmental harmony, interfere with business, or suppress property values could be deemed a threat to public order. In Japan, Christians have enjoyed a large measure of freedom since World War II. Christianity was first introduced into Japan by Jesuits in the sixteenth century and, at the time, it flourished. But in 1614 the authorities began an extermination campaign against believers. They were given the choice of renouncing their faith or dying. "Hidden Christians" remained secretly in remote areas, and their descendants exist as the "Kakure" to this day. (Mary Adamski, "Japan's 'Hidden Christians' Are the Subject of a Documentary," *Orange County Register*, May 20, 1996.) The next growth of Christianity came in the 1860s during the Meiji dynasty. There was relative freedom of worship but, during Japan's militarization in the twentieth century, Christians were required to subordinate their faith to the requirements of Imperial Shinto. Regrettably, Japanese church leaders also supported the military occupation of Korea and helped in enforcing the same demand on Korean Christians, many of whom died rather than submit. The first clear statements of repentance for this, and for the Japanese conduct of the war in general, appeared in a variety of church statements in 1995, on the fiftieth anniversary of the end of World War II. (Personal interview with Yoshiaki Yui, head of Japan Evangelical Christian Association's Social Action Commission, June 1995.) At present, the Christian community has two main concerns. First is the growth of government support for Shintoism, manifested in visits by government officials to the Yasakuni Shrine. The second is increased controls on religion in the wake of the nerve gas attacks on the Tokyo subway system, reportedly the work of the Aum Supreme Truth cult. The proposed new "fundamental law of religion" contains the restrictive stipulation that "religion is an internal affair of individuals." This could undercut any external religious behavior whatsoever. (Noriyoshi Mizufune, "Japan's Faithful Under Threat," *Far Eastern Economic Review*, April 4, 1996.)

63. The ongoing research on this period conducted at Yale University puts the figure at about 1.5 million.

64. A good survey of these developments is given in *Freedom in the World, The Annual Survey of Political Rights and Civil Liberties, 1994–1995* (New York: Freedom House, 1995), pp. 168–170.

65. A survey is given in Andrew Wark, "Cambodia's Church Comes to Terms with Its Past," *News Network International*, January 21, 1994.

66. Kim A. Lawton, "Abducted Relief Worker Faced Threats, Forced Labor," *News Network International*, June 14, 1994.

67. Andrew Wark, "Protestants Worry About Future Religious Climate," *News Network International*, December 8, 1994.

68. Andrew Wark, "Mom Barnabus," *News Network International*, January 21, 1994.

Chapter Six

1. Kent R. Hill, *The Puzzle of the Soviet Church: An Inside Look at Christianity and Glasnost* (Portland: Multnomah, 1991), p. 77.

2. *The Tablet*, December 23/30, 1995, pp. 1643–1644.

3. Jane Ellis, *The Russian Orthodox Church: A Contemporary History* (Bloomington: Indiana University Press, 1986), p. 313.

4. Dimitry V. Pospielovsky, "The Russian Orthodox Church in the Post-Communist CIS," pp. 41–74 of Michael Bordeaux, ed., *The Politics of Religion in Russia and the New States of Eurasia* (Armonk: M.E. Sharpe, 1995), p. 52. A survey of religion in the earliest years of glasnost is given in Michael Bourdeaux, *Gorbachev, Glasnost, and the Gospel* (London: Hodder and Stoughton, 1990).

5. Yves Hamant, *Alexander Men: A Witness for Contemporary Russia* (Torrance, CA: Oakwood Publications, 1995).

6. Pospielovsky, op. cit., p. 70.

7. John Dunlap, "The Russian Orthodox Church as an 'Empire-Saving' Institution," pp. 15–40 of Bordeaux, *The Politics of Religion*.

8. Lee Hockstader, "A Church's Painful Revival," *International Herald Tribune*, April 17, 1996; Paul Glastris, "A Mixed Blessing for the New Russia," *U.S. News & World Report*, June 24, 1996.

9. "Bosnia Serbs Hail Russian Nationalist," *Washington Post*, February 1, 1994.

10. Dunlap, op. cit., p. 19.

11. Pospielovsky, op. cit., p. 61.

12. Pospielovsky, op. cit, p. 55.

13. Michael Bourdeaux, "Glasnost and the Gospel: The Emergence of Religious Pluralism," pp. 113–127 of Bourdeaux, op. cit., p. 117. Bourdeaux also provides a partial list of mission agencies he regards as being very responsible in their work.

14. Personal interview, Minsk, April 26, 1993. Metropolitan Filaret of Minsk should not be confused with Metropolitan Filaret of Kiev.

15. Bourdeaux, op. cit., p. 118.

16. Pospielovsky, op. cit., p. 63.

17. Bourdeaux, op. cit., p. 123.

18. "Patriarch Blocks Last-Minute Drive for New Religious Freedom Law," *Keston News Service*, December 1995; *Liberty News*, vol. 1, May/June 1996, p. 3. See also Edmund Doogue, "Roman Catholic Warns about Russia's Religious 'Barbed Wire Fence,'" *ENI Bulletin*, May 23, 1995, p. 17; Philip Walters, "The Defrocking of Father Gleb Yakunin," *Religion, State, and Society*, vol. 22, no. 3, (1994), pp. 309–321; W. Cole Durham, Jr. et al. "The Future of Religious Liberty in Russia," *Emory International Law Review*, vol. 8, no. 1 (Spring 1994), pp. 1–66; Beverly Nickles, "Parliament Adopts Moderate Religion Amendment," *News Network International*, April 21, 1995; Lawrence A. Uzzell, "Yeltsin Statement Defends Religious Freedom," *Keston News Service*, November 22, 1996. On April 30, 1996, the Russian government also revoked the accreditation of the Jewish Agency and broke up one of its meetings in Pyatigorsk, see *Liberty News*, loc. cit.

19. Beverly Nickles, "Pentecostal Church Cites Increasing Harassment," *News Network International*, July 28, 1995.

20. "Religion Committee Chairman Killed in Auto Crash," *News Network International*, December 22, 1995; Michael Bourdeaux, "Death of a Deputy," *The Tablet*, December 23/30, 1995, pp. 1643–1644.

21. *The Tablet*, p. 1681.

22. For background, see David Little, *Ukraine: The Legacy of Intolerance* (Washington D.C.: U.S. Institute of Peace, 1991).

23. Jonathan Luxmoore, "Report Alleges Mafia Involvement in Patriarch's Death," *News Network International*, August 25, 1995.

24. A good survey is given by Bohdan Bociurkiw, "Politics and Religion in Ukraine: The Orthodox and the Greek Catholics," pp. 131–162 of Bourdeaux, *The Politics of Religion*. See also Little, op. cit.

25. Lauren B. Homer, "Religion and Law in the Ukraine," *East-West Church & Ministry Report*, Winter 1995, p. 2.

26. A good survey is given in Alexander F. C. Webster, *The Price of Prophecy: Orthodox Churches on Peace, Freedom, and Security* (Washington D.C.: Ethics and Public Policy Center, 1995), chapter 3, "The Romanian Religio-Political Symbiosis."

27. Webster, op. cit., p. 93.

28. Ibid. p. 94.

29. *Human Rights Watch World Report, 1996* (New York: Human Rights Watch, 1996), pp. 226–227. Willy Fautré, "Orthodox Militia Set Up to Terrorize Religious Minorities in Romania," *Compass Direct*, September 19, 1996. For other background on Protestantism in Eastern Europe, see Sabrina Petra Ramet ed., *Protestantism and Politics in Eastern Europe and Russia: The Communist and Post-Communist Eras* (Durham, NC: Duke University Press, 1992). Human Rights Without Frontiers and the Bulgarian Helsinki Commission have produced an excellent report, "Religious Minorities in Albania, Bulgaria, and Romania," *Human Rights Without Frontiers*, vol. 8, nos. 2–3, 1996.

30. *Human Rights Watch World Report, 1996*, pp. 208–209.

31. Jennifer S. Blandford, "Bulgarian Evangelicals Under Siege," *East-West Church and Ministry Report*, vol. 2, no. 2 (Spring 1994), p. 1.

32. Abdulfattah Amor, 1995 Report to the UN Human Rights Commission on Religious Intolerance, pp. 28–29.

33. Maryann B. Hunsberger, "Anti-Protestant Propaganda Restricts Religious Liberty," *News Network International*, August 17, 1994.

34. See Abdulfattah Amor, op. cit., p. 20; "Church Leader Fears Return of Totalitarianism in Belarus," *ENI Bulletin*, June 7, 1995, p. 16; Paul Marshall, "Political Uncertainty Clouds Future Religious Landscape in Belarus," *News Network International*, June 14, 1994; Willy Fautré, "Foreign Catholic Priests Denied Registration, Expelled," *News Network International*, February 6, 1996.

35. Willy Fautré, "UN Official to Investigate Charges of Religious Intolerance," *News Network International*, September 22, 1995.

36. Excellent background is given in *Greece: Religious Intolerance and Discrimination* (Brussels: Human Rights Without Frontiers, 1994). Under the dictatorship of General Mataxas (1936–1940), further restrictive laws on non-Orthodox were passed.

37. Kim Lawton, "Evangelicals Vote to Aggressively Resist Restrictions," *News Network International*, October 26, 1993.

38. *Greece: Religious Intolerance . . .*, pp. 23–26.

39. Kim Lawton, "Religious Minorities Allege Persistent 'Religious Racism,'" *News Network International*, October 26, 1993.

40. Lawton, op. cit.

41. op. cit., p. 8. See also *The Independent* (London), September 28, 1992.

42. *Greece: Religious Intolerance . . .*, p. 14.

43. See Rafik Osman-Ogly Kurbanov and Erjan Rafik-Ogly Kurbanov, "Religion and Politics in the Caucasus," pp. 229–246 of Bourdeaux, op. cit.

44. *Human Rights Watch World Report, 1996*, p. 198.

45. Felix Corley, "Recent Attacks Raise Concerns for Religious Minorities," *News Network International*, May 19, 1995.

46. Corley, op. cit.

47. Stephen F. Jones, "Georgia: A Failed Democratic Transition," Ian Bremmer and Ray Taras, eds., *Nations and Politics in the Soviet Successor States* (Cambridge: Cambridge University Press, 1993), p. 304.

48. Kim Lawton, "Protestants Allege Continuing Orthodox Attacks," *News Network International*, February 23, 1994.

49. Lawton, op. cit.; see also Abdulfattah Amor, op. cit., pg. 37.

50. Personal conversation with Ethiopian Protestants, Cyprus, December 1995. See also Nina Shea, "Letter to the Honorable Steven Coffey, deputy assistant secretary of state, Bureau of Democracy, Human Rights and Labor, Department of State," December 15, 1995. See also articles in *Feleg* (Addis Ababa), December 6, 1992 (1985 in the Ethiopian calendar).

51. There is comparatively little about persecution by Protestants in this book. One instance which might have been included is Northern Ireland. For most of this century, it certainly should have been included in such a book, since the Protestant majority has practiced pervasive discrimination against Catholics. And even now, the competing forces are largely identified by confessional background. However, the independence struggle seems to have moved, unlike many others in the world, away from religious identifiers. In the current negotiations, the question of political status seems to be paramount. As noted elsewhere, there are Protestant state churches in Western Europe. However, their discriminatory effects seem to be comparatively mild. In general, Protestants seem to have the best record in allowing religious freedom in recent decades, Catholics have the best record for solidarity with Catholic believers who are attacked, and the Orthodox have been the main victims of persecution.

52. James Walsh, "A Millennial Rending," *Time*, April 29, 1996.

53. Felix Corley, "Split Over Orthodox Loyalty Widens," *News Network International*, December 22, 1995.

54. Robert F. Goeckel, "The Baltic Churches and the Democratization Process," Bourdeaux, op. cit., pp. 202–225, p. 216.

55. Rebecca Schreffler, "Protestants Decry Continuing Discrimination by Catholics," *News Network International*, July 6, 1994.

56. *New York Times*, September 7, 1993.

57. Jane Ellis, op. cit., p. 482.

58. Jonathan Luxmore, "Non-Catholics Can Be Poles Too, Says Angry Lutheran Leader," *ENI Bulletin*, October 24, 1994.

59. Thomas S. Giles, "Concordat With Vatican Continues to Generate Controversy," *News Network International*, February 23, 1994.

60. See David Martin, *Tongues of Fire—The Explosion of Protestantism in Latin America* (Oxford: Basil Blackwell, 1990); David Stoll, *Is Latin America Turning Protestant?* (Berkeley: University of California Press, 1990).

61. Dafne Sabanes Plou, "Argentina's Protestants Battle for Equality with Roman Catholics," *ENI Bulletin*, June 7, 1995, p. 11.

62. "Argentina: Church and State Relations Excluded from Constitutional Reform," *News Network International*, August 17, 1994.

63. Djanira Blanco, "Court to Rule on Ban of Protestants from Military Bases," *News Network International*, February 10, 1995.

64. Djanira Blanco, "President Revokes Order Banning Non-Catholics from Bases," *News Network International*, April 7, 1995.

65. Kenneth D. MacHarg, "Rights Group Files Complaint to UN for Religious Discrimination," *News Network International*, July 28, 1995.

66. "Ecuador," *News Network International*, October 18, 1994.

67. There are, of course, violent attacks on Protestants, as well as Catholics and others throughout the region, by drug cartels, authoritarian governments, and guerrilla fighters. In Peru, the Shining Path guerrillas have targeted Christian leaders for assassination, and this has taken a brutal toll on the Quechua Tribes in the high Andes. Throughout Central America, authoritarian governments have targeted priests who work with the poor and campaign for human rights. I have not included these instances since, though they are clearly cases of persecution, they are not, in the sense I outline in Appendix C, cases of *religious* persecution because they involve people regardless of creed who are considered a barrier to those trying to hold or acquire power. Let me reemphasize that I am not focusing on the

suffering of Christians *per se*, nor on persecution *per se*, but on persecution *because of religion*. These brutalities grade into one another, of course, so the dividing lines I use are not strict boundaries but judgment calls.

68. Elisabeth Isais, "New Protestant Converts Pressured In Central Mexico," *News Network International*, June 16, 1995.

69. "Evangelical Church, Parsonage Destroyed in Acapulco," *News Network International*, November 1, 1994. See also Elizabeth Isais, "Five Towns in Mexico's Hidalgo State Persecuting Evangelicals," *Compass Direct*, July 25, 1996. Further attacks took place in September 1996 in Hidalgo and Oaxaca, "Religious Persecution Continues in Two Mexican States, *Compass Direct*, October 17, 1996.

70. Alan F. H. Wisdom, "Religious Freedom Hangs in the Balance," *News Network International*, April 12, 1994; Chris Woehr, "Exiled Christians Win Some Concessions Following Shootout," *News Network International*, August 17, 1994.

71. The preceding stories are reported in Elisabeth F. Isais, "Evangelicals Report Increasing Harassment in Oaxaca," *News Network International*, October 4, 1994; Chris Woehr, "Mayor Accused of Masterminding Attack on Christians Resigns," *News Network International*, October 18, 1994; Elisabeth Isais, "Protestants Continue to Face Harassment in Several Areas," *News Network International*, September 8, 1995; Elizabeth Isais, "New Catholic-Protestant Violence Claims Six Lives in Chiapas," *News Network International*, December 8, 1995.

Chapter Seven

1. "New Intolerance Between Crescent and Cross," *Wall Street Journal*, July 5, 1995.

2. Letter dated July 21, 1995.

3. I stress *Protestant*, since the Catholic record has been better. One can point to particular instances where Catholics have not dealt with these issues well, as I do in the section on "Peace with China and Islam." And American Catholics have often not responded where Protestants have been persecuted.

But this reflects that Protestants, who one would expect to be better informed on these matters, have not themselves raised them. There are also signs that several organizations, such as the National Association of Evangelicals and the Episcopal Church, are now addressing this issue in a more serious way. My purpose is certainly not to criticize or to malign these new efforts, nor what so many other Christians, as well as others, have done and are doing.

4. Letter dated August 2, 1995.

5. Dr. Frank Minirth, "Taking Care of . . . You," *Possibilities*, November/December 1994.

6. David F. Wells, *God in the Wasteland* (Grand Rapids: Eerdmans, 1994), pp. 114–115.

7. "The Cross Is a Minus Turned into a Plus," *Possibilities*, March/April 1991. Schuller does not imply that these blessings will be financial. Others are not so discreet. Television preachers such as Kenneth Copeland have no shame about promising big bucks for believers. He has tried his pitch in the Third World and, according to one ex-staff member, "is not so stupid as to promise them they're going to be millionaires, but maybe an extra donkey. . . ."

8. "If Madison Avenue executives were trying to attract people to the Christian life, they would stress its positive and fulfilling aspects. . . . Unfortunately, we . . . are so conditioned to . . . (this) that we are almost shocked when we learn that the first great principle of Christianity is negative. It is not, as some say, 'Come to Christ, and all your troubles will melt away.' It is as the Lord himself declared, 'If any man would come after me, let him deny himself. . . ,'" James Montgomery Boice, *Foundations of the Christian Faith* (Downers Grove: InterVarsity Press, 1986), p. 25.

9. Evangelical Christian bookstores offer an array, their subjects ranging from diet and fitness to angels. Large sections are devoted to counseling, marriage, family, and finance. Most of the fiction is romance, an escapist women's genre (sometimes called "sacred bodice-rippers") that has in recent years sent sales soaring, as witnessed by Christian best-seller lists. See *Christian Retailing*, September 11, 1995–April 8, 1996. During that same period the non-fiction bestsellers deal primarily with personal devotion, relationships,

families, and biblical prophecy. Not one title addresses matters beyond the United States.

10. John Seel, *No God But God* (Chicago: Moody Press, 1992), p. 66.

11. Paul Marshall, "Nationalism," World Evangelical Fellowship occasional paper, Wheaton, 1996.

12. (Dallas: Word, 1996).

13. (Colorado Springs: Focus on the Family, 1996).

14. In mid-1995, the Christian Coalition did write to President Clinton on this issue.

15. Howard Kohn, "Ideal Politics—Jim Wallis May Seem Like a Contradiction in Terms," *Los Angeles Times Magazine*, November 6, 1994.

16. Campolo continues, "Readers who are not from the United States may have to do some 'translating' to adapt some of this material to their own societal system. But, in the end, I am sure that Christians everywhere will fully understand the issues this book examines." Tony Campolo, *Is Jesus a Republican or a Democrat?* (Dallas: Word, 1995), p. xix.

17. I have used the term *fundamentalist* here since many conservative American Christians are quite happy to have the term applied to them, and use it themselves. By evangelicals, I mean Protestant Christians with a high view of biblical authority and a stress on personal faith. By fundamentalists, I mean those with a literal view of Scripture and a pronounced anti-intellectualism. By charismatics, I mean those who stress God's ongoing supernatural work in the church exemplified in healing and "speaking in tongues." In this chapter, I have usually lumped them together as "evangelicals," since that is a common collective designation, and the trends I am describing are common to all three. Nevertheless, there are many important differences between them, particularly about prophecy, and since they involve up to 30 percent of the U.S. population, they should not be slurred over in loose designations such as the "Christian Right."

18. Mark A. Noll, *The Scandal of the Evangelical Mind* (Grand Rapids: Eerdmans, 1994), p. 140.

19. Dave Hunt, *Global Peace and the Rise of the Antichrist* (Eugene, OR: Harvest House, 1996), pp. 219ff.

20. Hal Lindsey, *Planet Earth—2000* A.D. (Palos Verdes: Western Front, Ltd., 1994), p. 196.

21. Chronicles (2 Chronicles 26:17) describes how *God* brought up the King of Babylon against Israel. And Isaiah describes this as *God* giving Israel into Babylon's hand (Isaiah 47:6). But Babylon was described as doing evil, enslaving a people, and burning down the house of God. The prophet Jeremiah, in turn, denounced Babylon for its misdeeds. Some might protest that their aim is not to support anyone whose action may inadvertently have the desired end result, but rather to support those who are consciously trying to achieve what God has said will come about. But this too is a questionable procedure, clearly at odds with the Bible itself. It describes many instances of people doing evil, which evil was nevertheless turned to use by God. But it is not seen as justifying the actions.

22. Paul Marshall, "Follow Commandments, Not Prophecies in the Middle East," *Christian Week*, April 30, 1991.

23. Hunt, op. cit., pp. 37, 43.

24. Hunt, op. cit., pp. 43, 74, 98, 105, 110.

25. The book never made the best-seller lists given by most newspapers, since those newspapers rarely survey the outlets through which many Christian books are sold. This is another illustration of the secular ignoring of religion I describe in the next chapter.

26. Lindsey, *Planet Earth. . .* , p. 279.

27. "Christians give about 25 percent of their charitable donations to 'needy people in other countries.'" George Barna, *The Barna Report* (Ventura: Regal Books, 1993), p. 105.

28. One current example of these ongoing conflicts is the worldwide attention on the activities of the Toronto Airport Vineyard, where unusual charismatic manifestations have taken place (*Christianity Today*, January 8, 1996, p. 66). Toronto pastor John Arnott has written a highly-promoted book on the subject, *The Father's Blessing* (Orlando: Creation House, 1995). Another

is the fervent debate around the joint Catholic and evangelical convergence in the Declaration, "Evangelicals and Catholics Together." ". . . typically from the margins of evangelicaldom, the attack on ECT shows no signs of abating. Articles and books keep appearing. . . ." "While We're At It," *First Things*, March 1996, p. 75.

29. Kent R. Hill, *The Puzzle of the Soviet Church: An Inside Look at Christianity and Glasnost* (Portland: Multnomah, 1991), p. 175.

30. Interview with Doug Sutphen, East Gates founding president, April 1996.

31. Evangelical organizations have not been immune to maintaining diplomatic silence in order to safeguard access for Christian work. Billy Graham's trip to the Soviet Union in 1982 was widely criticized for downplaying religious persecution. After a trip to North Korea, the Billy Graham Evangelistic Association published a booklet [*North Korean Journey* (Minneapolis: World Wide Publications, 1994)], which passes over government repression.

32. The full name is the National Council of Churches of Christ in the United States of America, but National Council of Churches (NCC) is a more common designation.

33. Raymond L. and Rhea M. Whitehead, (New York: Friendship Press, 1978).

34. Whitehead, op. cit., pp. 21, 41, 43. Similar views are given in Ward L. Kaiser, ed., *China: People-Questions* (New York: Friendship Press, 1975), especially in the essay, "Religion: China," by Donald MacInnis, pp. 16–19. MacInnis was formerly director of the China Program of the NCC.

35. Peggy Billings, *Fire Beneath the Frost* (New York: Friendship Press, 1984).

36. Billings, op. cit., pp. 20, 21, 35.

37. *Religion and Democracy*, September/October 1988, p. 4.

38. Mary Lou Suhor, "Introduction," to Ward L. Kaiser, *Cuba: People-Questions* (New York: Friendship Press, 1975).

39. "Cuba Courts Black Churches," *Information Digest*, August 3, 1984; see also Fred Barnes, "The Jackson Tour," *The New Republic*, July 30, 1984.

40. Armando Valladares, "For the Record," *Washington Post*, July 17, 1983.

41. *New York Times*, June 21, 1984.

42. Robb and Robb, op. cit., p. 95.

43. *New York Times*, June 24, 1984.

44. Arie R. Brouwer, "Some Essential Elements of Ecumenical Credibility," speech to Governing Board of the NCC, May 13, 1987.

45. See, for example, "Resolution on Religious Intolerance in the USSR," February 22, 1968; "Violation of Religious Freedom and Human Rights," February 14, 1972; "Resolution on Reaffirmation of the National Council of Churches' Concern for Soviet Christian Refugees Residing in the Moscow U.S. Embassy," May 10, 1979; "Resolution on an Expression of Concern for Prisoners of Conscience in the USSR and Czechoslovakia," November 10, 1979; "Resolution on the Denial of Religious Liberty in Albania," May 12, 1983. There have also been a series of resolutions on Turkey, in 1955, 1957, 1979, and 1985. Its positions on China have been less forthcoming, perhaps because of the NCC's association with the China Christian Council and the Chinese Christian Three-Self Movement, both of them government-sponsored bodies representing only a minority of the Christians in China.

46. For further background, see K. L. Billingsley, *From Mainline to Sideline: The Social Witness of the National Council of Churches* (Washington, D.C.: Ethics and Public Policy Center, 1990); A. James Reichley, *Religion in American Public Life* (Washington: Brookings Institution, 1986); *A Time for Candor* (Washington: Institute on Religion and Democracy, 1983); Joshua Muravchik, "The National Council of Churches and the USSR," *This World*, Fall 1984, no. 9.

47. Paul Marshall, "National Council of Churches Soft-Pedals Cuban Religious Persecution," *News Network International*, November 17, 1995.

48. Gail V. Coulson, *The Enduring Church: Christianity in China & Hong Kong* (New York: Friendship Press, 1996).

49. Coulson, op. cit., pp. 32, 35, 36, 40, 42.

50. Albert M. Pennybacker, "Testimony Before the House Subcommittee on International Operations and Human Rights," February 15, 1996.

51. See Paul Marshall, "On the Universality of Human Rights," in Luis E. Lugo, ed., *Sovereignty at the Crossroads: Morality and International Politics in the Post-Cold War Era* (Totowa: Rowman and Littlefield, 1996), pp. 277–297.

52. Deacon Vladimir Rusak, "Open Letter to the Archbishop of Canterbury at the World Council of Churches, Vancouver Assembly," July 1983.

53. In this section, I have concentrated on U.S. Christian bodies, but it is important to consider the WCC here as well. NCC member bodies usually seek to coordinate their work with the WCC. We should also note that other bodies relating to the WCC, such as the British Council of Churches, have a better record.

54. After its Secretariat for Religious Liberty fell vacant in 1967, the NCC simply allowed it to wither away.

55. An excellent outline of these events is contained in Michael Bourdeaux, "The Russian Church, Religious Liberty, and the World Council of Churches," lecture given to the Royal Institute of International Affairs, London, October 29, 1984, published in *Religion in Communist Lands*, vol. 13 (Spring 1985), pp. 4–27.

56. Michael Bourdeaux, "The Fifth Seal," speech to Symposium on "Freedom of Religion, Human Rights, and Detente," Vienna, May 1983.

57. Bourdeaux, "The Fifth Seal," pp. 24–25, 27.

58. He was released early under Gorbachev.

59. *National and International Religion Report*, March 26, 1990. For further critical background on the World Council, see Kent R. Hill, op. cit.; Ernest LeFever, *Amsterdam to Nairobi: The World Council of Churches and the Third World* (Washington, D.C.: Ethics and Public Policy Center, 1979); *Nairobi to Vancouver: The World Council of Churches and the World, 1975–1987* (Washington, D.C.: Ethics and Public Policy Center, 1987); J. A. Emerson Vermaat, *The World Council of Churches and Politics: 1975–1986* (New York: Freedom House, 1989).

60. See "Cadres of the Church and Legal Measures to Curtail Their Activities," *Religion in Communist Dominated Areas*, XIX: 9–11 (1980), pp. 149–161.

The remaining sections of the Furov Report appear in RCDA XX: 1–3 (1981), pp. 4–19 and XX: 4–6 (1981), pp. 52–68.

61. The following material is derived from Alexander F. C. Webster, *The Price of Prophecy: Orthodox Churches on Peace, Freedom and Security* (Grand Rapids: Eerdmans, 1995).

62. Webster, op. cit., p. 38.

63. Webster, op. cit., p. 71.

64. Webster, op. cit., p. 57. This did not, however, stop him later in the year from deposing Father Gleb Yakunin from the priesthood on the grounds that he held elective office.

65. For example, in its presentation to the meetings of the United Nations Human Rights Commission in Geneva in February 1996, the WCC had a golden opportunity to raise the matter of religious persecution. It chose instead to focus on U.S. racism, a matter on which it had, with the aid of the NCC, spent months of hearings. Items raised included California's Proposition 187 on illegal immigrants, the book *The Bell Curve* on race and intelligence, U.S. housing policy, and the results of the November 1994 Congressional elections. It included an accusation that the U.S. has political prisoners and claims that America is on the verge of race war. No doubt some of these things deserve attention and criticism. But one can only wonder what it means when *these* are the basic worldwide human-rights issues that an international Church thinks to raise. As it was, the WCC merely provided the opportunity for Sudan, China, and Cuba to sponsor resolutions against the United States. Paul Marshall, "WCC Racism Stand Gives New Ammunition to Rights Abusers," *News Network International*, April 7, 1995.

66. Coulson, op. cit., p. 40.

67. Herb Schlossberg recounts that in speaking "with the NCC's main specialist on Muslim-Christian relations, the latter was at a loss to suggest any sources of information on the Muslim persecution of Christians. . . . He knew of no current cases. . . ." In another conversation, "The NCC's specialist on Islam views the problems of Christians living in Islamic lands as not very different from those of anyone living where another religion is

dominant. . . . He is concerned that stereotypes about Muslims are being perpetuated and points out that in places like Syria and Iraq, Christians are not persecuted. . . . He says this is because they regard themselves as secular states. Of course, if they are secular states rather than Islamic states, you cannot use them to show how beneficent Muslim rule is toward Christians." Interview with Marston Speight, NCC specialist on Christian-Muslim relations and adjunct faculty member at Hartford Theological Seminary, August 19,1988; interview with Charles Kimball, Islamic specialist at the NCC, August 17, 1988. Herbert Schlossberg, *A Fragrance of Oppression: The Church and Its Persecutors* (Wheaton: Crossway, 1991), p. 194. See also C. M. Naim, "Getting Real About Christian-Muslim Dialogue," *First Things*, November 1995, p. 10–12.

68. Paul Marshall, "On the Universality of Human Rights."

69. Paul Marshall, "Recent Christian-Muslim Dialogues Raise as Much Fear as Hope," *News Network International*, December 21, 1994.

70. *Religion News Service*, December 21, 1995.

71. See letter by William Cardinal Keeler to Dr. Mohammad Aslam Cheema, president of the American Muslim Council, March 26, 1996; "Statement to the Press," March 28, 1996, signed by NCCB, NCC, and others; memo from John Borelli, secretariat for ecumenical and interreligious affairs, NCCB, May 4, 1996; quotations supplied by Steven Emerson. See Steven Emerson's "Stop Aid and Comfort for Agents of Terror," *Wall Street Journal*, August 5, 1996, and critical reviews in a letter from Ihrahian Hooper of the Council on American-Islamic Relations, *Wall Street Journal*, August 22, 1996.

Chapter Eight

1. The four "White Fathers" had been shot dead four days earlier: Alain Dieulangard, 75; Jean Chevillard, 69; Charles Deckers, 70; Christian Chessel, 36 (Chessel was buried in France). Responsibility for the deaths was claimed by GIA guerrillas, as retaliation for the deaths of four terrorists who had been shot after hijacking an Air France airliner twenty-four hours before. Muslims such as those who attended the funeral, led by local Berbers, are

known to disagree with the agenda of the Muslim militants. Barbara Baker, "Security of Christians Deteriorates After Murder of Priests," *News Network International*, January 16, 1995.

2. *New York Times*, February 8, 1995.

3. *New York Times*, February 22, 1995; John L. Esposito, in his *The Islamic Threat: Myth or Reality* (New York: Oxford University Press, 1995), p. 180, gives a similar list. Bill Berkeley, in "The Longest War in the World," *New York Times Magazine*, March 3, 1996, pp. 58–61, described Sudan's Turabi as using Islam only as a "mask." Berkeley treats religion as a mere overlay to power struggles.

4. See *Newsweek*, April 1, 1996. This is also true of most books on East Asia, with the exception of Jim Rowher, *Asia Rising* (New York: Simon & Schuster, 1996).

5. Stephen L. Carter, *The Culture of Disbelief: How American Law and Politics Trivialize Religious Devotion* (New York: Basic Books, 1993), p. 10. See also John Pickering, "Christian Soldier in a Secular City: An Evangelical's Culture Shock," *Washington Post*, May 12, 1996.

6. James Finn, "The Cultivation and Protection of Religious Human Rights: The Role of the Media," pp. 161–189 of J. D. van der Vyver and J. Witte Jr., eds., *Religious Human Rights in Global Perspective: Legal Perspectives* (The Hague: Martinus Nijhoff, 1996), p. 188.

7. S. Robert Lichter, Stanley Rothman, and Linda S. Lichter, *The Media Elite* (Bethesda, MD: Adler and Adler, 1986); U.S. Civil Rights Commission hearings on religion, July 1, 1994; "Thin Skinned," *Commonwealth*, May 17, 1991, p. 309, quoted in Finn, op. cit., p. 186.

8. George Connell estimated a yearly attendance in 1993 of 5.6 billion at houses of worship, and 103 million at the three major professional sports leagues, *National and International Religion Report*, May 2, 1996. See the figures given in Thomas C. Reeves, *The Empty Church: The Suicide of Liberal Christianity* (New York: Free Press, 1996), pp. 50–68.

9. Quoted in Carl Horn, III, "Secularism and Pluralism in Public Education," *Harvard Journal of Law and Public Policy*, 7 (Winter 1984), p. 183.

10. *Christian Century*, November 1, 1995. I have used the summary given by Richard Neuhaus in *First Things*, February 1996, p. 85.

11. For example, the three current longest-held American hostages are Mark Rich, Dave Mankins, and Rick Tenenoff. They were abducted in Panama by Colombian guerrillas on January 31, 1993. We hear nothing about them. Does the fact that they were missionaries affect the lack of media coverage? See the *Los Angeles Times*, June 6, 1996.

12. Robert Audi, "The Place of Religious Argument in a Free and Democratic Society," *San Diego Law Review*, vol. 30, no. 4, Fall 1993, p. 667.

13. op. cit., p. 691.

14. John Rawls, *Political Liberalism* (New York: Columbia University Press, 1993), pp. 223–225. I am grateful to Professor Patrick Neal for raising these issues.

15. op. cit., p. 254.

16. "Interview," *The Times Literary Supplement*, June 24, 1994, p. 14.

17. Stephen Carter, op. cit., pp. 6–7. For a good discussion of these themes, see Ian S. Markham, *Plurality and Christian Ethics* (Cambridge: Cambridge University Press, 1994); Philip L. Quinn, "Political Liberalisms and their Exclusions of the Religious," *Proceedings and Addresses of the American Philosophical Association*, vol. 69, no. 2, November 1995, pp. 35–56.

18. A *Theory of Justice* (Cambridge: Harvard University Press, 1971), p. 554.

19. (San Francisco: Harper, 1987).

20. op. cit., p. 7.

21. op. cit., p. 127.

22. John L. Esposito, op. cit., p. 31; see also pp. 39, 43. On p. 220 he does discuss the human-rights implications of *dhimmi* status in modern states.

23. (Syracuse: Syracuse University Press, third edition, 1991), p. 290.

24. In *The Islamic Threat*, p. 89, he refers, in relation to Sudan, to the "traditional Islamic legal punishment [of] . . . the death penalty for apostasy."

25. *Islam and Politics*, pp. 290–292.

26. He also has some peculiar ideas about Christian theology. *The Islamic Threat*, p. 33, says that, in Christianity, "the reward for martyrdom is paradise." This would be a surprise to most theologians. Further, on p. 210, he misstates the dispute over funding of Islamic schools in the UK. In fact, the newer Christian, Jewish, and Islamic schools *have all* been denied funding.

27. Esposito's purpose in *The Islamic Threat* is to counter perceptions that simply equate Islam with its more militant forms, and this goal shapes his book in a more apologetic way than might be the case if he were simply trying to give a straight overview. Nevertheless, the picture he gives is rather too rosy.

28. (Washington, D.C.: United States Institute of Peace, 1992).

29. (Berkeley: University of California Press, 1993), p. 184.

30. U.S. Civil Rights Commission hearings on religion, July 1, 1994.

31. A good survey of the anthropological disputes is given in Thomas N. Headland, "Missionaries and Social Justice: Are they part of the Problem or Part of the Solution?," *Missiology: An International Review*, 24 (April, 1996), pp. 167–178, quotations on p. 168. See also Thomas H. Moore, "Frontier Missions and Their Critics," paper presented at the Canadian Anthropology Society Annual Conference, Vancouver, May 6, 1994.

32. Juergensmeyer, op. cit., p. 29.

33. Lamin Sanneh, "Christian Missions and the Western Guilt Complex," *The Christian Century*, April 8, 1987, pp. 330–334; *Translating the Message: The Missionary Impact on Culture* (Maryknoll: Orbis Books, 1989). A good survey of missionary linguistic work is given in Lowell Weiss, "Speaking in Tongues," *Atlantic Monthly*, June 1995, pp. 36–42.

34. Leo Strauss, "An Epilogue," pp. 99–129 of Hilail Gildin, ed., *Political Philosophy: Six Essays by Leo Strauss* (Indianapolis: Bobbs-Merrill, 1975), p. 129.

35. Edward Luttwak, "The Missing Dimension," pp. 8–19 of Douglas Johnston and Cynthia Sampson, eds., *Religion: The Missing Dimension of Statecraft* (New York: Oxford University Press, 1994), p. 9.

36. Luttwak, op. cit., pp. 9–10.

37. The analyst was Earnest R. Oney, see James E. Bill, *The Eagle and the Lion: The Tragedy of American-Iranian Relations* (New Haven: Yale University Press, 1988) p. 417, referred to in Luttwak, op. cit., p. 12.

38. Luttwak, op. cit., p. 11.

39. See also Barry Rubin, "Religion and International Affairs," pp. 20–34 of Johnston and Sampson, op. cit. These authors do not refer in this context to the Indian subcontinent. However, it is probably not insignificant that the "Hindu block" represented here has in recent years been involved in war on all of its frontiers.

40. These themes are similar to Samuel Huntington's "The Clash of Civilizations," *Foreign Affairs*, Summer 1993, pp. 22–49, but one does not have to accept all of Huntington's views to realize some of their salience. See also Michael A. Sells, *The Bridge Betrayed: Religion and Genocide in Bosnia* (Berkeley: University of California Press, 1996).

41. A good discussion in relation to Europe is given in William Pfaff, "The Absence of Empire," *The New Yorker*, August 10, 1992. *The Economist* also suggests that the boundary of Eastern Europe may be best understood by "religious identification," November 16, 1996, p. 50.

42. See also Larry Diamond, "Is the Third Wave Over?" *Journal of Democracy*, vol. 7, no. 3, July 1996, pp. 20–37; David Westerlund, *Questioning the Secular State: The Worldwide Resurgence of Religion in Politics* (New York: St. Martin's, 1996).

43. In this respect, the rapid spread of Protestantism in Latin America should receive far more attention in international studies than it has. See, for example, Henry Higuera, "Latin America's Reformation," *The National Interest*, Fall 1990, pp. 91–95. Sociologist David Martin calls it "perhaps the largest shift in religious faith in the world today."

44. Quoted in Natan Lerner, "Religious Human Rights Under the United Nations," pp. 79–134 of J. D. van der Vyver and J. Witte, op. cit., p. 83.

45. This myopia also affects other treatments. For example, of the seventeen chapters of Louis Henkin and John Lawrence Hargrove, eds., *Human Rights: An Agenda for the Next Century* (Washington, D.C.: American Society of International Law, 1994), not one is devoted to the subject of religion and

human rights. Roger S. Clark points out that the human-rights literature "is surprisingly sparse on the issue of religious intolerance." See Robert S. Clark, "The United Nations and Religious Freedom," pp. 197–225 of *New York University Journal of International Law and Politics*, 11 (1978), p. 197. I am grateful to Natan Lerner for these references. See p. 81 of Lerner, op. cit., and also Lerner's own discussion.

46. Meanwhile, the U.S. Report to the UN Human Rights Commission's 1995 hearings lumped together religion with the rights of migrant workers and minorities. Subsequently, the United States' speech before the Commission ignored the religious element and focused only the latter issues.

47. Jeff Jacoby, "Civil Rights Groups Yawn at African Slavery," *Orange County Register*, April 4, 1996.

48. loc. cit.

49. Minoo Southgate, "Slavery Ignored," *National Review*, October 23, 1995, pp. 26–29.

50. op. cit.

51. op. cit.

52. op. cit. This was also said by Cotton in a personal interview, January 23, 1996.

53. Paul Sieghart, *The International Law of Human Rights* (New York: Oxford University Press, 1983), p. 324.

54. (New York: Amnesty International, January 1995); see also *Sudan: Monitoring Human Rights* (London: October 1995).

55. Personal interviews with Bishop Taride Taban, Diocese of Torit Sudan (Catholic), Bishops Daniel M. Zindo, Diocese of Yambi, Nathaniel Garang, Diocese of Bor, Benjamin Ruati John, Diocese of Ezo (Episcopalians), South Sudan, May 2, 1996.

56. Morton A. Winston, "Amnesty International Testimony" before the House Committee on International Relations, Subcommittee on International Organizations and Human Rights hearings on "Religious Intolerance," February 15, 1996.

57. *Amnesty International Report, 1995* (New York: Amnesty International Publications, 1995).

58. *Human Rights Watch World Report, 1996* (New York: Human Rights Watch, 1995); see especially pp. 257–263.

59. "Sasser Helps Smooth U. S.-China Ties as He Pushes Strong Business Agenda," *Wall Street Journal*, September 17, 1996. The words in quotes are the *Journal's* summary of Mr. Sasser's remarks, not his own words. The same article also reports that Mr. Sasser has arranged for $450,000 from U.S. corporations to pay for renovations to the U. S. Embassy Building.

60. Nina Shea, "Testimony of Puebla Program on Religious Freedom of Freedom House" before the House Committee on International Relations Subcommittee on International Operations and Human Rights hearings on "State Department Country Reports on Human Rights Practices for 1995," March 26, 1996. The State Department can also be quirky. Its 1995 report on Syria complains that "there are no laws mandating access to public buildings for the disabled." As *The New Republic*, March 13, 1995, comments, "Of course, they don't have government-funded healthcare for torture victims either."

61. Lerner, op. cit., p. 134.

62. Carter, op. cit., p. 22.

Chapter Nine

1. Michael Horowitz, personal letter, April 9, 1996.

2. See Steve Bruce, "Protestant Resurgence and Fundamentalism," *The Political Quarterly*, 61 (April/June 1990), pp. 161–168.

3. Arend Theodor van Leeuwen argues that both Judaism and Christianity have contributed greatly to the development of "secularism," not in the sense of privatizing religion, but in the sense of allowing social institutions to develop free from the direct power of religious authorities. See his *Christianity in World History: The Meeting of the Faiths of East and West* (New York: Scribners, 1969).

4. Samuel P. Huntington, *The Third Wave: Democratization in the Late Twentieth Century* (Norman: University of Oklahoma Press, 1991). Some thoughtful essays on this are given in Douglas Johnston and Cynthia Sampson, eds., *Religion, The Missing Dimension of Statecraft* (New York: Oxford University Press, 1994). Huntington, in a famous article, has also elaborated a theory of the place of "civilizations," largely based on religious background, on the dynamics of present and coming world conflict. One does not need to accept all of his theses in order to appreciate the fact that religion is a key variable in both world conflict and in the possibilities of ameliorating that conflict. See Samuel P. Huntington, "The Clash of Civilizations," *Foreign Affairs* (Summer 1993), pp. 22–49; "The West: Unique, Not Universal," *Foreign Affairs*, November/December 1996, pp. 28–46; *The Clash of Civilizations and the Making of World Order* (New York: Simon and Schuster, 1996). See also David Westerlund, ed., *Questioning the Secular State: The Worldwide Resurgance of Religion in Politics* (New York: St. Martin's, 1996); various essays in the Summer 1996 issue of the *Journal of International Affairs* on "Religion: Politics, Power, and Symbolism." Huntington, in "The West . . . ," p. 31, notes that "In Islam, God is caesar; in China and Japan, caesar is God; in Orthodoxy, God is caesar's junior partner." This pithy formulation gets to the heart of the matter.

5. Quoted in A. A. Vasiliev, *History of the Byzantine Empire, 324–1453*, 2 vols. (Madison: University of Wisconsin Press, 1952), vol. 2, p. 396. The reference is given in Alexander Webster, "Crusading for Humanity? A Response to James Turner Johnson," pp. 145–151 of Luis E. Lugo ed., *Sovereignty at the Crossroads? Morality and International Politics in the Post-Cold War Era* (Totawa: Rowman & Littlefield, 1996), p. 149.

6. The Baroness (Caroline) Cox and John Eibner, Christian Solidarity International, "Evidence on Violations of Human Rights in Sudan," Report to United Nations Human Rights Commission, Geneva, April 1996.

7. Personal conversation, June 2, 1996.

8. Personal interview, July 1992. Several passengers in his vehicle had already been shot by guerrillas when a military gunship strafed the convoy. Whose bullets killed him cannot be determined. A popular biography is given in W. Terry Whalin and Chris Woehr, *One Bright Shining Path* (Wheaton: Crossway, 1993).

9. "Religious Freedom: Some Principles Informing Christian-Muslim Dialogue," a report prepared by a Working Party convened by Christians Relating to Islam, London, June 1995. "Some Suggestions for the WCC's Discussions with Muslims," A contribution by a Working Party convened by Christians Relating to Islam, London, June 1995.

10. Quoted in *The First Freedom*, January-June 1996, p. 4.

11. Roy Maynard and Paul Marshall, "Going Nowhere: Illegal Chinese Immigrants Find Lady Liberty Inhospitable," *World*, August 13, 1994, pp. 14–15; Paul Marshall, "U.S. Refugee Policy Sends Human Rights Message to China," *News Network International*, July 26, 1994; plus personal interviews with attorneys for the detainees in York County, Pennsylvania, June 1994; *Washington Times*, September 4, 1996. In 1996 Congress passed the Illegal Immigration and Immigrant Responsibility Act, Section 601 (c) reinstating coercive family planning as a criterion for refugees.

12. Nina Shea, *In the Lion's Den* (Washington, D.C.: Puebla Program, 1996), pg. 4. An expanded version of this will be published by Broadman and Holman in early 1997.

13. Letter by Nina Shea to Honorable Steven Coffey, deputy assistant secretary of state, March 18, 1995. Richard Land, "Testimony on behalf of the Christian Life Commission of the Southern Baptist Convention" to the House Committee on International Relations Subcommittee on International Operations and Human Rights hearings on "Religious Intolerance," February 15, 1995.

14. "Support Grows for Kuwaiti Christian Sentenced to Die," *The Times* (London), July 8, 1996. At the time of writing the State Department has also refused to take up the case of Man Thi Jones as a case of religious persecution. Mrs. Jones, an American, was detained in Vietnam for giving orphans pens which had crosses on them. The Department is aiding her as an individual but refusing to realize this is a human-rights issue with Vietnam. See "Christian Symbol Lands American in Vietnam Jail," *Washington Times*, November 19, 1996.

15. In Poland, in the lead-up to the fall of Communism, U.S. Embassy officials met with union activists, but their contacts with the Catholic Church, the

central institution in Polish society, were much more scarce. One small but useful step would be to have a religious attaché or equivalent in U.S. embassies, just as there are labor attachés and cultural attachés. See Edward Luttwak, "The Missing Dimension," in Johnston and Sampson, op. cit., p. 16. The same steps need to be followed within the U.S.'s domestic foreign policy apparatus.

16. A good survey of these developments is given in David Aikman, "Rescue to the Christians," *American Spectator*, July 1996, pp. 22–24, 82.

17. See "U.S. Policy Urged to Fight Persecution of Christians," *Washington Times*, September 8, 1996; "Senate Condemns Worldwide Human Rights Abuses Against Christians," *Los Angeles Times*, September 21, 1996; "Evangelical Christians Seek Action," *Washington Post*, September 22, 1996; "Evangelicals Press for Religious Freedom for Christians Abroad," *New York Times*, September 15, 1996; "From Ethiopia to China, the Lions Are Out There," *Los Angeles Times*, November 3, 1996; "Report Calls Persecution of Christians One of Biggest Untold Stories of Our Time," *Washington Times*, October 13, 1996. On the advisory committee, see Peter Steinfels' "Beliefs" column, *New York Times*, November 16, 1996; Laurie Goldstein, "U.S. Tabs Panel to Advise About Religious Strife," *Washington Post*, November 13, 1996. The notion of such a panel had earlier been criticized in an October 11 letter to President Clinton from, among others, Bill Bright, Charles Colson, Richard Neuhaus, James Kennedy, Diane Knippers, James Dobson, and Michael Novak. See Larry Witham, "Clinton Urged to Appoint Adviser, Not Panel, On Religious Persecution," *Washington Times*, October 21, 1996.

18. Caroline Cox and John Eibner, "Widespread Enslavement of Black African Southern Sudanese by Arabic PDF Militia," report of a visit by a Christian Solidarity International delegation to Bahr El Ghazal in Southern Sudan, October 23–28, 1995, p. 5.

Appendix C

1. See Natan Lerner, "Religious Rights Under the United Nations," pp. 79–134 of Johan D. van der Vyver and John Witte, Jr. eds., *Religious Human Rights in Global Perspective: Legal Perspectives* (The Hague: Martinus Nijhoff,

1996), pp. 91f, 115f. See also the comment by Special Rapporteur Benito that the right to change one's religion is "inseparable from freedom of thought, conscience, and religion," *Elimination of All Forms of Intolerance and Discrimination Based on Religion or Belief*, (UN Centre for Human Rights Geneva, 1989), p. 50.

2. The 1950 European Convention on Human Rights says in Article 9, "Everyone has the right to freedom of thought, conscience, and religion; this right includes freedom to change his religion or belief, and freedom, either alone or in community with others and in public or private, to manifest his religion or belief, in worship, teaching, practice, and observance." The 1969 American Convention on Human Rights says in Article 12:

   > Everyone has the right to freedom of conscience and of religion. This includes freedom to maintain or to change one's religion or beliefs, and freedom to profess or disseminate one's religion or beliefs either individually or together with others, in public or in private.
   >
   > No one shall be subject to restrictions that might impair his freedom to maintain or to change his religion or beliefs. . . .
   >
   > Parents or guardians, as the case might be, have the right to provide for the religious and moral education of their children or wards that is in accord with their own convictions.

   Article 13 states,

   > Everyone shall have the right to freedom of thought and expression. This right shall include freedom to seek, receive, and impart information and ideas of all kinds, regardless of frontiers, either orally, in writing, in print, in the form of art, or through any other medium of one's choice.

Appendix D

1. For an able discussion of these meanings see David Rieff, "An Age of Genocide," *The New Republic*, January 29, 1996, pp. 27–36.

2. While it is one of the worst human-rights violators in the world, there is no indication that Iraq singles out its Christian population for treatment any worse than it inflicts on the population in general. Indeed, there

have been signs that Saddam Hussein has given favorable treatment to Christian Iraqis. This does not seem to stem from any warmth toward Christianity or any desire for religious freedom, but from an attempt to counterbalance and undercut the country's Shi'ite population. A similar situation seems to pertain in Syria. Islamic activists opposed to the Ba'ath Party claim that it gives preference to Christians and other minority groups. See Mark Juergensmeyer, *The New Cold War? Religious Nationalism Confronts the Secular State* (Berkeley: University of California Press, 1993), p. 49. Islamicists may well be right in their accusations. This does not stem from any specific Syrian attachment to Christians, but simply because support for them undercuts Islamic extremism and thus strengthens the power of the regime. In turn, the Christians have no possibility of being in power themselves and so do not constitute a political threat.

3. For comments on this, see David Little, "Studying 'Religious Human Rights': Methodological Foundations," pp. 45–77 of Van der Vyver, op. cit., especially pp. 69f.

4. David B. Barrett, "Annual Statistical Table on Global Mission, 1996," *International Bulletin of Missionary Research*, January 1996. I have rounded out Barrett's figures to the nearest ten million.

Appendix E

1. Mark Juergensmeyer, *The New Cold War? Religious Nationalism Confronts the Secular State* (Berkeley: University of California Press, 1993), pp. 117–118.

2. Abdulfattah Amor, special rapporteur on religious intolerance, *1995 Report to the United Nations Commission on Human Rights* (Geneva: December 1994), p. 62.

3. Address of John Paul II to the Fiftieth General Assembly of the United Nations, October 5, 1995.

4. "Briefing" on "Report on Global Freedom of Religion or Belief," prepared for the U.S. Commission on Cooperation and Security in Europe by Michael Roan, W. Cole Durham, and Craig Mousin (The Tandem Project), Minneapolis, September 27, 1995, p. 3.

5. Summary of special rapporteur's presentation, "Conference on Freedom of Religion and Belief and the UN Year for Tolerance," London, September 18–20, 1995, given in Michael Roan et al., op. cit., p. 5.

Appendix F

1. A good exploration of Orthodoxy's political orientation is given in David T. Koyzis, "Imaging God and His Kingdom: Eastern Orthodoxy's Iconic Political Ethic," *Review of Politics*, vol. 55, Spring 1993, pp. 267–289.

2. See Chapters 2 and 3, on Islam.

3. See Chapter 3.

Appendix G

1. See report on recent research by Alexander Yakovlev, chairman of the Commission for Rehabilitating Victims of Religious Repression, into the NKVD and KGB archives, *The Tablet*, London, December 23/30, 1995, p. 1681.

2. Kent R. Hill, *The Soviet Union on the Brink: An Inside Look at Christianity and Glasnost* (Portland: Multnomah, 1991), p. 69.

3. Dmitry Pospielovsky, *The Russian Church under the Soviet Regime: 1917–1982*, 2 vols., (Crestwood, NY: St. Vladimir's Seminary Press, 1984), vol. 1, p. 53, quoted in Hill, op. cit., p. 75.

4. Hill, op. cit., p. 77.

5. Similar patterns were followed by other bodies such as the All-Union Council of Evangelical Christians-Baptists.

6. In the 1920s, the Communists also tended to support other Christian groups, especially the evangelicals, in hope of undercutting the position of Orthodoxy.

7. Pospielovsky, op. cit., vol. 1, p. 173–175, quoted in Hill, op. cit., p. 84.

8. *The Tablet*, December 23/30, 1995, pp. 1643–1644.

9. *The Tablet*, loc. cit.

10. Though the church hierarchy only paid 13 percent.

11. Hill, op. cit., p. 96.

INDEX

ABOUT THE AUTHORS

PAUL MARSHALL is Academic Dean and Senior Fellow in Political Theory at the Institute for Christian Studies, Toronto and Adjunct Professor of Philosophy at the Free University of Amsterdam. He is also an Adjunct Fellow of the Claremont Institute, Adjunct Professor at Fuller Theological Seminary, and Academic Advisor on Religious Freedom to the World Evangelical Fellowship.

He has testified on religious persecution before the Helsinki Commission of the U.S. Congress and lectured on human rights at the Chinese Academy of Social Sciences Beijing and also lectured in 15 other countries around the world.

He has directed a three-year research team studying "Pluralism" and is conducting a three-year study on "Human Rights Theories," both funded by the Social Sciences and Humanities Research Council of Canada.

Marshall is the author and editor of twelve books and booklets including *Human Rights Theories in Christian Perspective; Stained Glass: World Views and Social Science; Thine is the Kingdom: A Biblical Perspective on Government and Politics*, and *Labour Of Love: Essays on Work*. He has also published 300 articles. His "Calling, Work and Rest" was chosen by *Christianity Today* for the "Ethics" category of the best articles in theology in 1987 and his columns in *Christian Week* won the Canadian Church Press Award for the best columns in 1991. His work has been translated into eight languages.

Previous Visiting Professorships include Catholic University, Washington, D.C.; the Faculty of Law of the Free University, Amsterdam; Satya Wacana University, Salatiga, Indonesia; the European University for the Humanities, Minsk, Belarus, and an adjunct Professorship in Philosophy at Rutgers University. He has also been a Senior Fellow at the Institute on Religion and Democracy, columnist for News Network International, an exploration geologist in the Canadian Arctic, forest fire fighter in British Columbia, and advisor to the Council of Yukon Indians.

LELA GILBERT is the author and editor of forty books including works on religious persecution such as *Walking the Hard Road: The Story of Wang Ming Tao* and *Where the Brave Dare Not Go*. She also writes poetry and music and resides in California.